Meditation and Yoga in Psychotherapy

Meditation and Yoga in Psychotherapy

Techniques for Clinical Practice

Annellen M. Simpkins
C. Alexander Simpkins

WILEY

John Wiley & Sons, Inc.

Published by John Wiley & Sons, Inc., Hoboken, New Jersey.
Published simultaneously in Canada.

For general information on our other products and services please contact our Customer Care Department
within the U.S. at (800) 762-2974, outside the United States at (317) 572-3993 or fax (317) 572-4002.

Wiley also publishes its books in a variety of electronic formats. Some content that appears in print may
not be available in electronic books. For more information about Wiley products, visit our website at
www.wiley.com.

Library of Congress Cataloging-in-Publication Data:

Simpkins, Annellen M.
    Meditation and yoga in psychotherapy : techniques for clinical practice / Annellen M. Simpkins,
C. Alexander Simpkins.
        p. cm.
    Includes bibliographical references.
    ISBN 978-0-470-56241-3 (pbk.); ISBN 978-0-470-92055-8 (ebk); ISBN 978-0-470-92056-5 (ebk);
ISBN 978-0-470-92057-2 (ebk)
    1. Meditation—Therapeutic use. 2. Yoga—Therapeutic use.
    I. Simpkins, C. Alexander. II. Title.
    RC489.M43S557 2010
    616.89′165—dc22
                                                                                    2010023271
Printed in the United States of America

10 9 8 7 6 5 4 3 2 1

We dedicate this book to our family:
Alura, Anthony, Kira and Kaia Aguilera, and
C. Alexander Simpkins Jr.

And to R. Joanne Jao who helped us bring these methods to you.

Contents

Preface

We can have cognitions about our emotions and have emotions about our cognitions, but to exert control over either of these requires an additional set of capacities—those that enable self-direction.
(McCloskey, Hewitt, Henzel, & Eusebio, 2009, p. 73)

We live in challenging times. Powerful forces swirl about, pushing against the fabric of the world, changing it. Blown by these winds, we are hurled into an unknown future. We often feel that our lives are beyond our control, that all we can do is suffer the pushes and pulls of fate. Yoga offers hope. There is a way to take hold of and define our direction, and it is open to everyone. Though at times the path may be uncertain, lost in the ever-changing chaotic world, our way can be clear, anchored in the internal world. We can gain freedom and wisdom through training our consciousness, and with its development, we shape our destiny.

Many people think of yoga as simply being a set of postures, but the tradition includes much more. It offers a long-lived method to overcome suffering and reach higher consciousness developed through the body (the temple of the soul), the breath (the lord of the mind), and the mind (the lord of the senses) (Iyengar, 2001). Yoga uses each of these tools, and through their practice improves regulation of the mind-brain-body system.

It enhances self-direction through self-awareness. The result is an accessible set of invaluable interventions for overcoming psychological problems.

HOW YOGA CAN HELP THE THERAPEUTIC PROCESS

Therapists go through extensive training, and, as a result, they usually know what clients need. They are fully capable of sensitively guiding their clients through procedures that should help them resolve problems and grow. But sometimes even the experienced therapist using the most appropriate technique finds the intervention does not work. The client may sincerely try to comply, but simply cannot. This problem may stem from the fact that the client, who is untrained in psychological matters, is often out of touch with deeper emotions and doesn't know how to access them. Ask the simple question, "What are you feeling right now?" Most people will respond with a judgment such as "I'm good" or "I feel lousy." And they have no idea that this response is an abstraction from what is actually going on in their emotions at that moment.

Clients often lack the tools they need to link their attention to their thoughts, emotions, behaviors, and sensations, and yet, we frequently ask them to do so as part of therapy. Furthermore, they lack objectivity. When people are disturbed by conflicts, they have increased difficulty in focusing their attention, let alone holding it steady and observing what is there. The mental skills they lack are the very tools they need to overcome their problem and end their suffering.

We would not expect someone to be able to read if they didn't know the alphabet, understand how words are formed, or recognize the connection between words and meanings. Similarly, we will better help clients by teaching them to notice the signs they receive from their sensations and thoughts, to understand how these signs form patterns, and to read the meaningful connection between patterns and conflicts.

Yoga offers distinctive methods to address these deficits and build fundamental skills. Each step of yoga practice dispels illusions and resolves problems. Specific mental techniques begin with the simplest skills for paying attention, moving the body, and noticing breathing. Included are diverse meditative methods for cognition and emotions that develop a reflective ability, where consciousness becomes capable of observing itself objectively.

Facilitating Mind-Brain Change

The brain can be mobilized for healing as well. Contemporary neuroscience research has found that patterns of brain functioning, beginning with neuronal connections at the synapses are intimately involved in conscious experience. The brain responds to experience all the way down to the neuron. Many parts of the brain play a role, with multiple systems working together to facilitate control and regulate functions. Imbalances in any of these systems can lead to psychological problems. Yoga methods offer experiences to foster the healthy, natural rebalancing of the mind-brain system that clients need to alter psychological disturbance. The yoga framework integrates seamlessly with traditional therapeutic techniques by activating the mind and brain to undergo healthy change.

Fostering Human Potential

Clients develop the tools they need to succeed in treatment and make the best use possible of therapeutic interventions. When yoga methods are integrated into psychotherapeutic treatments, clients increase awareness and self-control, but what they gain goes far beyond rudimentary skills. The ultimate goal of yoga is more than just resolving problems: It seeks optimal functioning, higher consciousness, and spiritual enlightenment. Yoga's refined methods activate the natural abilities within for truly knowing oneself deeply. With self-knowledge comes a broader perspective that transcends problems as it develops attuned wisdom. And as skills improve, there comes a point when the mental processes are freed. Spontaneous meditation at the highest levels leads to happiness and bliss—what the ancients call Samadhi, enlightenment.

Through yoga practice, clients galvanize their intuition. They generate positive unconscious processes and make them available for conscious direction. They tap into the reservoir of inner truth, long extolled by the ancients as the means to revealing nature's deepest secrets. These time-honored and well-researched techniques will help clients gain mastery of their mental and physical well-being as they express their human potential in meaningful lifeworks and relationships.

For the purposes of psychotherapy, deliberate focused practice leads to effortless actualizing of potential. Positive psychology encourages directing therapy toward the good life (Kasser, 2004). Yoga's higher aims could be interpreted as a way of discovering the good life, found in the good *within* rather than searching for it *outside* of the self. Nothing stands in the way of higher functioning when clients can renounce their deluded thinking using tools that make it possible to truly let go of problems. Motivations are changed as well, so that people find reward in living a healthy life, their best life, and in a finely tuned mind, body, and spirit. What results is a deep and pervasive feeling of freedom and happiness.

YOGA'S POPULARITY

A recent "Yoga in America" market survey lends support for therapists to incorporate yoga and meditation into their therapy. Collected by the Harris Interactive Service Bureau for *Yoga Journal*, this 2008 survey found that 6.9% of U.S. adults, or 15.8 million people, practice yoga (*Yoga Journal*, 2008)—and interest is growing. The survey also found that nearly 8% of Americans, or 18.3 million people, who do not currently practice yoga say they are very or extremely interested in yoga and plan to start practicing soon. This figure is triple the number from a 2004 study. Another relevant finding was that 49.4% of the current practitioners began yoga to improve their overall health. This number was only 5.6% in a 2003 study, indicating that more people today are aware of yoga's health benefits. With an ever-growing body of research on yoga's use with a wide variety of problems and the growing interest in yoga, therapists can consider adding it as a helpful therapeutic tool.

ABOUT THIS BOOK

The book is divided into three parts. Part I covers research. Therapists want to know that the methods they use have been tested, and yoga has been under the microscope of scientific inquiry for many decades. Chapter 1 provides efficacy studies as well as investigations into the factors that may account for yoga's healing effects. Chapter 2 covers the latest neuroscience findings, showing how the brain and larger nervous system are altered by yoga methods.

Part II describes yoga. First, in Chapter 3, readers will enjoy sharing in the rich heritage of great writings by yoga masters throughout history, who have helped shape the discipline, along with a description of the many types of yoga that can be used for therapy. Chapter 4 explains the philosophical and psychological principles on which yoga is based. Interestingly, modern neuroscience is finding that many of these ancient theories seem to accurately reflect how the mind-brain-body system works. Therapists are trained to understand the therapeutic methods they use. Similarly, meditation methods should not simply be followed without understanding them. This book provides readers with the philosophical assumptions, rationales, and effects of yoga methods, so that therapists will not only learn what to do but also understand how, when, and why to use a particular technique.

Part III describes applications to common psychological problems. We provide cases to illustrate and exercises that therapists can do with clients. We address the person doing the technique directly, so that therapists can easily apply the exercises or clients can readily try them. The instructions can either be used directly as written or be individualized to suit the client's situation and personality, as well as to fit with the therapist's approach. We encourage creative individualizing of these methods to make them most helpful.

Books on meditation often promote only one meditation method, such as mindfulness or breathing, but experienced therapists would never use the same method with every client or problem. Similarly, people respond to meditation differently, finding some meditative skills easier and more helpful than others. The methods provided in Part III offer a range of techniques to give therapists many tools for the diversity and uniqueness of clients. Flexibly meeting the special needs of each person is one of the hallmarks of an effective therapist, so we offer a variety of methods and guide in how to creatively individualize techniques for best results.

At many points, we have included simple postures to be used as a focal point for meditation. Therapists who include active bodywork in their therapy may find the postures helpful. Those who do not use body movements can substitute simple sitting, lying down, or standing upright when varied postures are offered. In the integration of meditative focus with awareness of breathing and body positioning, just sitting in a chair can be transformed into a seat for healing.

Appendix I includes fundamental stretching exercises. We advise careful stretching before performing physical activity. Therapists should encourage clients to check with a medical doctor before engaging in any of the yoga movements included in this book.

Appendix II is a brief tour of the brain so that even readers who are unfamiliar with neuroscience will have a deeper understanding of how yoga alters the nervous system. Then therapists can add the dimension of brain change into their assessments and treatment plans.

We have incorporated practices that therapists can readily integrate into traditional psychotherapeutic treatments. We have also used only those methods that have multiple studies from several different investigators for a larger evidence base from scientific research. Yoga includes philosophical principles, traditions, styles, and techniques beyond the scope of this book. Readers may be motivated to use this book as a foundation for further study, which may be available in your community.

This book draws from our decades of practice, teaching, writing, and applying meditation to therapy. Over many years, we have developed a diverse collection of methods for working with people of all ages and with many different problems. Our sources for the book include traditional texts, modern interpretations, meditation research, neuroscience findings, illustrative legends, stories, and case examples.

May these methods inspire your own work, so that you continue to evolve and reach out to help your clients, for you are the source to inspire them to turn to the deepest wellsprings within.

Meditation and Yoga in Psychotherapy

PART I

EFFICACY AND NEUROSCIENCE RESEARCH

1

Efficacy

The world is ready to give up its secrets if only we know how to knock, how to give it the necessary blow. The strength and force of the blow come through concentration. There is no limit to the power of the human mind. The more concentrated it is, the more power is brought to bear on one point. That is the secret.

(*Vivekananda, 1953, p. 582*)

Nathan seemed to be a client with a great deal of potential. Although his mother died when he was very young, he had grown up in a loving home with a caring, committed father. He had excelled in high school as captain of the football team and as a National Merit Scholar. He was accepted into so many great colleges that he could not decide which one to choose. So, over spring break, he and his father embarked on a driving trip together to visit each college. The trip was fun, a shared adventure. By the last days of the trip, they were a little behind schedule with two schools left to visit. Nathan urged his father to drive straight through to the next college without stopping. It was late at night as they approached their destination. Nathan drifted off to sleep for just a few minutes. He awoke in a hospital, with no memory of what had happened. He was informed that they had been in a car accident. His father had died, whereas he survived. He recovered after a short stay in the hospital.

He felt overwhelmed by guilt over not staying awake to help keep his father alert and for having urged his father to continue driving that night. He began to dread the nearness of death, and going to college had a new meaning for him: The thought of it made him anxious.

Nathan had been to several therapists who had offered him various treatments, such as catharsis, desensitization therapy, and cognitive restructuring. He said that although each treatment was helpful in general, therapy could not remove that terrifying feeling that hung over him. So, he tried to not think about things too deeply, to help himself cope. As a result, this complex, highly intelligent young man simplified his life and worked only when he had to, at menial jobs. He lost interest in going to college, and instead, engaged in daring, dangerous extreme sports to escape his feeling concerning death. As he put it, "When I'm completely absorbed in what I am doing, with my life on the line, I really feel alive, and lose my feeling of fear about being near death." But a recent brush with death while attempting an extreme sport convinced him that this was probably not the best way for him to lose that feeling. He realized that he should attempt to change, so he decided to try a different therapy, a meditational one.

Nathan found relief as he learned to work with his mental faculties. He practiced yoga meditation and enjoyed the feeling of control he gained. He could then apply his attention fully to his therapeutic concerns, allowing him to address his problems at a level he never could before. He also appreciated yoga's integration of postures with breathing exercises, which allowed him to control his tension and fear. Then he could do some further analytical work, to help him come to terms with his guilt feelings, the meaning of college for him, and of his life in relation to his father's death. Soon, Nathan was able to ease his anxiety, engage in his life fully, and move forward. We heard from him a few years later, that he had gone to college and was pursuing a career in bioengineering. He continued to participate in sports, now as part of a college team, without the need for extreme risks.

Another client was in his early forties. He was short, with a stocky build, which had earned him the nickname "Tank." Unlike our client Nathan, Tank was unskilled. He had little education and low motivation. He lived with his sister and grandmother, barely getting by. He felt lethargic and spent much of his time sitting on the couch, watching television. He complained of feeling bored, but he could not think of anything he wanted to do. He did not say or do too much until something got him annoyed. Then he was prone to angry outbursts, which he claimed were not a problem to him, but they were a problem to everyone in the family, who wanted him to change. So, he grudgingly agreed to try psychotherapy.

From the very beginning phases, we could see that Tank was lacking in mental tools. He could barely hold his attention on what we were saying. Nor could he reflect on his own experiences. Clearly, Tank needed to build some skills. He began by turning his attention to breathing. He was truly amazed the first time he noticed the sensations of his breathing. He told us, "I never knew you could do that!" Tank's reaction is a reminder not to take for granted self-awareness skills. Although anyone can learn to access their attention, they may not automatically do so.

Gradually, building slowly along the way, Tank learned many of the exercises in this book, which helped him improve his attentional focus. He could turn his attention inward to his sensations or outward, extending his attention as he chose. As he became more capable of being self-aware, he was able to address his anger problem, which involved resolving some of his frustrations and resentments.

In time, Tank began to feel interested in the world around him. He took a trip to the local zoo. This was a big step for him, because he rarely went anywhere. Not only did he enjoy the animals, but he was even more interested in looking at the plants. We encouraged him to go to the public library to take out a book on gardening. He did, and he then followed the directions for planting a small garden. His attentional skills sharpened, as he learned how to follow his thought into action, right in his own backyard. His self-confidence improved as well, and he enrolled in a gardening class at the local nursery. Eventually, he got a job working for a landscape company. His family told us that his temper problem was greatly improved. "Now he's even nice to be around!" his sister told us. When we last saw him, he was happy, with a healthy curiosity about the world, and he had the mental skills to pursue his interests as they arose.

Yoga has stood the test of time as an approach that fosters transformation. Modern psychotherapists need to know that the methods they employ that seem sound conceptually have also been tested empirically. Interest in meditation has increased dramatically in the West over the past 50 years. In response, scientific research on yoga and meditation methods first gathered momentum during the 1960s. Over the past two decades, the number and quality of studies have increased significantly. Research on meditation's efficacy, along with neuroscience's evidence of real and positive effects on the brain have made it viable to include yoga in psychotherapeutic treatments. Therapists can now feel confident that these methods have an ever-growing scientific basis for helping with a wide variety of problems.

This chapter covers some highlights from the many research projects that have been done. Researchers are measuring the general effects of yoga when used therapeutically and what problems yoga can best address. Another type of research is investigating the healing factors involved. What makes yoga an effective method of treatment? How is it working? Both efficacy research and healing factors research are covered in this chapter, and the neuroscience findings are discussed in Chapter 2.

EFFICACY STUDIES OVERVIEW

Meditation and yoga were largely unknown in the West before the 1960s, except for a few isolated cases. It was not until meditation was popularized in that decade that it became broadly practiced in the West. Transcendental Meditation was one of the first meditation methods to be performed en masse, and the Transcendental Meditation organization, recognizing the importance of scientific verification, sponsored many scientific studies, some of which are included in this chapter. Although the quality of the studies may have varied, the sheer number and consistent results encouraged further investigation.

Efficacy studies usually compare yoga treatment to no treatment or to an alternative approach. These projects cover the effects of various forms of short-term yoga treatments. Some of the treatments involve postures combined with simple breathing awareness and meditative quieting. Other studies utilize more varied breathing exercises, at times combined with mantras (chanting a simple sound) and mudras (making a simple hand gesture) performed in a sitting position. And some yoga research is based solely in the use of meditation. All of these studies fall under the category of yoga research.

Neuroscience has been another boon to meditation research, offering strong scientific evidence for how meditation and yoga alter the nervous system in general and specific regions of the brain in particular. Taken together, the meditation and yoga research provides an ever-growing body of evidence that there is a scientific basis for using these methods in therapy.

Considering the positive findings from the use of different types and combinations of yoga techniques, it is clear that therapists have a rich source for methods to add into treatment. For example, you might want to incorporate a set of breathing exercises, simple postures, meditation, or any combination of these methods integrated together. The choice of technique should be tailored to fit the client's problem as well as the individual needs, and we will guide this process in Part III.

Some General Effects

Yoga fosters certain general effects. Researchers have found that yoga meditation has a positive influence on health. A summary of medical research on yoga over a 10-year period found that yoga can provide measurable health benefits for people who are healthy as well as those who suffer from musculoskeletal or cardiopulmonary disease (Raub, 2002).

A study performed at two companies tested managers and employees who practiced meditation regularly. The participants improved significantly in overall physical health, mental well-being, and vitality when compared to control subjects with similar jobs in the same companies. Meditation practitioners also reported significant reductions in health problems such as headaches and backaches, improved quality of sleep, and a significant reduction in the use of alcohol and cigarettes, compared to personnel in the control groups (Alexander et al., 1993).

Studies of many different forms of meditation have found that the practice improves the quality of life in terms of better memory and productivity, reduced anxiety, improvements in hypertension and sleeplessness, as well as converting loneliness, usually felt as a troubling emotion, into solitude, which can be a source for personal growth and even enlightenment (Dhar, 2002). Several studies found that Transcendental Meditation (TM), a practice that involves focusing attention using a mantra, led to overall psychological health (Alexander, Rainforth, & Gelderloos, 1991). A meta-analysis of 42 independent studies considered the effects of meditation on a general increase in self-actualization. The researchers found that meditators had markedly higher levels of self-actualization as compared with other forms of relaxation (Alexander et al., 1991).

Many different yoga methods have been studied and compared over the recent decades. A healthy group of men and women, ages 18 to 30 years old, participated in a three-month-long course in yoga. The first 30 days they practiced yoga breathing exercises, and then the last two months they added a series of yoga postures. Both the women and men showed positive improvements and reductions in risk factors for metabolic and cardiovascular diseases, as measured by reduced levels of total cholesterol and triglycerides following the breathing segment of the study. The subjects maintained that improvement when measured following the addition of postures in the third month of the study (Prasad et al., 2006).

Even in the midst of difficult circumstances, yoga can help people to cope better and experience improved mental and physical well-being. For example, individuals who have had HIV/AIDS learned breathing combined with meditation methods. Of the 47 subjects who completed the study, all showed marked improvement in their feelings of well-being right after the program. In follow-up interviews with the participants, subjects described having made positive life changes, even though their quantitative measures indicated that they were under increased stress (Brazier, Mulkins, & Verhoef, 2006).

Improved Memory and Intelligence

The ancient yogis believed that yoga techniques combining stimulating postures with calming relaxation meditations would bring about a state of mental balance. Recent studies have found that this claim may be true. The researchers measured the peak latency and peak amplitude of P300 auditory event-related potentials in 47 subjects, before and after these combined yoga practices. P300 is an indicator of cognitive processing. The results showed an enhancement of the P300, indicating that the combined practice of stimulating and calming yoga methods enhanced cognitive functioning (Sarang & Telles, 2006).

Studies were performed to test memory. For example, college students instructed in meditation displayed significant improvements in performance over a two-week period on a perceptual and short-term memory test involving the identification of familiar letter sequences presented rapidly. They were compared with subjects who were randomly assigned to a routine of twice-daily rest with their eyes closed, and with subjects who made no change in their daily routine (Dillbeck, 1982). In several studies, university students who meditated regularly showed significant improvement compared to control subjects on intelligence measures over a two-year period (Cranson, Orme-Johnson, Gakenbach, & Dillbeck, 1991; Dillbeck, Assimakis, Raimondi, & Orme-Johnson, 1986).

Large-Scale Studies: The Maharishi Effect

Under the guidance of the founder of TM, the Maharishi Mahesh Yogi (see Chapter 3 for details on the Maharishi and TM), and his organization, a group of large studies were performed in varied locations around the United States between the years of 1976 and 1993. The Maharishi pointed out that people have seen for millennia that meditation can help individuals. He sought to validate scientifically that the practice of meditation could change a whole society. In an address given by the Maharishi, he said:

> *When the number of people practicing the Transcendental Meditation program rises to about one per cent of a city's population, the one per cent effect comes into play immediately. Crime, illness, and all other negative aspects of social life diminish sharply, and an influence of coherence and harmony spreads throughout society.*
>
> **(Mahesh, 1990, p. 32)**

This phenomenon became known as the Maharishi Effect. During periods when large-scale Transcendental Meditation groups numbering more than 1% of the population were holding regular meditation sessions, researchers did find a statistically significant reduction in the rate of fatalities resulting from automobile accidents, suicides, and homicides in the United States (Dillbeck, 1980).

This TM project also investigated the effects of meditation on violence. Meditation is known to produce a feeling of inner peace and well-being. Some of these large-scale studies seem to bear out this time-honored claim. Four thousand practitioners of Transcendental Meditation assembled in Washington, D.C. from June 7 to June 30, 1993. The local police monitored the crime rate for the district. Statistics revealed that the crimes decreased 15% during this period and stayed lower for some time after the 21-day event (Hagelin et al., 1999).

Another large-group meditation study revealed a distinct improvement in the quality of life in Rhode Island. Crime rates dropped, auto accidents decreased, and there were fewer deaths resulting from cigarette smoking and alcohol consumption (Dillbeck, Cavanaugh, Glenn, Orme-Johnson, & Mittlefehldt, 1987). Meditation has even been shown to help in a wartime situation. There was a reported decrease in hostilities during the Lebanese war from collective meditation sessions (Abou-Nader, Alexander, & Davies, 1990; Davies & Alexander, 1989).

EFFICACY STUDIES FOR SPECIFIC PROBLEMS

A great many studies have been performed to test the efficacy of the use of yoga for specific problems, both physical and psychological. Yoga has been tested for high blood pressure, memory loss, movement disorders such as Parkinson's disease, and addictions, as well as for most psychological problems, including stress, anxiety, and depression. It has also been found to be helpful with children and problems of aging.

Research on Yoga for Stress

Yoga and meditation are effective ways to combat stress. Yoga exercises can help a person to take the steps needed to dramatically alter the brain's stress response, changing the mind-body balance for more comfortable coping. We present a few examples of the kind of research that is being done that shows how yoga is an effective treatment for stress.

The ability to focus attention can be helpful for better toleration of stress. Vaitl and Ott (2005) found that all altered states involve changes in the focus of attention. These changes can vary from a narrow focus of attention to a broad, extended awareness that includes all in a single grasp. Control of attention span has been shown to have many therapeutic applications, with stress being one of them.

For example, an experiment performed by Hempel and Ott (2006) tested 31 students before and after they underwent a 10-week yoga program. They found that narrowing the focus of attention using yoga methods brought significant improvement in handling an induced stressor, as indicated by psychological and physiological measures. The subjects scored higher on the TAS, a test that measures the ability to become absorbed, indicating focus of attention. The subjects also had greater baroflex sensitivity (BRS), which is responsible for maintaining a stable blood pressure. In addition, the subjects showed a more flexible cardiovascular responsiveness, which is linked to higher absorption (Kumar & Pekala, 1988). Thus, yoga training, which develops an improved focused use of attention and greater absorption of attention, proved helpful for tolerating and handling stress more comfortably and flexibly.

Therapists often help families who are coping with the stress of caring for an elderly loved one. The situation is demanding for the caregivers on many levels, from practical matters to emotional discomfort that must be tolerated. One study provided family caregivers a 6-session yoga meditation program to help with stress in caring for a family member suffering from dementia. The researchers found a statistically significant reduction in depression, anxiety, and improvement on perceived self-efficacy. Those caregivers who meditated longer had greater improvement in depression. They also reported that the majority of subjects felt the program helped them in their physical and emotional functioning (W. Thompson, Thompson, & Gallagher-Thompson, 2004).

One way to begin the process of establishing efficacy for a treatment is to compare it to a treatment that has already been shown to be effective. A group of researchers in Sweden did just that. A yoga treatment based on Kundalini yoga methods was compared to a stress management program based on cognitive behavioral therapy (CBT). The pool of 33 subjects was drawn from a large Swedish company. All subjects were given 10 sessions over a period of four months. The results showed that yoga was equally effective to CBT for stress management. All subjects showed significant improvement in psychological effects, such as self-rated stress and stress behavior, anger, exhaustion, and quality of life. Both groups also improved equally on physiological measures of blood pressure, heart rate, urinary catecholamines, and salivary cortisol. The researchers concluded that, similar to CBT, yoga shows promise as a method for stress reduction (Granath, Ingvarsson, von Thiele, & Lundberg, 2006).

Yoga for Anxiety

The many studies on yoga for anxiety offer optimism in integrating yoga methods into treatments for anxiety problems. In giving people specific things to do, yoga can be reassuring and helpful for people who feel anxious. Here are a few examples of the kinds of studies being done.

A yoga technique that combined postures with prone meditation has recently been found to improve performance on attention tasks and reduce state anxiety better than simple relaxation performed lying down (Subramanya & Telles, 2009).

Yoga treatments have been studied for particular types of anxiety problems. Obsessive-compulsive disorder (OCD), which has a strong anxiety component, can be difficult to treat, but with the addition of yoga techniques, treatments can become more effective. Eight adult subjects who were diagnosed with OCD were given a specific yoga breathing pattern to practice for OCD and several others for generalized anxiety. They also received a one-year follow-up course of therapy. They all showed significant improvement on the Yale-Brown Obsessive-Compulsive scale that compared them before treatment and at 3, 6, 9, and 12 months. They also showed improvement on anxiety, global severity, and stress indexes (Shannahoff-Khalsa & Beckett, 1996).

Yoga was also used with a group of women who were experiencing anxiety and stress. The subjects underwent a program of Iyengar yoga classes involving postures that the Iyengar system identifies as reducing anxiety and stress. The subjects attended two 90-minute sessions per week for eight weeks. As compared to the control group, the subjects showed significant reductions in anxiety, stress, fatigue, depression, headaches, and back pain, along with significant increases in well-being (Michalsen et al., 2005).

Posttraumatic stress disorder (PTSD) is another problem that brings clients to psychotherapy. Yoga treatment for veterans who suffered from PTSD was studied with a group of 62 outpatient veterans, 90% men. They participated in five 90-minute sessions given once a week and were measured pre- and posttreatment. The treatment consisted of mantra practice and one-pointed awareness. Following treatment, all subjects showed significant improvement in all the outcomes, including anxiety, stress, anger, quality of life, and spiritual well-being, with the largest improvement being for anxiety and well-being. The study found additionally that stronger results were associated with greater frequency of practice (Williams et al., 2005).

Yoga is often used as an adjunct to more conventional therapeutic methods, and we encourage this most of the time, but occasionally studies find that yoga can be used alone. Chronic fatigue syndrome and anxiety are sometimes diagnosed together. In a study of 155 subjects who suffered from chronic fatigue syndrome, several treatments were compared. Participants from a chronic fatigue syndrome clinic were offered treatment. Yoga was one of the treatments, and standard psychological support was another. After a two-year follow-up, those who did yoga had the strongest results, leading the authors to recommend yoga as a promising treatment for chronic fatigue syndrome (Bentler, Hartz, & Kuhn, 2005).

Thus, yoga can be effective for the treatment of anxiety in women and men, and it can be used for many different types of anxiety problems. It is often even more effective when combined with conventional therapy, and so can be a welcome addition to existing treatment programs.

Yoga for Depression

Yoga has been studied as a complementary treatment for people suffering from depression. A search for studies that used yoga techniques for depression was made in 2004. This meta-analysis uncovered five projects that used different types of yoga interventions. The severity of the depression ranged from mild to severe. All five studies found that yoga was helpful and had no adverse effects. For example, a study with severely depressed subjects showed improvement using rhythmic breathing and relaxation exercises (Khumar, P. Kaur, & Kaur, 1993). Another study gave depressed subjects classes in postures alone and found that the subjects' mood improved after performing the set of postures (Shapiro, Cook, Davydov, Ottaviani, Leuchter, & Abrams, 2007). The recommendation by these authors was that further investigation of yoga as a therapeutic method for depression is warranted (Pilkington, Kirkwood, Rampes, & Richardson, 2005).

Yoga and Meditation for Addiction

Yoga has been researched in the treatment of addictions for several decades. Now, many studies show success applying the different forms of yoga to treat addiction. One study performed by the Harvard Medical School found that yoga was as effective as traditional psychotherapy in assisting clients who were part of a methadone program (Shaffer, LaSalvia, & Stein 1997).

Research that combined psychiatric treatment with yoga for alcohol and drug addiction was performed using yoga and relaxation in the treatment of alcohol-dependent women (Nespor, 2001a, 2001b). This researcher incorporated yoga practices of meditation, postures, breathing, and attention to the yamas and niyamas, to help people overcome their addictions.

A meta-study of the use of Transcendental Meditation for preventing alcohol, nicotine, and drug abuse showed effectiveness in recovery and relapse prevention (Niranjanananda Saraswati & Alexander, 1994). Some of the studies found that TM helped remove the motivation for using the drug. Treatment also helped reduce stress and strengthen the subjects' ability to handle the withdrawal process.

Herbert Benson is a prominent researcher who has studied the use of meditation for alcoholism and found that TM brought about several physiological changes that resulted in decreased sympathetic nervous system activity. His studies showed that meditation practice did result in decreased drug and alcohol use (Benson, 1974).

A group of well-known researchers in the science of TM reviewed 24 studies on the use of TM for treating and preventing substance abuse. The studies included heavy substance–using prisoners, patients in treatment programs, and noninstitutionalized subjects. The researchers concluded that meditation improved some of the underlying factors involved in chemical use and led to stress relief, increased self-esteem, personal empowerment, and general improvement in health (Gelderloos, Walton, Orme-Johnson, & Alexander, 1991).

Even the famous founder of the Iyengar system of yoga addressed the problem of addiction in his book, finding that the regular practice of yoga could help overcome addiction and prevent its recurrence (Iyengar, 2001).

Yoga and Meditation Research for Aging

Yoga and meditation have been researched extensively for problems related to aging. Meditation may actually help lessen the negative effects of aging. One recent study performed by a large group of investigators (Lazar et al., 2005) showed that people who meditate over many years have an increase in the thickness of certain important parts of the cerebral cortex. This study compared typical Western subjects who were skilled in insight meditation with a control group of people with no meditation or yoga experience. The meditators had a daily routine that included career, family, friends, and hobbies along with daily meditation. The researchers found distinctive differences in the cortical thickness of older meditators from older non-meditators. Although the average cortical thickness did not differ, areas involved with sustained attention, sensing of inner experiencing, increased spontaneity, and visual and auditory sensing were thicker in the meditators. Normally, the entire frontal region of the cortex gets thinner as people age, but the older meditators retained thickness in these key frontal cortex areas. The average cortical thickness of the 40- to 50-year-old meditators was similar to the average thickness of 20- to 30-year-old meditators. Nonmeditators of all ages had less thickness in these brain areas. The investigators concluded that regular practice of meditation slows the rate of degeneration of these important areas of the brain.

Studies that have compared meditators to nonmeditating controls for benchmarks of aging have discovered that meditation seems to slow down the aging process in many respects. One study found that long-term meditators (five years of regular meditation) were physiologically 12 years younger than their chronological age, as measured by reduction of blood pressure, better near-point vision, and improved auditory discrimination. Short-term meditators were physiologically five years younger than their chronological age for these factors. The study controlled for the potentially confounding effects of diet and exercise (Wallace, Dillbeck, Jacobe, & Harrington, 1982).

Another meditation study compared the sleep patterns of young people, age 20 to 30 years, to middle-aged people, age 31 to 55 years. Each age group had meditators who used either Sudarshan Kriya Yoga (SKY) or Vipassana meditation compared with nonmeditating controls. Whole-night polysomnographic recordings were carried out in 78 healthy male subjects belonging to control and meditation groups. Polysomnography records brain wave changes (electroencephalogram, EEG), eye movements (electrooculogram), muscle tone (electromyogram), respiration (electrocardiogram, ECG), and leg movements while subjects were sleeping. Sleep patterns were comparable among the younger controls and the young and middle-aged meditation groups. Slow-wave sleep showed a 3.7% decline in the middle-age controls, but no such decline appeared in the middle-aged meditators. The authors concluded that meditation practices help retain slow-wave sleep and enhance the REM (rapid eye movement) sleep state in middle age. Meditators appear to retain a younger biological age as far as sleep is concerned, showing the benefits of meditation for antiaging (Sulekha, Thennarasu, Vedamurthachar, Raju, & Kutty, 2006).

Another large sleep study compared sleep patterns of 120 residents in an elderly care facility. One group given an herbal Ayurvedic treatment was compared to a yoga group who performed yoga postures, meditation, breathing, and received lectures on yoga philosophy. After six months, the yoga group showed a significant increase in the number of hours slept and had improvements in feeling rested. The herbal treatment group had no significant change (Manjunath & Telles, 2005).

Studies show that spirituality may literally help with mild cognitive impairment, the symptoms of early Alzheimer's disease. This study scanned 15 subjects who were experiencing memory loss and mild cognitive impairment pre- and posttreatment. All subjects received Kirtan Kriya yoga meditation involving repeated chanting of sounds and finger movements designed to help the mind focus and become sharper. They found increased blood flow as revealed in SPECT (single photo emission computed tomography) scan, with greater activation in the posterior cingulate gyrus, one of the first brain areas to degenerate with Alzheimer's disease (Newberg, Wintering, Khalsa, Roggenkamp, & Waldman, 2010).

Meditation was shown to reduce the activation of the sympathetic nervous system. An overly activated sympathetic nervous system is one of the markers of stress and risk for cardiovascular disease. Elderly subjects with congestive heart failure listened to a 30-minute-long audiotape for meditation twice a day for 12 weeks. They also had one weekly group meeting. The meditators were compared to a control group that had weekly meetings but no meditation tape. The meditation group had significant reduction in their sympathetic activation, measured as improved levels of noradrenaline, as compared to the control group, who had no change (Curiati et al., 2005).

Yoga Research With Children

Therapists and educators are often looking for nonpharmacological interventions to use with children. With yoga's potential to provide natural change, interest in yoga is on the rise, and research to test its effectiveness is being done. A yoga program for children tested 48 fifth-grade students, before and after yoga training. The program involved breathing exercises combined with imaginative journeys and yoga postures. The children had increased emotional balance, along with a reduction of fears, feelings of helplessness, and aggression. The participants also performed the exercises after school, helping them to have even better control over their negative feelings (Slueck & Gloeckner, 2005). Another extensive study was performed in six elementary schools located around the United States. A yoga program was provided followed by surveys from students, teachers, and parents. The study found that yoga practice had a positive influence on academic achievement, general health, and interpersonal relationships in kindergarten through fifth-grade students who participated (Buckenmeyer & Freltas, 2007).

Yoga is being increasingly researched as an adjunct for treating children with common childhood problems, such as ADHD, autism, anxiety, and depression. It has also been tested to enhance learning ability. For example, one study performed on boys diagnosed with ADHD showed improvements in their symptoms and attention following regular yoga practice (Jensen & Kenny, 2004). Another research group (Galamtino, Galbavy, & Quinn, 2008) reviewed 24 studies that used yoga with children who had different types of problems. All of the studies used breathing, meditation, and postures together as the intervention. One group of studies they reviewed showed improvement for healthy children on attentional tasks, motor performance, memory, and motor speed. Ten of the studies investigated cardiopulmonary effects, with significant improvements. Some of these studies showed reduced levels of fear, anxiety, and feelings of helplessness in traumatized adolescents. Children who were hospitalized for adjustment disorder and depression were also improved after yoga therapy. Even problems with asthma were improved. In general, the researchers recommended that yoga could be used as an adjunct for treatment of children.

FACTORS OF HEALING

If yoga helps enhance functioning and diminish problems, how does it work? Investigators have been attempting to uncover the healing ingredients that might be responsible for yoga's effects. These studies have found certain mechanisms underlying the effects, and we include a few of the possible mechanisms embedded in the methods.

Spirituality

One possible healing ingredient of yoga may be that it fosters a feeling of spirituality. Spirituality is wired into our brain, according to University of California at San Diego researcher Vilayanur Ramachandran. He has postulated that we may have neural circuitry in the limbic system and temporal lobes that is activated during experiences of spirituality (Ramachandran et al., 1999). Therapists who are sensitive to the spiritual dimension may offer clients additional ways to intensify the therapeutic process, giving it a more deeply felt personal significance.

A group of researchers set out to compare the results from a secular form of meditation with a spiritual one, using mantra meditation. One group of participants was taught a spiritual meditation technique that focused on the mantra "God is love" while the other group used the mantra "I am happy." Both groups practiced their mantra 20 minutes a day for two weeks and then returned to be tested. Each group performed their mantra for 20 minutes and then placed their hands in uncomfortably cold water. The spiritual group was able to withstand the discomfort twice as long as the nonspiritual group. The spiritual group also reported feeling less anxiety, having a more positive mood, and feeling a greater sense of spirituality. Interestingly, both groups had a similar decrease in heart rate (Wacholtz & Pargament, 2005).

Absorption

One healing ingredient that makes meditation so effective is its ability to foster absorption. Yoga has made the training of absorption into a highly refined science, with specific exercises for narrowing and opening attention. Recent findings show that absorption plays an important role in the psychobiology of self-regulation (Vaitl & Ott, 2005), which is a primary component for healing, according to attachment theories of therapy (Johnson, 2008). Typical brain activations and inhibitions in the cortex have been correlated with high and low absorption and different brain patterns as measured on EEG. Those subjects with high scores had changes in the occipital region, indicating a more flexible attentional style (Davidson, Goleman, & Schwartz, 1976), a useful trait to foster in people who are undergoing psychotherapy. Yoga training's ability to foster absorption may account for its effectiveness in psychotherapy.

What is absorption? Absorption is the ability to fully engage mental and emotional processes in an object of attention. Absorption occurs spontaneously, but it can be trained. Everyone has natural moments of absorption when they are so involved in something that time slips away and everything else becomes background. The object of absorption can take many forms.

It might be interpersonal, such as a significant other. It can also be something found in the environment, such as a piece of art, a game, or a beautiful flower. Another source for objects of absorption are experiences within, such as a deep feeling of inner calm while resting in a comfortable bed or a peaceful feeling of warmth, sitting in front of a campfire.

Absorption includes two components: openness and focused attention. Openness is the component of sincere involvement in an experience. Yoga fosters this openness in the early steps, where practitioners are encouraged to engage in the process with pure and sincere intention. Attention is the means for engaging involvement and openness to situations that will foster absorption. Yoga trains attention directly, and these methods form part of the core of the practice.

Self-Regulation

Yoga breathing has been studied for its effects on a wide variety of clinical problems (Brown & Gerberg, 2005). One of the well-documented effects is that yoga helps balance the autonomic nervous system responses. Through the practice of yoga breathing techniques, an overactivated nervous system can be returned to balance, and in this way will enhance well-being.

A second important benefit that comes from balancing the autonomic nervous system is better self-regulation. When people are angry, stressed, or anxious, the sympathetic and parasympathetic nervous systems are overactivated. By developing deliberate methods to calm these systems and return them to balance, people gain control over their responses. This ability to self-regulate can bring a strong sense of mastery. Psychological problems become easier to tackle, with the confidence that it is possible to voluntarily effect what has previously been experienced as an involuntary reaction. For example, one study showed that yoga practice reduced blood pressure and had positive effects on hypertension (Sung, Roussanov, Nagubandi, & Golden, 2001). One client of ours who lowered her elevated blood pressure using meditation methods gained a more generalized sense of mastery over her reactions, and then she was able to face the ways she was sabotaging her interpersonal relationships. With that willingness to take responsibility instead of simply blaming others, she took further steps toward change.

Self-regulation is helpful at any age. An increasing number of seniors have experimented with some kind of yoga to help improve their health, but they gain another important ability: self-control. One study tested the impact of a six-week yoga intervention on the psychological health of senior citizens with a mean age of 77. The subjects did a gentle form of yoga where participants sat in chairs, meeting for 45 minutes once a week for six weeks. Participants were also encouraged to practice at home each day. Yoga subjects improved over an exercise group and no-treatment control group on measures for anxiety, anger, depression, well-being, general self-efficacy, and self-efficacy for daily living. The researchers concluded that changes in self-control were associated with general self-efficacy and trait anxiety changes, and they proposed that self-control is the mechanism underlying the impact of yoga on psychological health (Bonura, 2007).

The Dual Action: Relaxation and Activation

Many studies have shown that meditation can produce deep relaxation. For example, a comprehensive meta-analysis (Dillbeck & Orme-Johnson, 1987) found 31 physiological studies that compared meditation to resting with the eyes closed. The study evaluated three key indicators of relaxation and found that meditation provided a deep state of relaxation, even deeper than simple eyes-closed rest.

That meditation produces relaxation is not surprising, but what is less obvious is that meditation also produces activation. This dual pattern of physiological activity and relaxation was first observed in the 1950s in studies of seven experienced yogis. A combination of brain waves including recurrent beta rhythms of 18 to 20 hertz, generalized fast activity of small amplitude as high as 40 to 45 hertz, and slow alpha rhythms were both seen at various stages of the yogic meditation (Das & Gastaut, 1955). A modern EEG study found similar results. Yoga meditators had an increase in the faster beta wave activity that is typically associated with wakefulness and alertness (Schneider & Tarshis, 1986). In addition, the meditators showed an increase in slower alpha and theta wave activity, which is associated with relaxation (Bhatia, A. Kumar, Kumar, Pandey, & Kochupilla, 2003). These studies clearly show that meditation entails both relaxation and alertness. Typically, when people are attentive, they are correspondingly stimulated, but in meditation, people seem to be able to remain calm even though they are highly aware. Staying alert and relaxed at the same time has many potential benefits for improving performance in varied situations and handling challenges well. Further research will undoubtedly explore the potentials and limits.

CONCLUSION

All of these studies indicate the many dimensions of yoga and meditation and how it can be helpful for therapy, but efficacy is not the only basis for yoga's usefulness to therapy. Research in neuroscience shows how yoga changes the brain, adding evidence for its therapeutic effect, as Chapter 2 describes.

2

Yoga and the Brain

We cannot look upon man as a physical machine to which spiritual life is attached from outside. The body is the instrument for the expression of spiritual life. So, instead of renouncing the material basis, the Yoga accepts it as part of the spiritual problem.

(Radhakrishnan, 1977, Vol. II, p. 352)

THE RELATIONSHIP BETWEEN MIND AND BRAIN

Yoga has been addressing the relationships between mind, brain, and body for thousands of years. Through careful training, they can be linked together. The material and spiritual, brain and mind become inseparable.

Science seems to be reaching similar conclusions. Neuroscience research makes it clear that real changes in the brain continue to take place throughout life, and these changes can have lasting effects on cognitions and emotions. The influence is bidirectional between brain, body, and mind. The findings of neuroplasticity, for example, clearly show that the mind and environment can influence the brain, and we know that the brain can have a strong influence on the mind, body, and environment. Therapists who understand how the brain, mind, body, and environment interrelate together will have more techniques and methods to help clients change (C. A. Simpkins & Simpkins, 2010).

Neuroscience findings about the brain have convinced contemporary philosophers that the brain and mind are not separate, but instead that the material or physical brain is primary in the mental processing we call *mind*. These philosophical positions are based on new neuroscience evidence indicating that brain pathways and functions can activate mental processes. In addition, research has shown that the mind has just as strong an influence on the structure of the brain, with the opportunity for neuroplasticity and neurogenesis throughout life (described later in this chapter). So, the influence seems to go both ways, mind to brain and brain to mind. These back-and-forth processes facilitate therapeutic change.

If mind and brain are interrelated, what is the nature of the relationship? Some say mind and brain have identical qualities, so they must be the same thing. The mind literally *is* the brain, in identity theory (Place, 1999). The mind is a function of the brain, in functionalism (Fodor, 1983). And from another well-regarded point of view, eliminativism, there are only brain processes, beginning with activity in the neurons, which create the epiphenomenon we call the mind (Churchland, 1986, 1995). From the yoga point of view, mind and body are separate in nature. Through yoga practices, their activity can be harnessed together, to function as a unified system. Clearly, no matter which of these positions one takes, yoga's ancient wisdom offers insight.

Neuroscience can help us understand how yoga influences the brain and body. Some of the recent evidence for the positive effects of yoga and meditation are given in terms of how the mental practice alters the brain. These studies show what parts of the brain are changed by yoga. Understanding the interrelationship between mind and brain is helpful for recognizing the significance of these studies. In addition, having the data of the brain structures and functions that are affected helps in making clinical decisions about what practices to apply for different problems. For those who are not familiar with brain structures and functions, Appendix II: A Quick Tour Through the Brain, offers a guide to the relevant information about the nervous system.

OVERVIEW OF HOW YOGA AFFECTS THE BRAIN

Yoga has a profound effect on the brain, with research evidence to show how and where. We can consider the effects in a general sense and more specifically as the effects of a particular practice such as breathing, postures, or meditation. First is a discussion of the general effects of yoga on the nervous system followed by a description of the specific effects.

Fostering Executive Control

People regulate their behavior and emotions using executive control. The brain areas involved in executive control include the prefrontal cortex and the anterior cingulate gyrus. Through executive functioning, emotional centers in the limbic system can be calmed and balanced.

Yoga practices increase the executive functions in the frontal lobe of the brain. According to one model (McCloskey, Hewitt, Henzel, & Eusebio, 2009), the executive functions consist of 23 executive function capabilities, including initiating, modulating, focusing, sustaining, stopping, inhibiting, holding, and balancing. Yoga meditation trains all of these skills through its practices.

From Deactivation to Activation

One dimension of yoga's effects on the brain may be characterized as *not doing*, which is a form of deactivation. For therapy, this process gives clients clear methods to help them stop engaging in negative patterns. As they do so, they lessen the strength of stress-producing pathways and problematic rewards (secondary gain). Clients acquire tools for objectivity to help them recognize that some of their beliefs may not be true. The techniques offer definitive ways to help them turn away from illusions. The not-doing phase opens the way for more positive possibilities and clearer thinking.

The other side of practice involves *doing*. At these phases, practitioners learn to deliberately and consciously direct attention and hold it voluntarily on an object they choose. They develop more tools to help differentiate between false and accurate perception, clearing the way to perceive the world as it really is. At this phase, healthy habits begin to be established, activating a learning process. New associative links form. The yoga practices of voluntary focus and self-control build the capacity to take charge over behavior and cognition and guide it toward healthier adjustment. By disengaging from unhealthy patterns and encouraging new patterns to form, yoga facilitates the therapeutic process of change and growth.

Integration

At the most advanced levels of practice, an open form of meditation is practiced, which engages both doing and not doing, getting the unconscious working in conjunction with the conscious processes of executive control. More of the brain becomes involved through the meditative practice known in neuroscience as brain coherence. At the highest meditative levels, more of the brain is activated, and new capacities become possible. The practitioner develops a highly attuned awareness that is present in every aspect of experiencing, a consciousness that can respond more flexibly, become more aware of the self and others, and approach life with openness to a spiritual dimension.

Yogis seek higher truth. Clients seek therapeutic truth. After therapeutic truth is found, clients will experience a realistic conception of themselves and their world. As a result, their responses will be in harmony with their embodied situation as it unfolds.

THE NEUROANATOMY OF YOGA

Yoga can be analyzed into its fundamental elements of practice: breathing, postures, mantras, and meditation. Western neuroscientists have studied each of these elements separately to offer theories and research that show how the brain is affected by these yoga practices. With the mounting evidence from neuroscience that the nervous system is an interactive network of emotions, cognition, and behaviors, we find that higher brain systems interact closely with lower brain functions when breathing, moving, and speaking. With such closely integrated sets of systems, clinical work can intervene at any of these levels. Yoga offers a method for all of the levels, with highly refined techniques for each. Therapists gain more options to help clients with some of their most challenging problems.

Breathing

Breathing is a combination of voluntary and involuntary processes. It involves a complex group of feedback mechanisms in the autonomic nervous system.

The brain stem, endocrine system, and cortex are involved. Pranayama elicits a decrease in oxygen consumption, heart rate, and blood pressure, while it increases parasympathetic activation combined with increased alertness and reinvigoration (R. Jerath, Edry, Bames, & Jerath, 2006).

Research shows that breathing is highly linked to the limbic system. This close interrelationship can be clearly recognized when feeling a strong emotion that is usually accompanied by an increase in breathing rate. The relationship goes both ways (Ley, 1999). For example, deliberately slowing down the breathing rate can calm an emotional reaction and return the autonomic nervous system to balance. One group of researchers proposed that slow, deep breathing could reset the autonomic nervous system by synchronizing neural elements in the heart, lungs, limbic system, and cortex (Jerath et al., 2006).

The vagus nerve is the tenth cranial nerve and has long been known to be involved in respiratory function. Hering and Breuer proposed the first theory of the vagus nerve's involvement in regulating breathing in 1868, which spurred a significant line of research (Steffensen, Brookhart, & Gesell, 1937). The vagus nerve originates in the medulla and extends down the neck, into the chest and abdomen, conveying sensory information to the brain about the state of the body's internal organs (viscera). Today we know that the vagus nerve has both sensory and motor attachments, with a complex neural network of connections and feedback mechanisms involved in breathing.

The polyvagal theory is a contemporary view that explains how breathing interrelates with emotions and cognition, and thus helps explain how breathing meditations found in yoga affect feelings and thoughts. According to the polyvagal theory, breathing is connected to our advanced cognitive and emotional capacities. Human beings have a large brain, resulting in a greater need for oxygen. Through evolution, human beings developed a more sophisticated nervous system for providing the amount of oxygen needed to sustain a large brain. Thus, our respiratory system prompted the development of advanced abilities for orienting, paying attention, and regulating emotions. The polyvagal theory views all emotions and interpersonal interactions as biobehavioral processes. In recognizing that the interaction between physiological and psychological processes goes both ways, psychotherapy can bring changes to the nervous system just as much as the nervous system can influence emotions, thoughts, and even social interactions (Porges, 2009).

Yoga breathing methods provide many powerful interventions for deliberately rebalancing an out-of-balance autonomic nervous system aggravated by mental or physical problems (Brown & Gerberg, 2005). Yoga includes varieties of breathing techniques, each with its own unique effect on the autonomic nervous system. One example of how this works is slow-paced breathing, which involves taking slower or longer breaths and increasing the length of time between breathing in and breathing out. This form of pranayama breathing increases inhibition in the lungs, activating the parasympathetic actions that bring about relaxation, lowered blood pressure, and slower heart rate (Pramanik et al., 2009). In addition, these parasympathetic calming responses synchronize the hypothalamus with the brain stem (Newberg & Iverson, 2003). Pranayama methods can be incorporated into treatment to deliberately foster an effect that is needed. People will appreciate having tools they can use to help themselves cope better and foster their own changes.

Postures: Standing, Sitting, and Lying Prone

We move through life in many postures, but they can be reduced to three basic body positions: standing, sitting, and lying prone. These positions combined with walking have been called the four dignities of man (Brooks, 1982). These dignities, and our ability to flow from one to the next, are our birthright, setting us apart from other creatures.

Much of the nervous system is involved in making coordinated, balanced movements, including the motor cortex, the basal ganglia, the cerebellum, the brain stem, and the spinal cord. To begin performing a movement, such as going into a yoga posture, the brain receives information about the current body position from the nerve cells in the extremities. Then the brain guides coordinated motion into the posture by sending messages to flex or extend, down through the spinal cord and out to the nerves in the muscles. Yoga postures can have a profound influence on experiencing by engaging so many different areas working together.

Different brain patterns emerge for varied body postures. Standing upright with feet together activates the anterior lobe and the vermis of the cerebellum, as well as the right side of the visual cortex in the occipital lobe. We would expect the cerebellum to be involved, because it is important for maintaining balance in an upright posture. If we shift weight to one foot, blood flow increases to the cerebellum on the opposite side to the weight-bearing leg. If we close our eyes while standing on both feet, the prefrontal cortex is activated (Ouchi, Okada, Yoshikawa, Nobezawa, & Futatsubashi, 1999).

Blood flow, measured by PET (positron emission tomography) scans, finds elevated rCBF (regional cerebral blood flow) in the cerebellum when standing as compared to sitting or lying down. The rCBF is lower in the frontal and parietal lobes when a person is sitting and standing more than when lying prone. All the data combined shows that the vermis area of the cerebellum is more active when a person is standing versus sitting or lying prone (Raz et al., 2005).

The neuroscience that distinguishes each position is often overlooked (Raz et al., 2005). Most fMRI (functional magnetic resonance imaging) machines take readings from people who are lying prone. EEG is usually done sitting upright. Evidence seems to point out that ERP (event-related potential) readings from EEG vary depending on whether subjects are sitting upright or lying down (Raz et al., 2000).

Yoga is performed in all three of these primary body positions, thereby taking advantage of the varied patterns of activations afforded by each position. Perhaps through the difference from one posture to another, client's responses become more flexible and varied, with new options opening to them.

Mantras

Mantras have been used as part of yoga meditation for thousands of years to stabilize mental processing, clear the mind, and raise consciousness. Mantras are words that are spoken (chanted), listened to, viewed as a written word, or just thought about. Recent neuroscience research shows different effects on the brain depending on whether words are heard, seen, spoken, or thought about, confirming their differential use.

PET scans of subjects engaged in chanting showed an increase in blood flow to areas of the left hemisphere involved in language processing. Hearing a mantra increased the blood flow to the auditory cortex in the temporal lobe near the junction with the parietal lobe. Silently reading a mantra showed more blood flow to the visual cortex in the occipital lobe and the association area for visual memory. Chanting a mantra sent more blood flow to the areas of the motor cortex associated with moving the mouth, as well as Broca's area for speech. When the mantra was just thought about, the limbic association areas were activated (Restak & Gruben, 2001). Mantra practice typically involves listening, speaking, reading, and thinking about the mantra, thereby engaging more of the brain to have a stronger mind-brain-body effect.

Conscious and Unconscious Attention

One of the most important tools of yoga is meditation, and the key component is attention. Typically, people have varying skills with their attention. The development of skill in its use is usually addressed only indirectly, such as paying attention in school or playing in sports. Yoga meditation trains the ability to be fully attentive and absorbed in several distinct ways. Direct, voluntary control of attention is achieved through the practices of breathing (pranayama), postures (asanas), withdrawing attention (pratyahara), and directing attention (dharana). In all of these practices, attention is focused on a chosen object, and the practitioner becomes deeply immersed or absorbed in the experience. As skills improve, a second level of attentional absorption is achieved, practiced in the open-ended form of meditation known as dhyana, which allows a free flow of attention in the present moment. Dhyana engages unconscious processes and tends to be spontaneous. In the unity of yoga practice, open, effortless meditation can occur in conjunction with focused attention, as for example, in an aware, effortless breathing. The ultimate goal in yoga is to deliberately direct processes until optimal, healthy functioning becomes effortless, the state of Samadhi.

Meditation researchers Lutz, Slagter, Dunne, and Davidson (2008) have investigated the distinction between these two general forms of meditation: voluntary focusing of attention on a chosen object and open-ended, attentive moment-by-moment awareness. They found different groups of brain areas are involved in each.

Brain Areas Involved in Focused Attention

Several distinct brain areas help coordinate selecting an object and focusing on it. Selective attention activates the temporoparietal junction, the ventrolateral prefrontal cortex, the frontal eye fields, and the intraparietal sulcus. Sustaining attention involves the right frontal and parietal areas and the thalamus.

The thalamus is the gateway to the senses, and researchers have found that a certain area of the thalamus, the lateral geniculate nucleus (LGN), helps direct attention to a relevant area in the visual field (Dantzker, 2006).

Another feature of focused attention, meta-attention, directs attention to the process of attention itself. Meta-attention is developed during meditation. During focused meditation, the meditator learns to notice when attention drifts away or turns to focus on something else. Some researchers call this aspect, *attention monitoring,* or *conflict monitoring* (Lutz, Slagter, Dunne, & Davidson, 2008). Attention monitoring is that aspect of the process that notices that the meditator is not paying attention, and when attention is found to be wandering, it is brought back to the object of focus. Unique brain areas become involved. The dorsal anterior cingulate cortex is activated during error detection and decision-making. The dorsolateral prefrontal cortex is activated in planning, organization, and regulation of thought with action.

Brain Areas Involved in Open Meditation

Focused attention uses a number of specific brain areas, but open meditation engages more of the brain. Open meditation, being unfocused and undifferentiated, is not processed top down or mediated by deliberate, higher level cortical activity. Instead, the brain goes through a series of more generalized brain states, where each state becomes the source for the next one, integrating together for regulating the meditative experience. This kind of open-ended attention can be measured using EEG. Experienced meditators evoke a measurable high-amplitude pattern of gamma synchrony, a dynamic and global reaction across the whole brain (Lutz et al., 2008). These highly synchronized brain states can be promising for promoting neuroplasticity and the ability to have new learning, especially for highly ordered cognitive and affective functions, because of the integrative and widely distributed neural processes that get involved.

The open form of meditation involves no particular attentional focus, and so it engages different brain areas from those activated by narrowed focus. Open meditation is correlated with greater activity in the right frontal lobe, an area that is typically associated with monitoring, vigilance, and disengaging attention from distractions. Open meditation also engages monitoring of ongoing body experiences such as perception of temperature and pain, processed by the anterior insula, the somatosensory cortex, and the anterior cingulate cortices.

This form of meditation reduces the need for voluntary attentional effort or control, while remaining focused and concentrated. Psychological tests showed meditators who had expertise in open forms of meditation could detect stimuli quickly with a more economical use of attentional resources than control subjects (Slagter, 2007). This has led researchers to characterize open meditation as a dynamical global state that is activated moment by moment rather than a top-down control as in focused attention forms of meditation (Lutz et al., 2008).

FROM MIND TO BRAIN: NEUROPLASTICITY AND NEUROGENESIS

Yoga influences the mind-brain-body system in many ways through the practice of techniques for thinking, breathing, body positioning, and meditation. All of these methods influence the brain, as has been described. Neuroplasticity is the brain's ability to undergo a change in the connections between synapses; neurogenesis is the growth of new neurons that takes place mostly during development, but can occur to some extent through out life. We can enhance or retard neuroplasticity and neurogenesis at any point by what we do and how we do it. Yoga techniques facilitate the potential for the brain to undergo real change from the level of neurons to structures and functions.

Neuroplasticity Occurs at the Synapse

Research on the neuron's ability to modulate the strength and structure of their synaptic connections in response to certain types of experience is often done at the neuronal level. Plasticity involves local synthesis of proteins at the synapses. The cells, in a sense, think globally but act locally (Shen, 2003). This means that the signal can be generated at the synapse and then travel to the nucleus. Once in the nucleus, the signal changes in gene expression. Then the signal travels back to the synapse with the new gene information to produce an enduring change in the strength of the synapse. Some of the mechanisms of synaptic plasticity involve synthesis of messenger RNA and proteins leading to growth of new synaptic connections (Martin, Bartsch,

Bailey, & Kandel, 2000). With plasticity occurring at the synapses, it becomes clearer why the possibilities for neuroplasticity and neurogenesis are much greater than had been previously believed (Martin & Zukin, 2006).

Neuroplasticity and Neurogenesis Occur at Any Age

The brains of laboratory animals were injected with a radioactive marker to observe neuroplasticity and neurogenesis at the neuronal level. But researchers could certainly not inject a human being's brain with a radioactive marker to find out if humans have neuroplasticity and neurogenesis. A marker, the molecule BrdU, was already being used with oncology patients to track the new growth of cancer cells. Since any cell that undergoes cell division incorporates the BrdU molecule, neurogenesis would be marked wherever it occurred. Terminal patients whose tumors were being monitored with the BrdU molecule agreed to donate their fresh brain tissue for observation upon their death. The patients in the study ranged in age from their late 50s to 70s. The brains of these patients did show measurable neurogenesis and neuroplasticity in the hippocampus. This research supports the idea that the human brain undergoes neurogenesis, which continues through old age (Gage, Eriksson, Perfilieva, & Bjork-Eriksson, 1998).

How Neuroplasticity and Neurogenesis Occur

Once it was understood that plasticity takes place at any age, researchers wanted to find out what brings it about. Researchers have measured a number of conditions that stimulate neuroplasticity and neurogenesis.

Enriched Environments

Enriched environments can influence the developing brain in positive ways. When rats are given a more enriched environment, shared with other rats along with ladders to climb on and wheels to spin, their cortices became thicker than rats living in simple cages with nothing extra. These differences are reflected in behavior as well. The rats from enriched environments perform better than deprived rats in learning tasks such as mazes. The synaptic connections become denser and the dendrite branching more complex. Furthermore, when animals are taken from the impoverished environment and placed into the richer one, they undergo a surge in neurogenesis, especially in the dentate gyrus area of the hippocampus involved in learning and memory (Briones, Klintsova, & Greenough, 2004; Greenough, Black, & Wallace, 1987).

Based in Greenough's animal research on the thickening of the cortex from enriched environments during early development, researchers tested the effects of an enriched environment on adult mice. They placed adult mice raised in the typical impoverished laboratory environment into an enriched environment for 45 days. Following this relatively brief period, the number of neurons in the hippocampus of these mice was far greater than the matched mice that remained in the typical laboratory cage (Kuhn, Dickinson-Anson, & Gage, 1996). Even an adult brain undergoes neurogenesis when given the right environmental stimuli.

Physical Activity

Physical activity stimulated neurogenesis, but better results on learning tests depended on physical activity *combined* with volition rather than just the physical activity alone (Begley, 2007). Mice who engaged in voluntary running on their exercise wheels showed more intelligent behavior and better learning ability than those who were forced to exercise in a tank of water, the water maze.

Remapping of the Sensory Cortex From Deficits

Another way that plasticity has been explored is by observing what happens when something goes wrong. Remapping occurs in the sensory systems of people who are born deaf. They do not lose all functioning in their auditory cortex as one might expect, nor does the auditory cortex become dormant. Instead, the brain remaps the auditory areas for more complex visual capabilities, putting the unused region to work (Bavelier et al., 2000).

Phantom limb pain is another example of cortical remapping. Amputees often experience a mysterious pain sensation in the amputated limb long after it has been removed. One researcher suggests that the reason these individuals continue to feel sensation is due to the neuroplasticity in the adult human brain (Ramachandran, Blakeslee, & Sacks, 1999). The brain represents the body on the somatosensory strip located in the parietal lobes. Input from the hand is mapped onto the brain next to input from the arm, next to input from the face. Following the amputation, patients experienced sensations in their phantom limb when their faces were stimulated by gently stroking with a forefinger. The brain had remapped the areas from the missing arm and hand onto the closest brain region, that representing the face (Ramachandran, Rogers-Ramachandran, & Stewart, 1992).

A group of researchers (Jenkins, Merzenich, Ochs, Allard, & Guic-Roble, 1990) gave monkeys a new sensory experience to see if that would alter the brain areas associated with that new experience. They positioned a 4-inch grooved disk near the cage and trained the monkeys to reach out to touch the disk as it spun. The animals learned that if they applied just the right amount of pressure, the disk would spin and they would be rewarded with a banana pellet. Comparing pre and post maps of the cortex, researchers found that the map had changed: the areas receiving signals from the fingers were 4 times larger. This was evidence that behavior could bring about a significant, measurable change in the brain's structure (Allard, Clark, & Merzenich, 1987; Merzenich et al., 1987).

Another technique, known as deafferentation, disconnected a nerve in part of the body of adult monkeys, such as the middle finger. At first, the researchers expected that once the nerve was cut, the corresponding cortex area would shut down. But in fact, they found that the cortical area devoted to the third finger did not stop functioning. Instead, the second and fourth fingers moved into the cortical area that had previously been used to respond to finger three. They also found that after extensive long-term deafferentations in adult primates, the cortical maps changed far more than was expected (Pons et al., 1991). The results of many types of experiments such as these, with small deafferentations in fingers and large ones with arms, showed that cortical plasticity was pervasive and over large areas.

Based on the work done with deafferentation of animals and the significant plasticity in affected brain areas, researchers have developed methods for working with stroke patients suffering from paralysis in one arm using Constraint Therapy (CT). The stroke patients who participated in the study were 54 to 76 years old. Their treatment involved constraining the "good" arm for 3 hours daily for 10 consecutive days, thereby forcing use of the afflicted arm. They combined this with a "transfer package" lasting 30 minutes each day to help the subjects transfer their gains to their daily activities. The study showed that not only did the patients improve the ability to use the impaired arm, but they also had measurable increase in gray matter in their sensory and motor areas (both primary and secondary cortices) for the affected arm as well as increases in both the right and left hippocampus (Gauthier et al., 2008).

Ways to Enhance Neuroplasticity and Neurogenesis

Thoughts, emotions, and behavior can influence neuroplasticity and neurogenesis. Ernest Rossi has been a strong spokesperson for the use of novelty and creativity in psychotherapy to stimulate neuroplasticity through neurogenesis at the level of gene expression. Genes do not exist alone; they are in a dynamic, nonlinear relationship with the environmental inputs and the larger brain functions. The genes actively respond to inputs from life experience. These changes can be immediate, moment-to-moment, occurring over hours to days, or they can take effect more slowly. According to Rossi, "conscious experience of novelty, environmental enrichment and voluntary physical exercise can modulate gene expressions to encode new learning and memory" (Rossi, 2002, p. 12). The processes of neuroplasticity and neurogenesis can be facilitated in therapy to overcome problems and create new potentials.

From all of these studies, it becomes clear that what we do has a strong influence on the brain. Yoga techniques add another dimension to treatment. In general, yoga provides a source for enrichment and novelty. Many forms of yoga practice may be new to clients. Drawn from a rich tradition, yoga broadens and sensitizes clients to enriching experiences. Yoga techniques present novelty and enrichment to clients while also helping them to notice the world around them more deeply and fully. Thus, in many ways, these practices can foster neurogenesis and neuroplasticity, making new learning more likely to occur.

Specifically, yoga methods help to rebalance the autonomic nervous system, a key ingredient of managing stress and emotional arousal. The development of attention can enhance cognitive processing and thereby assist in developing a more reality-based adjustment.

Memory and Learning

Learning and memory are other important aspects of yoga training. Yoga introduces new techniques to learn and routines to commit to memory through both conscious and unconscious processes. Stimulation of the nervous system through learning and memory brings profound changes to the mind and brain at many levels. Yoga enhances these processes, and later chapters will show how to bring it about during therapy.

Learning is one of the means for fostering neuroplasticity and neurogenesis in the brain's systems, and memory is how the learning is made more permanent. The brain can alter at any point in life, and so we can be optimistic about fostering growth and learning at any phase of life with clients. Neuroplasticity and neurogenesis involve the processes of learning and memory, because these processes create something new. Learning and memory have been studied in the brain, from the level of fundamental synaptic connections between neurons to the level of brain structures and systems.

Neuronal Level of Learning and Memory

Memory processing begins at the synapse with long-term potentiation (LTP). This memory processing at the synapse is based on (a) specificity, (b) cooperation, and (c) association. First, LTP tends to be specific to those synapses that have become highly active. Only these synaptic connections become strengthened. Second, axons that are located close together tend to work together cooperatively to bring about an even stronger LTP effect than would occur from one axon alone. Third, when a weak input is paired with a strong one, the weaker response is enhanced. Thus, memory can be enhanced all the way down to the neuronal level by specifically targeting certain skills to improve brain performance. Because neuroplasticity can occur at any age, even elderly clients may experience improvements in memory.

Structural Level of Learning and Memory

Neuroscientists have studied how learning takes place in the different brain structures. A conditioned link is made in the amygdala. The conditioned stimulus (CS) comes in through the thalamus and then goes directly to the amygdala, where it gets stored, as does the unconditioned stimulus (US). After pairing of the US and CS, cells are triggered to respond to the CS from the amygdala. Thus, the conditioned response (CR) is the result of a learning process that depends on the amygdala. Evidence suggests that synaptic plasticity within the lateral nucleus of the amygdala is responsible for storing memories of the CS-US association (Medina et al., 2002).

Systems Level of Learning and Memory: Conscious and Unconscious

Learning and memory are generally considered two separate but interacting systems, each with its own neural counterparts. One system is conscious, declarative, and semantic; the other is unconscious, nondeclarative, and implicit. These systems have their own unique logic: conscious recall for declarative and unconscious performance for nondeclarative. Differences between these two systems are found in terms of the cognitive tasks and brain areas involved Figure 2.1.

The senses take in a great deal of information, but consciousness is limited, only registering a few bits of information at a time in short-term

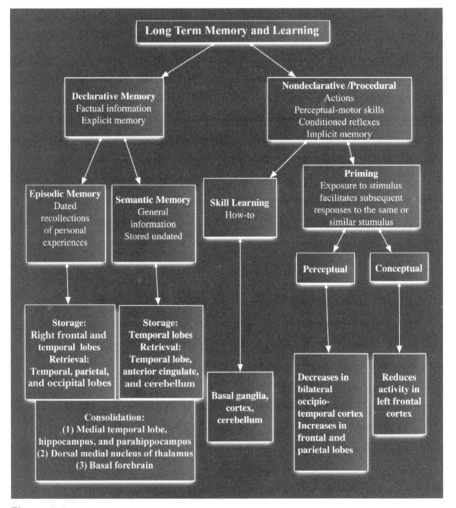

Figure 2.1

memory. Anything beyond 7 plus or minus 2 bits of information goes unnoticed consciously, but research shows that it is registered unconsciously. The unconscious continually absorbs much more information than consciousness perceives at any given moment, even from only a single presentation of an item. Although this unattended information remains outside of conscious awareness, it can influence our behavior, thoughts, learning, and emotions.

Researchers devised a way to test how unattended information is processed. This process is called priming. Priming research has shown us how stimuli that are not consciously attended to can enhance learning from unconscious processing (Mitchell, 2006; Squire & Kandel, 2000). Implicit memory is affected by priming. After having a recent experience with a primed stimulus, people show improved speed, accuracy, or efficiency in their ability to identify words or objects. We tend to respond more rapidly and fully to previously experienced stimuli than to completely new experiences. Dhyana meditation opens perception to receive and process information unconsciously.

Declarative Memory

Declarative memory is responsible for encoding, consolidating, and retrieving episodic and semantic memories. Encoding requires attention, and so it can be improved by attention meditations. Encoding of episodic memories tends to involve specific areas of the dorsolateral area of the prefrontal cortex in one of the hemispheres: Verbal episodic memory occurs on the left side. Nonverbal episodic memory involves the right side (Cabeza & Nyberg, 2000).

Consolidation of declarative memories involves three main areas (Zillmer, Spiers, & Culbertson, 2008). The hippocampus, the parahippocampus, and the medial temporal lobes consolidate declarative information and then send it to long-term memory for storage. Memory consolidation also engages a section of the thalamus, the dorsal medial nucleus. The basal forebrain, basal ganglia, nucleus accumbens, and amygdala are also involved in long-term memory consolidation. The basal forebrain structures actively output the neurotransmitter acetylcholine to the cortex, a process that is important for making memory structures function properly. The basal forebrain area also has strong links to the limbic system. Thus, the important link between memory and emotion is reflected in the brain systems involved.

Retrieval involves more brain areas. For episodic memories, the temporal, parietal, and occipital lobes are activated, as well as the cerebellum. Retrieval for semantic memory also involves large portions of the brain, including the temporal lobe, anterior cingulate, and cerebellum.

Nondeclarative Memory and Learning

There are three main types of nondeclarative memory and learning. Each type does different things, but all share the common feature of not being monitored consciously. Procedural knowledge is how to perform a yoga posture or a breathing exercise. Implicit knowledge comes from experience without being consciously aware of it, such as performing a long-practiced yoga routine without having to think about it. Habits may begin with deliberate learning but in time become unconscious. The nondeclarative areas involve the cerebellum and basal ganglia, both part of subcortical motor processing. Habit learning is processed by the caudate nucleus, located deep inside the brain and part of the basal ganglia.

Emotions have a strong influence on learning and memory. Just having an emotional response can increase or decrease the strength of learning. Evaluations of inputs, whether we like or dislike something, or whether an input is associated with a traumatic or uncomfortable past experience, will have a profound effect on how we learn and remember. Emotional learning is highly linked to the amygdala, and the response is often unconscious (Williams et al., 2005). Psychotherapy can draw on these emotional factors to facilitate therapeutic learning.

Evidence for the Distinctions Between Declarative and Nondeclarative Systems

Patients with severe long-term amnesias in the declarative systems can still improve on various kinds of nondeclarative learning tasks. Herbert Gustav Molafson (1926–2008), known as H. M., had lost his ability to acquire any new conscious learning or memories following surgery for epilepsy, but he did improve his skills on a procedural mirror-tracing task, offering evidence for unconscious learning and memory systems being separate from conscious ones (Schoville & Milner, 1957).

Comparative research with mice showed that different brain areas are involved in declarative and habit learning (Bear, Connors, & Paradiso, 1996).

In the declarative learning situation, finding food involved remembering where it had been located the day before. Memory was disrupted by damage to the hippocampus, showing that the hippocampus is involved in declarative learning and memory. To test habit learning, the food was located in the same place in the maze and never changed. Damage to the hippocampus made no difference in how well the mice found the food. However, damage to the caudate nucleus disrupted their ability to find the food even though they had learned where it was located. Thus, there are two distinct locations in the brain for the two different types of learning: habitual activities that we do the same way over and over and declarative learning that occurs as we learn and remember new information.

CONCLUSION

Many areas of the brain are activated when we breathe, go into a posture, and focus attention during yoga. Because so many areas and different patterns of brain activity are involved in yoga meditation, it has great potential to alter how people think and feel. Then problems can be approached from many possible directions and levels, offering a broad range of potential for therapy. Look to Part III for specific applications for using yoga to foster healthy mind-brain change.

PART II

WHAT IS YOGA?

3

Traditions

The powers of the mind are like rays of light dissipated; when they are concentrated they illuminate.

(*Vivekananda, 1953, p. 581*)

Yoga is the inner thread that runs through many great ancient traditions. As a practice that yokes or joins, yoga tended to integrate with other disciplines and be adapted to other contexts, melding with many philosophies and systems. Hinduism and Buddhism contain elements of yoga at their heart. Many great yogis taught that truth and wisdom could be found in a variety of viewpoints. What yoga offers is a set of methods to help people in finding those truths. As a result, the various paths were combined with yoga as a means of gaining higher consciousness. Originally, through Hinduism and Buddhism, and now as a discipline of its own, yoga reaches out to guide us today.

Dating back before recorded history, yoga was practiced as a method of mental and physical discipline. Focused concentration, deliberate placement of body positioning, and breath control were the doorways to higher consciousness. These practices are ageless and timeless, not limited by just one set of philosophical concepts. What makes yoga unique and enduring is that it is not only a philosophy but also a practical system. The result is that through the practice of yoga, people benefit, gaining health, self-discipline, and raised consciousness.

Several kinds of Hindu yoga developed in India. Certain sects of Buddhism also merged with yoga (e.g., Yogacara and Tibetan Buddhism). The Far East, Middle East, and Indonesia also received and developed yoga practices. Even Christianity has yoga-like rituals, such as the meditation on the Stations of the Cross. In being so adaptable, yoga can now be brought into psychotherapy, to help people develop the tools they need to succeed in the process.

TRACING YOGA'S ROOTS IN ANCIENT TEXTS

The practices of yoga are ancient. The first teachers of yoga did not communicate their techniques through writing. Instead, as gurus, they taught students directly. The tradition was passed along, teacher to student, until it was gradually recorded in texts. The ideas expressed in the ancient texts are likely to have evolved before recorded history. The guru tradition also continued through history, with masters who transmit yoga directly to their students, and some of the contemporary gurus are covered later in this chapter.

The Vedas

Yoga's root themes were first vaguely expressed in ancient texts. Gradually over time, references became clearer. The first definite references to yoga are found in the four Vedas (Rig, Yajur, Sama, and Atharva), ancient Hindu texts. The Vedas are among the earliest surviving writings of Indian thought, believed to be composed around 1200 BCE. However, they are considered wisdom that was heard, and so they may draw from older ideas. The word *veda* means knowledge. The Vedas address knowledge of God and serve as an important record of early spiritual traditions and rituals. Important yoga themes of sacrifice, discipline, and praise for virtue and beauty as personified in nature are also found in these pages.

The Rig Veda is the oldest of the four Vedas, and expresses spiritual knowledge in 1,028 lyrical hymns. It includes hymns that offer praise for the gods and their powers. The text reveals that these ancient people believed that health, wealth, and long life could be theirs through ritual fire sacrifices. Sama Veda rearranged the hymns for practitioners to sing mantras during rituals. Yajur Veda includes instructions for priests to guide in creating altars, preparing for prayers, and performing rituals and sacrifices. The Atharva Veda, the more recent veda (900 BCE), offers a variety of subjects, including magical spells and charms.

The Upanishads

Yoga was more explicitly referred to in the Upanishads, written between 800 and 600 BCE. The name means those who sat down near their teachers (*up*, near; *ni*, down; *shad*, sit), and these texts opened knowledge up to those who were willing to study with a teacher. The Upanishads is the first known Indian text to include philosophical wisdom. This book, directed to the priests, the Brahmins, goes further than simply presenting instructions for rituals. It also includes stories that explain the rationale for the rituals and the central concept of Brahman as the sacred power.

Four famous phrases have survived and are often quoted, known as the four Mahavakyas: Aham Brahasmi, *I am Brahman*; Ayamaatma Brahma, *The Self is Brahman*; Tatvamasi, *That Thou Art*; and Pryagnanam Brahma, *Consciousness is Brahman*. These four phrases concern the self, expressing the direct relationship of the self to God and the identity of God with knowledge: "The higher is at the same time the inner and yet the more inclusive" (Raju, 1948, p. 407). This key philosophical idea continues to be important today and is especially useful for clients who have lost touch with their deeper self (see Chapter 12). The Upanishads teach that through our consciousness, we can come to have knowledge of the true self, which leads to God. The doctrine should not be taken to mean that we are all that God is, giving us the personal power and direct identity of God. What it does tell us is that we do not have to turn outward to find God, The answer lies within, but beyond the individual self of the everyday world. We are all part of something greater.

The Bhagavad Gita

The most well-known, early systematic description of yoga is the Bhagavad Gita, *Song of the Lord*, the sixth book of the large Indian epic, the Mahabharata. The author of this epic is in question, but the mystic figure Veda Vyasa is traditionally considered to have written it. The Mahabharata is written as a poem, telling the story of a war between members of the house of Bharata. Although its exact date is unknown, the Bhagavad Gita was probably composed between the fifth and second centuries BCE and is written as a dialogue between a warrior, Arjuna, and his charioteer, the god Krishna. Arjuna is reluctant to enter into a battle that would require him to fight against his relatives. Krishna lays out yoga philosophy and the different branches of yoga as he guides Arjuna to engage in his role as soldier with devotion to God. Though the context of the Bhagavad Gita was a warrior one, yoga actually relates to all aspects of life. The teachings show how people can use yoga discipline to mold the clay of their lives and circumstances to become what they want to be.

The Vedanta

Yoga philosophy also draws from the Vedanta, the later literature of India. The Vedanta texts concern self-realization to gain understanding of reality, Brahman. Brahman is described as an intelligent principle that is the cause of the universe. We can transcend the confines of the individual self, from practices of the body, breathing, and meditation, to gain ultimate wisdom by merging with the greater cosmic consciousness, Brahmin. These texts offer persuasive arguments along with expressive metaphors that explain the philosophy and inspire devotion to higher values.

Patanjali's Yoga Sutras

Patanjali was the first to formally gather the practices of yoga into an ordered, consistent system in his famous *Yoga Sutras*. Patanjali's *Yoga Sutras* were probably written sometime between the second century BCE and the fourth century CE, most commonly thought to be around the third century CE. Some scholars believe that a professor of grammar and linguistics, also named Patanjali, wrote the sutras much later, but most scholars do not generally concede this claim. Although there may be some uncertainty about the identity and date of the author Patanjali, the centrality of the doctrine of the *Yoga Sutras* to yoga philosophy is not disputed. In a sense, Patanjali is the personification of the source of these writings, which gather and outline this ancient doctrine.

The passages of each sutra are quite brief. This is because the sutras were part of oral tradition, and thus were to be committed to memory by the student. Beginning soon after the sutras were put in writing, many complex commentaries both ancient and modern have been added, to fill out the terseness of the descriptive statements written by Patanjali.

The earliest commentary, known as the *Yoga Bhashya*, on the *Yoga Sutras* was composed by Veda Vyasa in the fifth century and provides a clear explanation of each limb in the system. Authoritative interpretations by the founders of the modern lineages of yoga help put the writings into perspective. For example, Krishnamacharya, the founder of many modern yoga schools, and his student, B. K. S. Iyengar, wrote books about the *Yoga Sutras*. And the contemporary luminary of philosophy, Barbara Stoller Miller (1940–1993), thought so highly of its importance that she worked on its explanation in a book up to the last moments of her life from her hospital bed. More continues to be written about the sutras, a deep wellspring of concepts and principles for living well. The *Yoga Sutras* allow for interpretation and use in many contexts. Though the background of the *Yoga Sutras* was Indian thought, the concepts can be adapted easily to many more frames of reference. And these concepts can be applied in psychotherapy.

After Patanjali's *Yoga Sutras*, in a direct transmission from guru to student and down a line of succession, the teaching continued. The first important written work to depict the postures used in Hatha yoga is known as the *Hatha Yoga Pradipika*. This book described the practices, including drawings of postures, but because it was not translated, the knowledge remained obscure, behind closed doors. Other texts followed, but most remained only in Indian languages. Today, many of the great Indian texts are translated into other languages, opening the way for anyone who is interested in delving deeper into the philosophical roots.

DIFFERENT FORMS OF YOGA

In the description of Reality as Satchidananda, *we posit three entities and unite them to arrive at a trinity. We say, "existence, consciousness, bliss," and then we say, "They are one."*

(Aurobindo in Chaudhuri & Spiegelberg, 1960, p. 300)

The many forms of yoga are distinguished by their philosophy and practices. But in the sense that Aurobindo reminds us of, these many forms of yoga are one when they become expressed in the mind and body of the practitioner who masters the skills. Some of the most commonly practiced forms of yoga are Hatha yoga, Raja yoga, Jnana yoga, Mantra yoga, Karma yoga, Bhakti yoga, Tantra yoga, and Kundalini yoga. Each yoga discipline was originally thought of as a separate way to follow, but today they tend to overlap in practice. Each type of yoga helps to concentrate attention toward a particular point of focus, bringing about self-discipline and leading to a state of Samadhi, enlightenment. All of these yoga practices have therapeutic applications and will be referred to in this book.

Hatha Yoga

Hatha yoga is best known to the West. As the yoga of health, Hatha yoga includes different types of postures, breathing methods, and meditation to enhance vitality and well-being. Most of the yoga schools that people attend in the West are offering some style of Hatha yoga. Today Hatha yoga often includes other forms in its practice, such as Raja yoga.

Raja Yoga

Raja yoga specializes in the development of the mind, consciousness, and character. The Sanskrit word *raja* means "royal." Rather than seeking wisdom through rational thought, Raja yoga practitioners use meditative methods and techniques of attention, concentration, and contemplation for discipline, control, and direction of the mind. Raja yoga includes many methods of meditation and concentration that lead to higher consciousness and enlightenment.

Jnana Yoga

Jnana yoga is the yoga of wisdom. The Sanskrit word *jnana* means "knowledge." Followers of this path contemplate, using conceptual, rational thought to turn the mind toward higher consciousness. With the use of meditation and reason, practitioners can recognize illusory thinking, set it aside, and get back to the roots to discover truth. Through this process, worries, fears, and doubts can be set aside. Thus, Jnana meditation methods are helpful as part of a therapeutic process. A renowned exemplar of Jnana yoga is J. Krishnamurti.

Mantra Yoga

Mantra yoga, the yoga of sound, uses repetitions of sounds, syllables, and phrases to bring about changes in consciousness. The root words combined from Sanskrit are *manas*, meaning "mind," and *tra*, meaning "tool." A well-known example of this is Transcendental Meditation (TM), founded by Maharishi Mahesh Yogi. TM trains students to meditate with their own personal, specially chosen mantra to bring about evolution toward enlightened consciousness. The use of mantras has been researched and can be helpful in giving attention an accessible point of focus for calming disturbances.

Karma Yoga

Karma yoga applies yoga to work and everyday life for achieving enlightened living and higher goals. The Sanskrit word *karma* means "to do." Karma refers to actions, fate, and destiny. This form of yoga is applicable for active people committed to occupations and families who would like to integrate yoga with their actual lifestyle. Karma yoga teaches how to maintain focus during action, even when circumstances are challenging. "The calmer we are and the less disturbed our nerves, the more shall we love and the better will our work be" (Vivekananda, 1953, p. 486).

Bhakti Yoga

Bhakti yoga of devotion and selfless love for a higher power is a philosophical method for finding enlightenment by living life devoted to higher values of compassion and charitable actions. The Sanskrit term *bhakti* means "devotion." Immersion in work devoted to others leads to focus away from the personal self and opening a connection to the deeper true self. Bhakti yoga may be expressed through committed relationship to others through a sincere charitable organization.

Tantra Yoga

Tantra yoga merges action with symbolism. The Sanskrit word *tantra* means "continuation, weaving together." Tantra techniques are ancient, and some form is found in many ancient cultures and traditions. Techniques that developed in India were also used as part of Hinduism. Around the seventh century, tantra was combined with Buddhism, most notably and highly developed as vajrayana, an important part of Tibetan Buddhism. Tantra includes many sets of techniques, usually action-oriented, to weave together mind and body. Tantra yoga seeks enlightenment through symbolic experiences, which may include sensual and emotional ones in relationship with a partner. During tantric rituals, couples learn to merge the other with the divine as they practice, and thereby link with the greater universe.

Yantra yoga is a method that is often combined with Tantric ritual. The Sanskrit word *yantra* is a combination of *yam*, meaning "sustain" or "hold," and *tra*, or "tool." Yantras are a type of mandala created with geometric patterns of symmetry. The patterns have sacred significance and are used as a focal point to help sustain or hold attention in meditation.

Kundalini Yoga

Kundalini yoga (Figure 3.1) is another tantric method that is being applied to psychotherapy today (Shannahoff-Khalsa, 2006). The Sanskrit word *kundalin*, the root from which it is derived, means "coiled, spiral, or ring." This form of yoga concentrates on the mind-body-spirit system in terms of the flow of prana energy and uses pranayama breathing methods to raise the energy through psychic centers located in the body.

Prana has three primary channels that the life-energy flows through: the first two are *ida* for the energy flowing in the left side of the body, and *pingala* for the energy in the right side of the body. Their Sanskrit root words relate to the terms for sun and moon. These energy pathways are often connected with the symbolic representation of many significant opposites, such as the two hemispheres of the brain. Thus ida, the left channel, is symbolically linked to the moon and the planet Mercury, with the corresponding meanings of coolness, white, the moon, quiet, and introverted. Pingala, the right channel, is linked to the sun and the planet Mars, with the corresponding meanings of warmth, golden-brown color, and extroverted.

Sushumna is the central channel for balanced energy that flows up the middle along the spinal chord. The Sanskrit word means "most gracious." Sushumna symbolizes the life-force and the universal light of higher consciousness. We access the energy within ida when we breathe through the

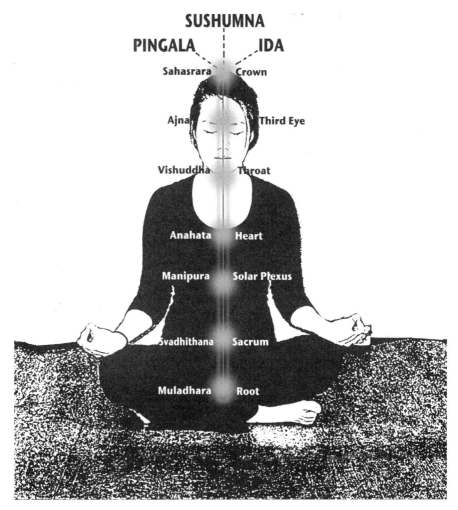

SUSHUMNA
PINGALA   IDA
Sahasrara   Crown
Ajna   Third Eye
Vishuddha   Throat
Anahata   Heart
Manipura   Solar Plexus
Svadhithana   Sacrum
Muladhara   Root

Figure 3.1

left nostril and pingala when breathing through the right. Breathing through both nostrils together, we access the balanced energy within sushumna. Thus, some of the breathing exercises in later chapters work with one nostril, then the other, or both together.

These three energy channels come together at seven different centers in the body, known as *chakras*, and are sometimes referred to as lotuses. The Sanskrit word *chakra* means "spinning wheel." Each chakra has a location in the body, a color, a number of lotus petals, and certain physical and psychological issues associated with it. Meditations are directed to a particular center of energy and moved up through the chain, to raise energy and connect with the universal principle of higher consciousness. Kundalini yoga refers to this process as raising the Kundalini energy, sometimes symbolized as a serpent, up from the bottom of the spine and out through the head.

Clients often find symbols a useful focal point to help evoke experiences that will enhance a direction, a tendency, or an adjustment goal that the client is working on. Chakras can be used as the symbols for focus. The seven chakras are as follows:

1. The *Muladhara chakra* (Figure 3.2) with four lotus petals is the root chakra, located at the base of the spine and associated with the color red. Often linked to sexuality, this chakra also symbolizes being stable, emotionally sensual, and spiritually secure.

2. *Svadhisthana chakra* (Figure 3.3) has six lotus petals and is found in the lower abdomen between the belly button and pelvic bone. It is orange and associated with relationships, emotions, creativity, and sexuality.

3. *Manipura chakra* (Figure 3.4) has 10 lotus petals and is positioned at the bottom of the rib cage. It is yellow in color, plays a role in digestion, and symbolizes self-esteem, energy, and personal empowerment.

Figure 3.2

Figure 3.3

Figure 3.4

Figure 3.5

4. *Anahata chakra* (Figure 3.5), the heart chakra with 12 lotus petals and found at the heart in the center of the chest, is green and symbolizes love, compassion, equilibrium, acceptance, and trust.

5. *Vishuddha chakra* (Figure 3.6) is the throat chakra with 16 lotus petals. It is located in the throat, with a light turquoise blue color, and symbolizes communication, expression, faith, and inspiration.

6. *Ajna chakra* (Figure 3.7) is situated above the bridge of the nose between the eyebrows, with two lotus petals, an indigo blue color, and symbolic issues of intelligence, intuition, and trusting inner wisdom.

7. The highest chakra, *Sahasrara chakra* (Figure 3.8), has 1,000 lotus petals, is located at the top of the head with a white or violet color, and is thought to be the chakra of pure consciousness. Here we find spiritual understanding and its expression in selflessness, devotion, and inspiration.

Figure 3.6

Figure 3.7

Figure 3.8

A chakra can also help to map a transition from one emphasis and concern in life to another, by contemplating and linking to the next chakra in sequence to incorporate its qualities. For example, chakras can be used to transition from a primitive overconcern with sensuality and sexuality in relationships to more mature emotions and creativity in relationships. This process can be symbolized as a journey from the Muladhara chakra to the Svadhisthana chakra. The chakras also include a mystical tradition with rich symbolism applied to complex healing rituals invoking the chakras as spiritual centers. Readers who are interested in delving deeper into the mystical elements of yoga spirituality will find a great deal of information, both ancient and modern, readily available.

INTRODUCTION TO THE WEST
THROUGH GREAT TEACHERS

Meditation was brought onto Western soil for the first time at the World Parliament of Religions. The conference was held in Chicago in 1893. It offered a forum for great leaders of religion, East and West, to meet and interact for the first time. Many great leaders from the East attended the conference, opening the first East–West dialogue.

Vivekananda: An Interface Between Science and Religion

The keynote speaker, Vivekananda (1863–1902) was a famous yogi who helped demystify the practices of the East and opened the way for Western scientific inquiry (Figure 3.9). Vivekananda thought that people become isolated in their own cultural traditions. It was his sincere belief that these ethnocentricities could be transcended. In one of his addresses at the Parliament, "Why We Disagree," he said, "I have to thank you America for the great attempt you are making to break down the barriers of this little world of ours, and I hope that in the future the Lord will help you to accomplish your purpose."

Figure 3.9

He was optimistic about scientific study of Eastern practices. In another paper read at the parliament, he said, "The Hindu is only glad that what he has been cherishing in his bosom for ages is going to be taught in more forcible language, and with further light, from the latest conclusions of science" (Vivekananda, 1953, p. 190). Following the Chicago parliament, Vivekananda made many appearances around the West. His teachings embodied a synthesis of science and religion, which did much to open the way for scientific inquiry into yoga and meditation.

Vivekananda spoke passionately of tolerance and acceptance of all religions. He encouraged people to embrace an experience of universal oneness, linking all nations, religions, and people together with love and compassion. His philosophy encompassed Karma, Bhakti, Raja, and Jnana yoga systems as applications of yoga for different types of people in various lifestyles. For example, he believed working people would be inspired by Karma yoga, while philosophically inclined intellectuals might prefer Jnana yoga. He wrote several books and lectured extensively, thoughtfully raising questions that are relevant to all humanity. Vivekananda devoted his life to guiding people toward higher truth: "I shall not cease to work. I shall inspire men everywhere, until the world shall know that it is one with God" (Vivekananda, 1953, p. 179).

Radhakrishnan: Think Deeply to Find Common Ground

Sarvepalli Radhakrishnan (1888–1975) was an accomplished scholar of both Eastern and Western traditions who built bridges between East and West (Figure 3.10). He was able to clearly express one in terms of the other, to make Eastern thought accessible to Westerners and vice versa. His volumes on Indian philosophy including Hinduism, Yoga, and Buddhism still speak to English-language readers, with their clear histories and accounts of the philosophical ideas, along with his own insightful analysis. His philosophical writings looked for interfaces between East and West. He wrote cogent commentaries on many of the most important Eastern classics, such as the Bhagavad Gita, the Upanishads, and the Brahma Sutra. He began his career as a university professor at the University of Calcutta and then became a professor of Eastern Religions and Ethics at Oxford University (1936–1939). Later, like Plato's ideal in the *Republic*, he became a philosopher-ruler, serving as the first vice president of India from

Figure 3.10

1952–1962 and then as president from 1962–1967. Radhakrishnan helped to open an intelligent dialogue between East and West, deeply influencing comparative philosophy.

J. Krishnamurti: Question Illusion to Find Truth

Jiddu Krishnamurti (1895–1986) was a Jnana yogi who became highly individualistic. He wrote influential books and spoke widely on college campuses, engaging many people in philosophical dialogues about seeking deeper truth and understanding (Figure 3.11). He masterfully showed how to question patterns of thinking that create illusory obstacles to enlightened experience and living. He pointed out a way to follow that involved sensitivity and awareness. He believed thinking and questioning deeply

Figure 3.11

leads beyond thought into deeper wisdom. This statement epitomizes his view:

> *No dynamic golden pill is ever going to solve our human problems. They can be solved only by bringing about a radical revolution in the mind and the heart of man. This demands hard, constant work, seeing and listening, and thus being highly sensitive.*

(Lutyens, 1970, p. 175)

Sri Aurobindo

Sri Aurobindo (1872–1950) was a Hindu who was raised and educated in England (Figure 3.12). His passion for India brought him back to his mother country where he involved himself at first in controversial political activity in support of Indian nationalism. But he changed, and his quest for nationalism became a purely spiritual one, instead. He spent his later years in an ashram that he founded, devoted to conceiving and expounding a deeply philosophical and integrative system of yoga. He believed that an evolutionary process leading to a pure consciousness-force exists, a supermind. Life, matter, and mind are all subordinate to supermind. "There is a double

Figure 3.12

movement at work in Reality, declares Sri Aurobindo—a descent and an ascent" (Chaudhuri & Spiegelberg, 1960, pp. 300–301).

Aurobindo inspired his followers to do more and to be more than they thought possible. A modern example is Sri Chimnoy, who challenged and broke many limits of strength and endurance. His feats are recorded in the *Guinness Book of World Records*. The famous architect and woodwork designer Nakashima, originally commissioned to build a structure at Aurobindo's ashram in India, ended up joining the community for two years (Nakashima, 1981), then finally returned to express his creative vision in wood. His organic style of woodworking expresses the unity of humanity with nature. As he said, "We woodworkers have the audacity to shape timber from those noble trees. In a sense, it is our Karma Yoga, the path of action we must take to lead to our union with the divine" (Nakashima, 1981, p. xxi). This sense of taking action in the world to find union with the highest potential is the path the client walks on the therapeutic journey. Aurobindo left a legacy through his many students and numerous books on philosophy and yoga of discovering one's personal unity through the course of life's endeavors.

Self-Realization Fellowship

Another early teacher of philosophical yoga was Paramahansa Yogananda (1893–1952), who came to Boston and founded the Self-Realization Fellowship in 1925 (Figure 3.13). His vision was one of spiritual unity, with God existing equally in the true self of all people. His system emphasized the religious application of yoga known as Kriya yoga. Some of the research projects cited in Chapter 1 used Kriya yoga techniques. Today the fellowship has its headquarters in Los Angeles, California. The founder of Bikram yoga, a popular form of yoga practiced widely today, is Bikram Choudhury, who was originally a student of Yogananda's brother, Bishnu Ghosh.

Figure 3.13

Hatha Yoga Grandmasters

Several grandmasters of Hatha yoga philosophy and yoga practice founded organizations that continue to spread their teachings today. These modern teachers have influenced contemporary theory and practice of yoga.

Sri Tirumalai Krishnamacharya (1888–1989) was a great Hindu master of yoga who taught and lived in India to the age of 101 (Figure 3.14). He instructed at the palace of the Maharaja of Mysore. His students passed down their own lineages of yoga, which continue to have a strong impact on many contemporary schools. He was a shining example of how yoga can keep people youthful and healthy throughout their lives. Photographs of him in his late seventies and eighties show him trim and fit, performing some of yoga's most challenging poses with grace, flexibility, and strength.

Figure 3.14

Figure 3.15

Krishnamacharya's younger brother-in-law, B. K. S. Iyengar (1918–), evolved a system of his own, which is widely taught, with a large number of postures and stretches (Figure 3.15). Although his roots are firmly in Krishnamacharya, he was sent away to teach early in his career, and so developed his system using his own body to research his methods. He introduced the pragmatic use of creative props, such as blocks and straps, to help students gradually ease into greater flexibility and move more easily into the poses. Showing how yoga can be done at any age, Iyengar has been teaching into his eighties at large seminars with students from countries all around the world. He continues to inspire people as an example of a healthy yoga life devoted to sharing his art with others.

Pattabhi Jobis (1915–2009), another student of Krishnamacharya, founded the Ashtanga system of yoga, which is popular with young, active students. According to Ashtanga's history, Krishnamacharya and Jobis discovered an ancient manuscript in a library, which Jobis used along with Krishnamacharya's teachings to develop this system.

Indra Devi (1899–2002), a Latvian student of Krishnamacharya, was the first woman yoga teacher. She taught at a time when women were not usually accepted as yoga students and certainly not considered capable of being

Figure 3.16

accomplished masters (Figure 3.16). In the 1960s, she was known as the woman who brought yoga to the Kremlin. She bravely taught in Vietnam during the period of the Vietnam War and later in India and Argentina. She also came to California and instructed many Hollywood celebrities, including Gloria Swanson, who posed for Devi's book on yoga, *Yoga for Americans* (Devi, 1959).

Swami Sivananda (1887–1963) was an idealistic Hindu medical doctor who found himself drawn to yoga and ultimately chose yoga as his life's work (Figure 3.17). Many of his students came to Europe and America. He founded the Divine Life Society and evolved an important system of yoga, Sivananda yoga, which continues to be widely taught. His prescription for a spiritual life was: "Serve, Love, Give, Purify, Meditate, Realize" (Vishnu-devananda, 1995).

Sivananda's students included Satchidananda (1913–2002) (Figure 3.18), who opened the famous Woodstock festival held in Woodstock, New York,

Figure 3.17

Figure 3.18

from August 15th to 18th, 1969. His inspirational words were said to set the unifying, spiritual tone for the memorable event.

> *The whole world is watching you. The entire world is going to know what American youth can do for humanity. America is helping everybody in the material field, but the time has come for America to help the whole world with spirituality also.*

(Satchidananda from www.integralyogaofnewyork.org)

Satchidananda founded the Integral Yoga Institute and created a system that combines yoga with the Western philosophy of pragmatism to encourage higher functioning in body, mind, and spirit. Lilias Folan, a former well-known television yoga teacher, was in this lineage as well.

Chinmoy Kumar Ghose, known as Sri Chinmoy (1931–2007), believed that an excellent way to practice yoga was devotion to intense physical activity, expressed as total immersion and focus in art and extreme sports (Figure 3.19). Samyama, the meditative last three limbs of Patanjali's system,

Figure 3.19

can be performed to develop the powers of the physical body, and a great deal can be learned about attention and concentration from such practices. Chinmoy became a shining example of selfless action and loss of the lower self that showed the world the untapped potential of focused concentration. Among many of his feats, Sri Chinmoy demonstrated exceptional acts of strength and endurance for the sake of yoga, such as ultra-marathons and lifting vast amounts of weight, even at an advanced age. His actions exemplified how the mental practice can expand the limitations of the body.

One of the most influential yogis of our time was the Maharishi Mahesh Yogi (1917–2008), founder of Transcendental Meditation (Figure 3.20). The Maharishi developed a method of meditation using Mantra yoga. In addition to his studies on violence, the Maharishi Effect, described in Chapter 1, Maharishi had a long and active career. He founded a university and sponsored numerous research projects, referred to in Chapter 1, which offered

Figure 3.20

scientific evidence of how yoga can be used therapeutically. His approach inspired and was practiced by many successful musicians, such as the Beach Boys, the Beatles, and other creative artists, bringing it prominently into the Western consciousness during the 1960s, 1970s, and 1980s. His extensive work showed how yoga can be interpreted and used to positively affect life in many ways.

This is only a selection from the large pool of influential yoga masters. Many other great and accomplished yoga teachers came to America and Europe, too numerous to mention, contributing their skill and wisdom to the world for the betterment of humanity.

CONCLUSION

Many paths may be followed to the destination. Yoga has many varieties of teachers, with individual emphases in teaching and practices. In each classical form, they seem distinctive and separate, but for therapeutic purposes, these methods can be integrated, sharing a common root in their sincere devotion to the enhancement of human potential. In the ultimate schema, all is truly one.

4

Philosophy

Indian psychology realized the value of concentration and looked upon it as the means for the perception of the truth. It believed that there were no ranges of life or mind, which could not be reached by methodical training of will and knowledge. It recognized the close connection between mind and body. . . . The Yoga system of philosophy deals especially with these experiences.

(Radhakrishnan, 1977, p. 28)

Hinduism provided fertile soil for the growth of human thought. Yoga philosophy evolved within this rich environment. Yoga was one of the six schools of thought that were established as part of the Hindu tradition. Nyaya was a form of logic; Vaieshika, an empirical approach based in an atomist conception; Mimamsa, an antimystical school; and Vedanta, the sophisticated and broad group of ideas that formed the foundation of modern Hindu thought. Samkhya, one of the six schools, was a dualistic philosophy of mind and matter that has been integrated in many respects with yoga. The Sanskrit root *yuj* for the word yoga is interpreted as having two meanings: *to yoke* and *to join*. The dualistic meaning of the word points to the two-fold nature of the yogic school, which ultimately resolves in a higher unity.

FROM SAMKHYA TO YOGA:
INTEGRATION OF MIND AND MATTER

Samkhya philosophy is ancient, and it proposed two primary principles of reality: *prakriti* and *purusha*. Prakriti is the material aspect of reality. The world that we experience is prakriti, the phenomena of matter, but the world is not just material. There is also purusha, consciousness, the light of intelligence within the realm of the mind. Purusha is the source of our deeper nature, the true self. The suffering people feel in life comes from identifying with prakriti and losing touch with the deeper spiritual nature of purusha. According to ancient Samkhya philosophy, these two principles can never be resolved into each other: the nature of reality is dual. Much like Descartes' idea of mind and body always being separated, purusha and prakriti are separate, and both are real.

Yoga philosophy introduced a way to integrate mind and matter: the ruling principle of Ishvara. The meaning of Ishvara varies depending on the school of thought, but for our therapeutic understanding, Ishvara can be thought of as similar to Aristotle's First Principles. There is cause and effect that organizes the universe. For example, scientists observed the way objects fall down when dropped, and from many careful observations and measurements, they derived the law of gravity. Each material event is caused, and inevitably leads back to a first cause, a supreme controller, or principle behind everything that exists.

In yoga philosophy, the universe is intelligently organized, flowing from its first principles of infinite wisdom. We partake of this wisdom through the purusha part of our nature. The method of yoga is a set of practices that allows us to transcend the constraints of the finite material prakriti and identify with the spiritual purusha consciousness that understands and partakes of the universal principles of Ishvara. Through the development of our purusha, unity is found between mind and matter. The way to truly understand the nature of the universe is found not by directing attention outward to the external world, but rather begins by turning the gaze inward to consciousness. "That, thou art" is the famous phrase from the Upanishads, described in Chapter 3. By immersing in consciousness, we become unified with universal wisdom and literally become it. The meaning can be given to the phrase, of *thatness*, which is the general focus of yoga: That we meditate; we are one.

THE EIGHT LIMBS OF YOGA

The eight limbs of yoga from Patanjali's system help us to master the relationship between the material and the mental, to direct focus toward consciousness, and to bring awareness of our true nature. Yoga, as Patanjali explained, is not just for a purpose but also is a philosophy of life. Like the framework of Aristotle's logical principles, yoga development follows a template whose clear path can lead the practitioner from the lower roots to the highest limb of enlightenment through healthy and wholesome practices.

Each limb helps gain control and restraint over outward projections on the material world, of everyday engagement in prakriti, the outer world of things and events. Through the process, consciousness identifies with the still, calm inner awareness that is purusha. This focus, brought about by yogic practice, leads to freedom from suffering, enlightened knowledge, and a life of blissful happiness.

In modern yoga philosophy, the *Yoga Sutras* of Patanjali have become fundamental to the fabric of yoga. The pattern woven with these sutras is a compass to orient most modern yoga approaches. His concepts and general descriptions, originally of Raja yoga, are now part of yoga systems today, in one form or another. The eight limbs are a way to gather the thoughts and actions of yoga together into categories for practice that make sense and have a directional quality, when considered as a sequential hierarchy. The limbs give firm support for the practitioner who can use them to climb the tree of yoga to the top. And like the limbs of an actual tree, each of the aspects of yoga is part of the whole, and can be emphasized, and perhaps even paused on for a time, to gain benefits on the climb. But the limbs lead toward the ultimate goal of yoga: freedom, *Samadhi*, enlightenment.

The eight limbs can be psychotherapeutic as they free clients from illusions they create through their projections onto their material world of interaction. They discover a center that is wise and attuned to their deeper nature. Clients get in touch with their own deeper nature to develop clarity of perception that helps them resolve their conflicts and find inner peace.

The Philosophy of the Eight Limbs

The *Yoga Sutras* can also be interpreted in terms of holistic philosophy, as a unified pattern. The integration of the limbs is a process. Each of the limbs is complete, necessary, and meaningful in itself, but practiced together they interact to create a whole. There is a feedback and feed-forward effect from each of the limbs, so that the unity created is a dynamic process, improving and evolving over time: From the interaction, each of the parts gets enhanced.

According to Patanjali, yoga is for the relief of suffering, but it also aims toward a higher integration that leads to the discovery of wisdom and true happiness. Yoga offers many ways to bring about relief and inspire wisdom. This two-sided approach fits with an implicit quality within psychotherapy's intentions: To cure psychological problems while also helping clients find happiness.

Yoga includes the body as part of its focus, as expressed in Hatha yoga. The body is the temple of the soul and is not to be neglected. The body becomes the vehicle to overcome suffering and discover enlightenment. Hatha yoga practices focus on the body and is well suited to overcoming physical discomforts and fostering physical well-being while also enhancing mental capacities. In the West, Hatha yoga has become almost synonymous with yoga itself, but as has been described, yoga encompasses much more, including the highly developed mental practices of breathing and meditation. The many types of yoga emphasize one aspect of yoga more than other aspects (see Chapter 3). For psychotherapeutic purposes, we draw from all of these components, to best help clients on many levels. All of the yoga approaches share in the central aim or goal of yoga: wholeness, balance, and ultimately integration through uniting with a higher consciousness of truth. These aims fit seamlessly with psychotherapy.

The Yamas and Niyamas

The yamas and the niyamas, the first two limbs, are ethical guidelines. The yamas are those things not to do, and the niyamas are those things to do. These practices are part of the structure of yoga, not just in terms of values as ethical and moral precepts and guides to everyday actions, but also in relationship to each of the other limbs as well. The themes of the yamas and niyamas resonate throughout the life of the practitioner and in every aspect of yoga. In Patanjali's writings, they are few, only five of each. Samkhya philosophy has many more. When yoga is blended with Western psychotherapy, the scope of the yamas and niyamas may be enlarged from their classical limits, but they should be based in the originals for their orientation and direction to retain their meaningfulness. For the purposes of this book, we will use Patanjali's formulation.

These broad guidelines of yoga are sensible. The point of these prohibitions and observances is to live in an ethical and healthy manner. The later limbs feed back to this earlier limb, and earlier ones form a basis for the later ones. For example, for meditation to bear its fullest fruits, the yamas and niyamas must be sincerely lived, not just thought about. The flow of yoga is continuous, giving direction and guidance to the life force, so in these ways, the yamas and niyamas interact with all of the other limbs. Without ethical guidelines to follow, the yoga practitioner could be hindered on the journey to enlightenment. Similarly, without guidelines for healthy psychological functioning, clients remain stuck in redundant patterns. The guidelines of the yamas and niyamas enhance development to facilitate the ultimate goal of yoga, enlightenment: Samadhi.

The yamas are also often referred to as the abstinences. They are ahimsa—nonharming, satya—not lying, asteya—not stealing, bramacharya—restraint, and aparigraha—nonattachment.

Ahimsa, the first yama, is nonviolence or nonharming. Not to harm is a natural, easily justified moral injunction and a rational one. It includes acts of goodness toward others and even extending compassion toward those who we feel have wronged us. This is paradoxical, but when practiced correctly can result in a positive and less stressful social environment. Ahimsa can be interpreted in many ways, for example, not to hurt others but also not to hurt oneself either, not just physically but also psychologically, emotionally, or perhaps financially as well. Nonharming is a useful ethical criterion of one's activities, leading to better behavior in the world. Ahimsa puts the brakes on such things, and when practiced, negative behavior is less likely. For psychotherapeutic purposes, where clients fail at stopping harmful behavior, psychotherapeutic work can begin.

Satya, the second yama, means to abstain from falsehood. This means to seek truth, to speak the truth, and to be truthful in deed. Psychological problems often involve self-deception or deception of others, a kind of falsehood. In a very deep sense, all psychotherapy seeks inner and outer truth, through living in congruence with the true self, as well as with others. By living in truth, mental health becomes possible, perhaps inevitable. Truth in speech is the narrow sense of satya, which translates as truth in dialogue. More broadly, satya involves accurately matching who you are within, your true self, with how you act in the world. When clients talk things out, they can come to better resolutions about matters and live true in thought, word, and deed.

Asteya, the third yama, means to abstain from stealing. Stealing is not just theft of property; it can be much more. For example, stealing need not be limited to actions; it may also be a wish, perhaps simply a wish to have something that is not one's own. Wishing to steal another's relationship, another's success, or even aspects of another's identity could fall under this category. The tendency should always be to return to the true self. Yoga encourages its practitioners to honestly be themselves and to honestly want what is one's own, not to want to be or have what belongs to others. By becoming and wanting only what is fully one's own, great potential can be realized with it.

Bramacharya—control, moderation, and restraint—is another yama that can be interpreted to guide lifestyle in many ways, whether as complete abstinence from sex or simply moderate restraint in general sensual pleasures, which means not to engage in promiscuous sexual relationships. In traditional times, chastity was practiced, and in India, the saddhu or wandering monk may live this way, but in the West, modern yoga does not restrict intimacy within committed relationships. This yama also leads to a concern for modesty in emotional matters.

Aparigraha, the fifth yama, is to abstain from greed and to cultivate detachment. This yama can lead toward a central value of Buddhism, nonattachment, which is important to coping with the problem of craving, the cause of suffering in life. This yama applies to action in general. Krishna explained in the Bhagavad Gita that action should not arise out of selfish motives or out of fear of consequences. Krishna encouraged Arjuna to work for the work itself and not to be concerned with the results of action. "Therefore, always perform the work that has to be done without attachment, for man attains the Supreme by performing work without attachment" (Bhagavad Gita in Deutsch, 1968, p. 49).

The niyamas are those things that one should do, also known as the observances. Again, there are five: *shaucha*—purity, *santosha*—contentment, *tapas*—austerity, *pranitara*—attentiveness to self-study, great literature, inner reflection on matters of meaningful spirituality, and finally, *Ishvara pranidhana*—devotion to higher value, whether God or perhaps an organizing spiritual principle.

Saucha or purity can be interpreted in many ways, not only in the literal sense of cleanliness, both inwardly and outwardly in the body, but also as purity and refinement of thought and speech. For example, from the outward physical perspective, saucha involves keeping the body clean, well groomed, and well dressed, going to the hairdresser or barber and dentist at appropriate times and so on. Inwardly, it means to ensure good physical health, correct regularity of toiletry to ensure good eliminative function, purity of food and drink for healthy digestion. Similarly, in thought and in speech, such practices as clearing the mind through meditation or focusing on the breath can serve this function. We see examples of purity expressed in many domains. For example, in the West, we have our scientific method, based in reductionism, attempting to purify philosophical claims and predictions about the world to empirically verifiable hypotheses with correlated observations. Pure mathematics is another way that this niyama can be expressed in thought.

Purity has a feed-forward–feedback effect, where its practice feeds back to becoming healthier, clearer, simpler, which feeds forward to a healthier lifestyle, a clearer proposition, or a simpler mathematical formula. The seventh and eighth limbs can be understood in these terms as well, because when you achieve enlightenment, it is a kind of purity of mind and spirit that feeds back into all aspects of life.

Santosha or contentment is a helpful attitude to cultivate. We often overlook the positive qualities of our lives, do not accept things, or fail to recognize how good some things are. The beautiful sky overhead, the comfortable chair that we sit in, the help others give us may never seem enough. Santosha encourages us to appreciate the goodness in our lives and be content with it. Much relief from suffering can be gained in this way.

Tapas or austerity involves a sincere concern to improve one's lifestyle and make the right efforts to do so. Tapas of the body involves caring about fitness, healthy habits, a clean body on the inside and outwardly as well, in terms of grooming, and so forth, and then doing something to bring it about. Tapas of the mind leads to controlling and refining thoughts, regulating emotions, and keeping the mind steady. All of the practices of yoga help to carry out tapas in everyday life.

Pranitara is a niyama we all should remind ourselves to return to: self-education and an effort toward self-improvement through learning. Through attentiveness to our studies, self-study, and reflection on higher spiritual matters, our thoughts and subsequent contemplations are elevated, and we can evolve to our full potential, as well as helping others to do so. One of the great strengths of yoga is the universality of its spirituality.

The fifth niyama, *Ishvara pranidhana*, is dedication to a higher power, whether this means surrender to God's will, letting go to nature's design, following the way of Daoism, or walking the middle path of Buddhism. Ishvara pranidhana reminds practitioners to orient their lives toward a higher principle, greater than just themselves or that of the phenomenal world. Isvara is the unifying principle within the nature of the universe, as described earlier, and so being dedicated to a principle found in all that is, elevates intentions to higher values. This niyama encourages you to make your best efforts wholeheartedly while letting be. Surrender to spontaneous unfolding of the present moment, being one with here and now, and staying in the here and now without concern for the future or past. The renowned Integral Yoga teacher Sachidananda told people to believe in Now. Be deeply one with your life as it is and have faith in it. Believe in believing itself, not just in a particular belief.

Applying the Yamas and Niyamas

The yamas and niyamas are intended not merely to present specific observances and injunctions but also to encourage living cooperatively in general. Practitioners are thereby freed to continue on an enlightened life, without hindrance. Although the yamas and niyamas are important in *what* they are, they are even more important in *that* they are. Their *thatness*, so to speak, is more significant than the specific virtue.

What does *thatness* mean? Sincerely committed gurus communicate the inner truths of yoga with correct, ethical actions. For example, when we drive a car in the United States, we drive on the right side of the road. But if we drive in England, and in some other countries whose rules of the road have been affected by England, we drive on the left side. Which side of the road we drive on may vary, but *that* we drive on the correct side of the road should not vary. And similarly, when the guidelines of these categories are applied, they can be adapted somewhat to the customs and conditions of the country and culture of the practitioner. There are some absolutes, but quite a bit can vary. In actual practice, many people individualize yoga creatively. If we were to visualize yoga's philosophical principles as a net, it would be a flexible net, but it would still be a net.

Asanas

Asanas, the third limb of Patanjali, refers to postures. All through life, we take on a posture of some sort. In the West, we lie in bed to sleep; we sit at the table to eat, work at a desk, or stand in an assembly. We use postures all the time, moment to moment, as part of our action. Action points toward goals, which are purposive and clear, but there is much more to body positioning. In yoga, the asana is a position, a posture of the body in space, with action, often with a symbolic as well as a practical meaning. For example, in an everyday context, the writer sits at her desk, with the work before her to do. This unified reality is important for bringing all together in the moment. As a result, body, mind, and spirit are accessible for the writing purpose. Setting herself in position, she is not doing anything else. The asana is part of attention to the matter at hand.

In Western culture, we use the equivalent of asana in many activities. For example, in a sport, body posture is part of learning to perform the sport well. The tennis player is taught to address the ball, racquet in hand, set to fully engage in the swing. The Olympic diver gets set on the springboard before the dive, in good posture and balance. Similarly, in each religion, the counterparts of asanas are used, often without recognition. People kneel in church at certain key moments, bowing their heads, and stand attentively at others, not only as part of participating in the mass, but also to receive and share in spiritual experiences. Postures parallel the concept in Eastern religions. So, the physical reality of placing the body in an asana can be used deliberately to engage physical, mental, and spiritual dimensions.

The spiritual dimension can be deliberately activated by postures, breathing, visualization, thoughtful contemplation, and conscious immersion in the process toward enlightened living. Posing the body and mind in a yoga asana tends to induce a setting that permits the practitioner to have useful experiences for learning from the symbolic interaction by confronting personal feelings about doing it. For example, struggling with the difficulty or discomfort of the pose, at first, becomes an opportunity to learn about oneself and grow. Experiences are teachers, a path to walk on and find the higher self. Later, after extending limits, the practitioner simply experiences the asana and its results in sequences known as a routine. But in pursuit of the higher goals of meditation, the primary asana is simply to sit upright with spine straight, in good posture cross-legged, still and at ease.

Pranayama

In yoga philosophy, the outer world is filled with flowing prana energy, as well as the inner world of the body and mind. And the Universe breathes with relation to the life within it. The next limb, Pranayama, involves focusing attention on breathing, and then deliberately using breathing patterns and rhythms of breath for the control, direction, and distribution of prana, or vital energy.

Pranayama includes using various rhythms and patterns of breathing for specific purposes within the body, such as calming down or energizing. Through the practice of pranayama, breath can be directed and circulated for health and well-being to access higher states of consciousness. The practitioner gains access to specific states of emotional functioning by voluntarily and consciously using breathing rhythms associated with specific patterns of breathing that usually take place involuntarily and unconsciously. We breathe differently when we are angry than when we are quietly resting. We breathe in patterns according to the need we have. This natural link is used in yoga as a stepping stone to desired states. In the context of psychotherapy, the deliberate body postures and breathing patterns bring emotions with their corresponding mental states into consciousness for therapeutic work.

Pratyahara

Pratyahara is the limb that follows pranayama. When attention is focused on breathing, a figure-background switch from outward toward the world to inward toward the body's inner realm of experience becomes possible. Pratyahara is traditionally thought of as restraint: Withdrawing from engagement through the senses with the general outer world.

But pratyahara is also a form of renunciation, an important aspect of yoga. Renunciation is a continuing theme throughout all of yoga, in balance with the efforts made to accomplish goals. For every step forward, there is a sense of leaving the previous step behind. The ability to renounce allows the yogi to be free of concern for many of the potential distractions of life. For example, the yogic interpretation of altruism is that it involves renunciation, not only of selfishness but also of self-centered action, to unify with a higher intention: Identity with the deeper Self, which encourages action for the benefit of others. Psychotherapy takes a moderate road to renunciation. For clients, renunciation can become integrated into treatments by offering a way to disengage and disentangle from unhealthy patterns, emotions, or behaviors, thereby opening clients to being able to engage in positive relationships and meaningful endeavors. So, clients do not need to renounce the world, but do need to renounce their own entrapments.

Dharana

Dharana, the sixth limb, is one-pointed focus of attention, also known as concentration. This one-pointed focus of attention that is developed through yoga helps make unusual abilities available to the yogi. Because the yogi has withdrawn from the distractions of the senses, concentrated awareness is available to direct to a selected area, such as the pattern of breathing established in pranayama. Again, this limb interacts with all of the earlier ones. For example, nonharming moderates the use of these patterns, and the focus here is on oneself. Then, as a result, healthy, adaptive practice is followed, and new potentials become possible.

Dhyana

Dhyana, the seventh limb, follows Dharana. Now that the yogi is focused intently on inner matters, contemplation begins with a free play of thought, feeling, and experience on and around the object of attention. Yogis believe that direct perception of the object can take place, without the interposition of the senses. Union, joining with the object, occurs, leading to Samadhi, the eighth limb. The last three limbs—dharana, dhyana, and Samadhi—are considered as a three-sided unity, known as *samyama* (Figure 4.1).

Through the practice of samyama, sometimes called making samyama, enlightened consciousness emerges.

Eastern Yoga Parallels With Western Plato

Yoga involves the pursuit of the Good, when conceptualized in Western terms, and though many people may differ in their perception of what the good is, none differ in that it exists and is worthy of pursuit. Plato left Athens and journeyed for many years after Socrates was put to death, searching for comfort, before returning. There is a theory that he might have gone to India, where he learned about yoga. Whether this theory is true or not, we can find overlaps with yoga in Plato's later theory, expressed in certain

Figure 4.1

dialogues, especially the Phaedo, in which he describes the last hours that Socrates shared with several of his followers.

Concern for a higher perception, beyond the senses and the limitations of the body, was important to Plato, in a similar way to how higher consciousness is valued in yoga. Plato was committed to the correct use of the mind in the search for truth, which is of the essence for yoga as well. Plato portrayed Socrates as unconcerned about being sentenced to death, because he believed that his soul would continue in the quest for truth. Instead of fearing dying, Socrates told his friends and students that he felt truly happy in his last few days of life. He looked forward to being free to seek truth, unhindered by the limitations of his senses. And Socrates felt detached from his desires and motivated by the quest for liberation, committed to philosophy and a true, ethical life.

INTEGRATION

Chapters 3 and 4 have described the historical roots and traditional theories of yoga that have led to the rich collection of techniques and methods. Chapters 1 and 2 discussed scientific inquiry into the factors making yoga effective for therapeutic applications, such as control of attention, alteration of breathing, which is connected to emotions, thoughts, and behavior, and holding the focus on the body and mind. What is primary for psychotherapy is not just a specific posture or breathing technique. Rather, *that* the client moves into poses, *that* she alters her breathing, *that* he focuses his mind at will. In short, *that* she does it, *that* he experiences, and *that* she transcends the usual consciousness. These qualities impact the therapeutic process. Actively engaging the client in the process will have a profound effect. From continually attending to the contents of cognition, the mind becomes steady and achieves the ability the yogis call *constant concentration* or *Samadhi*.

Samadhi comes in many forms. For example, as you read this book now, you focus your mind deeply on the ideas presented until the form of the book disappears and all that remains is the meaning. In a small way, this is an experience of Samadhi. Therapeutic Samadhi focuses deeply on the psychological problem as it manifests in emotions, body experience, and behavior. Gradually, patterns emerge until the client discovers the motivating meaning, the deeper insight that frees. The problem drops away, and the client is healed. Religious Samadhi, often portrayed in yoga literature, is an experience of unity with God that comes from a similar use of the mind. And indeed, once freed of their conflicts, clients may have a deep spiritual experience.

Ultimately, there is a transformation of the self-identity. The client no longer identifies herself as just an individual self, alone, but instead recognizes in a felt, experiential way that she is not isolated but partakes in Existence with a capital "E." All existence is manifested in each individual, and all individuals partake of existence. With correct practice of the eight limbs, anyone can be enlightened. As Vivekananda stated, "Samadhi is the property of every human being . . .. When [meditation methods are] faithfully practiced, they will surely lead to the desired end. Then will all sorrows cease, all miseries vanish. The seeds of actions will be burnt, and the Soul will be free forever" (Vivekananda, 1953, p. 617).

CONCLUSION

Human beings around the world have asked many of the same questions: How are we related to the world? How can we truly know ourselves? How can we find happiness? Yoga offers its answers to these questions, often with a familiar ring to Western ears, and at other times with answers that add new tones and melodies. We in the therapeutic community can harmonize these healing sounds with our therapeutic methods, to help clients transform at a profound level. Including yoga philosophy helps clients to direct their gaze inward to uncover the roots of conflict and transcend them. Engagement in the methods brings the discovery of true nature and a sense of being at home and at peace.

5

Practices

Spirit without mind, spirit without body is not the type of man, there-
fore, a human spirituality must not belittle the mind, life, or body or
hold them of small account: it will rather hold them of high account, of
immense importance precisely because they are the conditions and instru-
ments of the life of the spirit in man.
(Aurobindo in Chaudhuri & Spiegelberg, 1960, p. 99)

Recent neuroscience findings indicate the brain, mind, and body function together in a unified system. Each emotional response travels through neurological pathways, built into our physiology at fundamental levels (C. A. Simpkins & Simpkins, 2010). Patterns of thought or feeling are expressed in brain activity and body posture. Everything we think, feel, and do, our cognitions, emotions, and behaviors, are embodied.

Experience-based neuroplasticity has shown that things we do can influence how the mind-brain-body system functions, changing the brain, which also changes the emotions and thoughts. Thus the practice of the eight limbs of yoga, which works with the body and mind, affects the brain-mind-body system for the better.

This chapter offers a framework for practice that can be applied with most forms of therapy and even generalized to many activities of life. The framework develops a quality of attention combined with body poise, free of distractions, focused, and balanced. Approaching activity in such a state, the practitioner will gain more from the therapeutic experience. Indeed, the yoga framework can be used to approach life in general. Each endeavor becomes an object to be viewed through the clear lens of yoga consciousness, self-aware and ready for action. Then, much more becomes possible as the brain is enhanced, the body improved, and the mind sharpened. The meditative exercises here form a preliminary basis for practice. They are drawn from Patanjali's eight limbs, including pranayama (breathing), asana (postures), pratyahara (withdrawal), dharana (concentration), dhyana (contemplation), and leading to the subsequent experience of enlightenment (Samadhi). For therapeutic purposes, the goal is therapeutic integration, for clients to overcome their problems and develop their capacities fully. Chapters in Part III show how to expand these methods further with specific techniques to address particular problems.

INTEGRATING YAMAS AND NIYAMAS AS A THERAPEUTIC TOOL

Early cognitive behavior therapy revolutionized therapy practice by recognizing that emotions, behaviors, and thoughts are interrelated. By becoming aware of, evaluating, and replacing problematic thoughts, feelings, and behaviors, a more reasonable, functional, and healthy pattern emerges. People feel better, and the legacy of research stands behind this approach. Yoga offers broad criteria to add to the usual rational ones, which can aid in replacing faulty patterns while also stimulating healthy functioning. Just as clients learn to reexamine their thoughts and behaviors through the lens of reason, they can look into yoga philosophy's crystal lens for a vision, with guidance from the yamas and niyamas, to foster emotional comfort, psychological well-being, and the pursuit of a healthy and meaningful life.

Putting yoga philosophy into practice begins with the process of assessing thoughts and behaviors in terms of guidelines for what is helpful and what is harmful, and what should be done and what should not be done. Cognitions and behaviors are also directed in the best possible directions.

When clients begin any form of therapy, they have in essence taken on many of the issues raised by the yamas, because the therapeutic process guides toward many of its principles, such as to prevent harming oneself or others, to stop being false to oneself and others, and to halt engaging in criminal activity, promiscuity, or greed. Therapy points clients with the niyamas when it helps take care of the lower needs for cleanliness, nutrition, to become more self-aware, to control unhealthy impulses, and to always be open to learning and growing. The niyamas help clients recognize that they can draw from a wellspring deep within, beyond their everyday functioning, for strength and wisdom greater than just their own.

At first, clients may be unable to relate to the yamas and niyamas, and this is part of what the therapeutic process is all about. But as they move toward healthier fulfillment, they come to recognize the inherently unsatisfying quality of the secondary gain they might be receiving from their self-destructive activities. They add awareness of their thoughts and actions and the means to do something to remodel them in a more positive, healthy way.

The yamas and niyamas offer codes of conduct people should reject or adopt. Although modern psychotherapy is neutral about what people should and should not do specifically, we have learned from studying the brain that some habits and actions will foster healthy functioning and others will hurt it. In addition, positive psychology research has found distinctive links between values and well-being (Sagiv, Roccas, & Hazan, 2004). The ancients knew the truth of this insight, recommending that people should be clean, stay in shape, and continue to learn. When people are disturbed, they may neglect some of these seemingly rudimentary habits for healthy living. Milieu therapy in treatment facilities often fosters such habits using reinforcement and other incentives. Therapists should guide clients to make commitments toward these healthy and fulfilling life changes, as they will strongly enhance progress.

ASANA POSTURES

Posture becomes perfect when the effort to attain it disappears.
(Patanjali's Yoga Sutras *in Christensen, 1997, p. 6*)

We express emotions and attitudes in how we hold our body. When people stand tall with their shoulders back, they may be expressing feelings of confidence and strength. Or when clients come into the office with shoulders slumped forward and eyes turned down, they may be feeling sad or insecure. The experienced clinician knows that body language is an important dimension and considers the body as part of making a diagnosis. This mind-body link can be extended into treatment by taking on a posture deliberately.

The practice of yoga teaches us how to listen, feel, and sense. Using a simple asana posture can gently and gradually point to the fundamentals of breathing, sitting, standing, and moving. Attention comes back into focus, an essential for many clients who are dissociated from their everyday actions and yet caught up in repetitive concerns.

Attitudes can be encouraged and even adopted physically first, thereby paving the way for an easier cognitive or emotional change. Some of the attitudes that can be encouraged with a posture are calm and relaxation, flexibility, strength, and courage. All of these qualities will help clients face the therapeutic process and engage in it more fully and easily.

During therapy sessions, clients typically sit up or lie down. Some simple yoga asanas can be introduced to offer another source for healthy input into the client's life. Each asana can embody a healthy psychological attitude that gently adds to what already takes place during therapy. The practice also provides opportunities for experiences of mastery, especially if the therapist carefully uses only postures the client can easily perform. Other nonspecific benefits of feeling good, gaining flexibility, and enjoying the practice makes a gentle asana routine a positive addition to treatment.

General Guidelines for Asanas

One of the qualities of asana practice that makes it so helpful to therapy is that, much like therapeutic change, what begins with making an effort ultimately becomes effortless. The best asana positioning is natural, effortless, aligned with gravity, free of excess tension. It models being comfortable with yourself as you move through life.

Asana practice involves more than simply moving the body into a posture and holding it there. Each asana contains three aspects to the pose: moving into the pose, holding the pose, and then coming out of it again. By noticing these three phases, attention becomes focused better, with improved awareness in general. Each of these phases of movement should be performed smoothly, calmly, slowly, and with balance and poise.

Two qualities are important to develop when performing asanas: *sthira*, alertness, and *sukha*, relaxation. "These qualities can be achieved by recognizing and observing the reactions of the body and the breath to the various postures that comprise asana practice. Once known, these reactions can be controlled step-by-step" (Paganjali's *Yoga Sutras*, in Desikachar, 1995, p. 180). Learning to be both alert and relaxed while in an asana may generalize to how clients carry themselves in everyday life.

Asanas can be divided into several basic categories: sitting, standing, and lying prone. Yoga also includes inverted postures, but these are not included here. Clients who want to go further with yoga practice can be encouraged to take a regular Hatha yoga class where more advanced asanas are performed.

Introducing Asanas Into Therapy

Performing complex poses is not necessary for a therapeutic effect. One purpose of asanas for treatment is in how the attention is directed and kept on breathing and movement, unifying thought and action together. Attention skills sharpen by having an accessible object for attention to place its focus, and the asanas offer this point of focus. This skill is invaluable for therapeutic progress. When clients can stay focused on the work from a poised, aware center, they will handle their problems realistically and address their conflicts efficiently.

To introduce asanas into therapy, begin with the simplest sitting (Easy Pose) or sitting in a chair (Chair Sitting), standing (Mountain Pose), and lying prone (Savasana) poses. The client already stands, sits, and lies prone, so the attention to these natural postures can be used with anyone, even those who might not be interested in yoga practice. We provide the basic positions, performed in the yoga way, first sitting position, then standing, and finally lying prone. The chapters in Part III expand these basic skills with short asana routines to add for treating specific problems. Routines can also be practiced between sessions if the client would like to have something tangible to do at home.

Sitting Asanas

Therapy is most often performed in a sitting position, so sitting asanas are the most natural place to begin. When people feel emotionally disturbed, they are often uncomfortable with their sitting posture. They lose concentration and feel awkward. Turning attention to sitting can start a process toward feeling more comfortable in general.

Today we are more accustomed to sitting in chairs, so some people might feel intimidated by having to sit on the floor. For those who are not able to sit comfortably cross-legged on the floor, or who may not want to, sitting postures can be adapted to chair sitting, so long as the body is positioned correctly. A chair-sitting adaptation is given here.

Beginners who decide to sit on the floor will find it easier to use a firm cushion that will raise the hips 3 to 6 inches. This takes the strain off the lower back and makes sitting on the floor more comfortable. Eventually, seated asanas can be performed without a pillow.

Easy Pose, Sukhasana

One of the easiest sitting positions is called easy pose (Figure 5.1). The easy pose is very similar to the cross-legged position most people used as a child when sitting on the floor.

Come into the pose by drawing your left foot in until the heel is as far under your right thigh as possible without forcing it. Then draw the right foot under the left thigh in the same way. Bring your hands to rest on your knees. Your legs will be crossed at the ankles. Most important is that you keep your spine, neck, and head balanced and held upright. Once in position, hold this pose as you remain alertly aware of your body, but at the same time relaxing any unnecessary tensions. Perform several complete breaths (instructions for breathing are given in the pranayama section of this chapter), staying alert and relaxed. Eventually, the pose should feel easy and natural to maintain over an extended time. When you are finished, carefully come out of the pose, remaining aware as you move your legs apart and stand up to finish.

Chair-Sitting Position

Many asana positions can be modified for sitting in a chair (Figure 5.2). *Choose a stable, four-legged chair to use or a sturdy living room–type chair. Make sure the area around the chair is clear and safe. To perform the sitting pose*

Figure 5.1

in a chair, apply the same steps of coming into the sitting pose, maintaining it with breathing, and then coming out of it. When performing a yoga pose sitting in a chair, sit toward the edge of the chair as pictured. Keep your spine, neck, and head upright just as in the floor-sitting positions. Make sure your thighs are parallel to the floor and your lower legs are perpendicular to the floor. If the chair is too high to do this, you may need to place a book or pillow under your feet on the floor to raise them up. Let your hands rest on your knees, with your arms away from your rib cage.

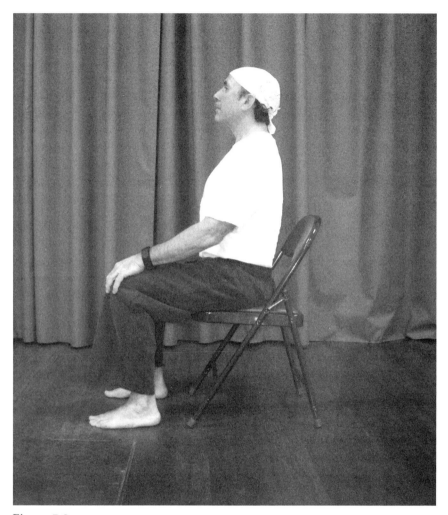

Figure 5.2

Pelvic Pose, Vajrasana

Pelvic pose, vajrasana, is a kneeling position (Figure 5.3). Once again, perform this sitting pose by attending to coming into the pose, maintaining the pose with breathing, and mindfully coming out of it again.

To find this position, kneel on the floor and then sit upright back on your heels. You might find it more comfortable by placing a small cushion under the backs of your legs or your shins to sit on. Some people may prefer this position to cross-legged ones, whereas others may have the opposite reaction. Let your body be your guide as to how to sit most comfortably.

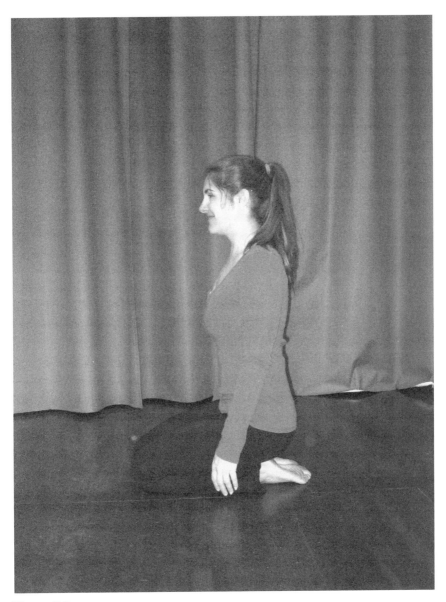

Figure 5.3

Standing Asanas

Much of life is spent standing. We balance upright and walk from the standing position. Our spine keeps us upright, giving us support. We gauge where we are and orient perceptually from our height. And so, it is logical that standing asanas are important.

Standing asanas help clients in many ways. The standing postures build strength, coordination, and flexibility. Having improved body alignment and poise helps clients develop a feeling of well-being and confidence. Vitality is enhanced as well. Another primary benefit is balance and centering. For clients who have a poor sense of their own self-support or have difficulty self-soothing when they are upset, standing asanas may offer an indirect sense of taking responsibility for oneself, with a strong base in "standing on one's own two feet," as the expression goes.

Finding a Balanced Mountain Pose, Tadasana

People often neglect their posture and then find themselves developing habits that can cause aches, pains, and fatigue. Poor posture often forces you to fight against gravity, thereby dissipating energy. When you can stand straight with your feet firmly on the ground, legs under you, spine straight, and head centered, gravity becomes an ally. Alignment is natural, and standing becomes effortless. A fundamental position for standing asanas is standing aligned, with attention directed to standing (Figure 5.4).

Stand with feet together, ankles touching, and arms at your sides. Stand up straight yet relaxed. Keep your shoulders from slumping, and do not let your back hunch.

Let your weight be evenly balanced between your two feet, and balanced front to back. If the balance point is not readily apparent, close your eyes use this additional tool for finding your standing pose aligned with gravity. Rock very gently from side to side and feel the balance point shifting from one leg to the other. You will notice a place exactly between your two legs where balance is effortless and shared by both legs. Stand for a moment or two as you sense this point. Next, try rocking very slightly forward and back. You will feel your muscles tighten up as you shift forward and backward. Notice the point in the middle where your muscles relax. Find the place between side to side and forward and back where you are most relaxed and balanced, aligned with gravity. Now with your body standing comfortably straight, you are firm like a mountain. In this position of balance and alignment, perform several complete breaths. Try to be alert and relaxed at the same time. If you notice some tension in an area, try to relax it. When you feel ready, come out of the posture, keeping attention focused.

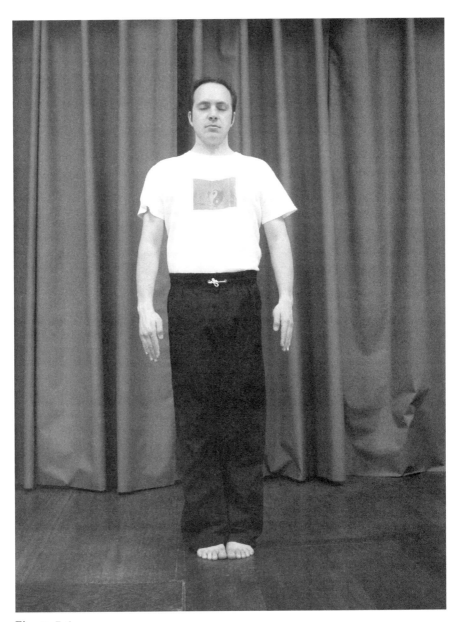

Figure 5.4

Lying Prone

Life is always in relationship. When lying down, there is a relationship to the supporting surface. Many of the prone asanas can be performed more easily because of the support given by the floor. People can learn about themselves through this relationship. Several of the classic prone postures can be used for calming. Savasana and crocodile poses can relax the body from head to foot.

Corpse Pose, Savasana

The *savasana* pose (Figure 5.5) can help you to rejuvenate and revitalize. Being very restful, savasana can help bring about a feeling of well-being.

We rarely think of lying down as more than the act itself, but a prone position can also become a yoga asana. Begin by paying attention to how you go into the prone position. As you lie down on your back on the floor with legs extended and arms at your side, palms facing down, let your body be relaxed, and your attention focused on the movement. Try to move smoothly and slowly into this posture. Once in position, let your feet move apart and rotate outward slightly. Close your eyes. Breathe comfortably, performing several complete breaths. Scan your body with your attention and let go of any unnecessary tensions. People often express extra tension in the muscles of the face, stomach, neck, shoulders, and back, so let any unnecessary tightness go. Try to relax as deeply as you can. Rest in this position for a few minutes.

If you feel tight in your lower back in this asana, you can modify it by raising your knees while leaving your feet flat on the floor. You may want to put a pillow under your knees and let your legs extend comfortably. This tends to let the lower back flatten, allowing it to relax deeply. As you feel the back muscles let go, you

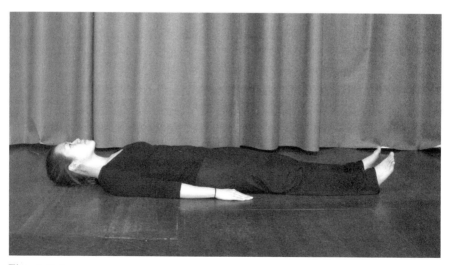

Figure 5.5

may be able to extend your legs flat into the savasana pose. If not, use the modified position to allow yourself to relax as much as possible. When you feel ready, come out of the position in the opposite way of how you went into it, continuing to be aware throughout the entire process.

Crocodile Pose, Makarasana

The Crocodile pose (Figure 5.6) is also a relaxation posture, performed lying on your stomach. According to Indian folklore, the crocodile is considered one of nature's most extraordinary creatures, because it can be comfortable on the earth as well as in the water. Thus, this pose symbolizes the ability to be fully relaxed under any circumstance. The Crocodile pose can be helpful to the digestive system, massaging the abdomen slightly. Some people may find this pose more comfortable than savasana. If so, use this one, instead, for deep relaxing.

Perform this posture using the same steps as in savasana: slowly going into the posture, breathing while holding the position, relaxed and alert, and slowly coming out of it. Lie face down on the floor with your legs stretched apart at a comfortable distance and your heels facing in and toes pointing out. Bend one arm to make a resting place for your forehead, placing the hand on your opposite shoulder, forming a triangle. Let the other hand come across your body at shoulder level

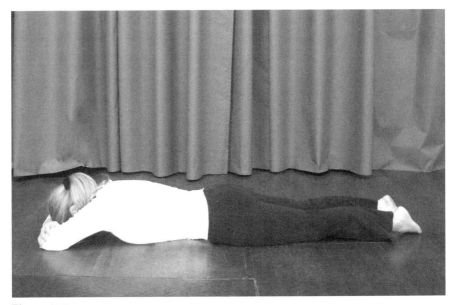

Figure 5.6

and grasp the opposite shoulder. This position keeps your arms from moving. Once you are in position, let your body relax completely. Gently breathe in and out, as you let go of any unnecessary tensions. Try to keep your inhale and exhale approximately the same length. Remain resting in this position for several minutes.

PRANAYAMA BREATHING

When this prana has become controlled, then we shall immediately find that all the other actions of prana in the body will slowly come under control.

(*Vivekananda, 1953, p. 595*)

Practicing the yamas and niyamas sets in motion a process of examining one's life. By initiating the intent toward self-awareness, the therapeutic venture begins. Asana practice focuses attention on the body and mind in action. But simply turning attention outward toward behaving in the world does not get at the source of action. Breathing is an internal activity that forms a bridge between outer and inner world. It is readily accessible to everyone, and so is used in yoga to guide the practitioner toward awareness of inner experiencing. It can help clients walk across the bridge to innermost feelings and thoughts that are driving their conflicts.

The breathing techniques of pranayama have a primary place in yoga as one of the eight limbs of yoga. *Prana* in Sanskrit means "vital life force" or "breath," and the Sanskrit *Ayama* means "to suspend or restrain." Thus, the term *pranayama* means a way to restrain the vital life force, the breath. Each person has a flow of prana that can be raised, lowered, and directed. Through skilled, deliberate methods, pranayama brings breathing under conscious control. Yoga breathing practices influence both mind and body for optimal functioning. These breathing techniques enhance self-control in general and the regulation of emotions and thoughts specifically.

Anatomy of the Breath

Breathing can be divided into four parts. First is the inhalation, *puraka*, when the air is brought into the body. Next comes held-in-breath, *kumbhaka*, a moment between breathing in and out. Exhalation, *rechaka*, lets the air out, followed by a pause, or held-out breath, *shunyaka*, before the pattern repeats again.

After years of disciplined pranayama practice, accomplished yogis can vary their breathing at will. The process starts with gradual changes to normal breathing and builds from there. By making gentle adjustments in the pattern, timing, and force of different parts of the cycle of breathing, practitioners can gain voluntary control over what usually seems to be an involuntary process.

Preliminary Guidelines for Breathing

Here are some guidelines to offer to clients. Take time in performing any of the breathing exercises. People often need to warm up just as they would in any physical exercise, so encourage patience in allowing time to settle into the exercise. Do not breathe deeper than is normal and comfortable. If clients have any blood pressure health concerns, have them check with a medical doctor to ensure that it is safe for them to work with their breathing patterns.

Always breathe through the nose. Introduce the idea that as clients begin to perform a breathing exercise, they will need to pay attention to the sound of the air moving in and out along with the feeling of the air and the movement in their body. As they begin to explore breathing, they will notice that there are many interesting aspects to each breath, with great potential to alter breathing for the better.

If a client begins to feel dizzy or uncomfortable with an exercise, stop for a few minutes until the dizziness goes away and try again. Beginners sometimes experience a slight dizziness. Do not ever push anyone too hard or too fast. If dizziness persists, clients should be encouraged to check with their medical doctor. Be especially careful if the clients have any blood pressure issues, to monitor carefully and continue checking with their doctor, and always moderate practice so that unhealthy effects do not occur.

Developing Awareness

Breathing is usually an unconscious process that takes care of itself, but in leaving the breathing process involuntary and unconscious, people often form poor breathing habits, which may be a reflection of their inner distress. Conscious awareness can help to gently redirect breathing in new and better habitual ways. Its regular practice will lead to greater vitality and calm and thereby initiate a change in one source of disturbance. The first step in pranayama is conscious awareness of breathing. So, begin by turning attention to breathing.

The body responds best to gentle, gradual extension of its capacities, and thus control of breathing must always be done carefully and gradually. Ultimately, the breath happens of itself naturally. The practitioner just helps the process along without forcing anything, by deliberately enhancing the natural potentials of the body with corrective techniques.

The First Breathing Exercises

Yoga concentration begins as an inner experience. Two time-honored methods are counting the breaths and listening to the breaths. Experiment with both of these exercises to see which seems more natural. For those who are new to meditation, try doing each of these exercises for a brief time. Set a timer for 1 minute and then begin. As the client becomes comfortable with a short time, he or she will be able to increase the duration for longer periods. Do not force it, but be persistent.

Focus on Breathing: Counting the Breaths

Sit cross-legged on a pillow on the floor or on a chair if you find sitting on the floor uncomfortable. Keep the back relatively straight and head facing straight ahead so that the breathing passages are open. Close your eyes and begin silently counting each breath. Consider the entire breath—inhaling, holding, and then exhaling—as one breath. Count up to 10 and then begin again. If your attention wanders away from the count, gently bring it back as soon as you notice. Over time, you will be able to stay focused on your breathing at will.

Listening to Breathing

Some people find listening to breathing comes easier than counting the breaths. Sit comfortably and close your eyes. Pay close attention to the sound of the air as it enters your nose. Keep your attention focused on the quiet between inhaling and exhaling, and then listen carefully as the air exits again. Keep focusing attention on the sound of breathing. If you get distracted, gently bring your attention back to the sound of your breathing.

You can hear your breathing more easily by placing your hands lightly over your ears. Notice how the sound becomes more pronounced. After you have done this for a short time, you will become sensitized to your breathing sounds, making it easier to stay attuned.

The Complete Breath

The complete breath is one of the cornerstones of yoga, used in conjunction with most of the postures. It can be performed standing, lying down, or sitting. A complete breath naturally brings about movement of the chest, rib cage, diaphragm, and abdomen. When done correctly, the complete breath fills the lungs, expanding them forward, sideways, and backward.

Without realizing it, people often get into the poor habit of holding their chest, rib cage, diaphragm, and abdomen rigid while breathing. Such inflexibility prevents a full breath from happening. As a result, energy becomes blocked or even stuck, resulting in discomfort and even illness. The complete breath initiates a process to free breathing as it frees the body. The complete breath uses all of the respiratory muscles optimally. By involving the breathing processes in this way, unnecessary tensions are released, and energy flows naturally and fully.

For a standing complete breath, you can use your arms to help. Stand with your feet together, hands at your sides, and palms facing in toward your body. Let your head sag forward slightly and exhale. Slowly begin inhaling as you raise your arms out from your sides, arms straight with palms up. Let your lungs be completely filled with air when your hands meet up above your head. Hold for a moment and then slowly begin exhaling as you lower your arms. All of your air should be expelled when your arms are back down at your sides.

The complete breath can also be done sitting. Find a comfortable seated posture. Begin by inhaling. When you are first learning, in order to feel the motion as you breathe, place the palms of your relaxed hands on your upper abdomen. Your hands should move with your abdomen as your lungs fill with air. Exhale and let your abdomen deflate, keeping your hands in place.

Expanding the abdomen is just part of the complete breath. The diaphragm, rib cage, and chest are also involved. Place your hands on your diaphragm/rib cage area to feel this part of the breath. As you inhale again, notice how your diaphragm naturally expands downward as your ribs spread outward. Your chest also expands, and your shoulders rise slightly. The complete inhale, done correctly, will bring about movement in your abdomen, diaphragm, ribs, chest, and shoulders. Note the moment between inhaling and exhaling, and then begin to do the opposite, to exhale by relaxing your chest first, then your rib cage, and finally, lightly tighten your stomach muscles to help push the last bit of air out. Your chest and rib cage contract, and your shoulders drop with exhalation. One complete sequence—inhale, hold, and exhale, with one following the other—makes up a complete breath.

Inhalation and exhalation should be evenly timed, with a slight pause. You may want to count to four as you inhale and then four as you exhale. You can breathe for up to six counts. Do what feels comfortable. More advanced breathing exercises add a short pause between inhalation and exhalation, but at first the pause is minimal.

Work to keep the time that you spend inhaling and exhaling equal. This may mean shortening exhalation or lengthening inhalation. Try this out for yourself. Listen to your own inner rhythms. Even though you are deliberately trying to breathe in a certain way, keep it as relaxed and natural as possible. You should not feel like you are forcing your breathing to be longer or shorter. Breathing should not be strained, hard, or sudden. As your breathing becomes more balanced and comfortable, you may feel more relaxed and calm as well.

Activate the Kundalini

Kundalini energy is believed to be the natural energy stored at the base of the spine in the root chakra, the Muladhara, in a coil. Activating the Kundalini will give a feeling of energy to the whole body. Once you become comfortable with this exercise, you will be able to direct your energy to different chakra energy centers to enhance therapeutic work (see Figure 3.1).

Begin sitting in easy pose, with your spine fairly straight and eyes looking straight ahead. Breathe comfortably, balanced between both nostrils. Perform this breathing for several minutes until you are able to allow the air to flow through both nostrils evenly. Recall that when you breathe through both nostrils together, you are activating the central life force in the Sushumna channel that flows through the center of the body along the spinal cord. As you continue breathing comfortably, visualize energy flowing up the left side of your spine, rising up from the root chakra. Follow the energy as it flows all the way up through each chakra to the top of the forehead, the Sahasrara chakra. Then, visualize the energy flowing from left to right at the center of the forehead and then flowing down the right side of the spine, back to the root chakra. Now imagine the energy flowing around, under the root chakra, to the left side, and then back up again through your body. Repeat the circle flowing around naturally and comfortably for several minutes.

MEDITATION

Breathing and postures can only take clients partway along the path to becoming more self-aware. Often people do not actively direct their thinking but are, instead, the passive recipients of thinking processes, pulled in one direction or another by the objects of thoughts. The practices of Pratyahara, Dharana, and Dhyana put practitioners back into the driver's seat of their cognitive processes. This is an invaluable tool for anyone, and especially for clients who struggle with uncontrollable thoughts and feelings.

Pratyahara

Pratyahara is the withdrawal of perception from the outer world and turning attention inward. Traditionally, pratyahara involves withdrawing the senses and withdrawing the prana, energy. The two work together. Pratyahara can be understood by considering two sides: not-doing and doing. Withdrawing from involvement in outer, less important concerns, the not-doing side, conserves energy and frees consciousness for constructive use, the doing side.

Pratyahara discipline applies to many activities beyond the purely meditative context. One example of this is Method Acting, founded by Constantin Stanislavski, which teaches actors to withdraw their attention from the external world, the audience, and center their attention on their experience on the stage in the play.

This practice is particularly applicable to psychotherapy, where clients need to stop engaging in problematic behaviors, thought patterns, and emotions, freeing their energy for healthy behaviors, thoughts, and emotions. Variations on pratyahara can be helpful for many psychological problems, as will be seen in Part III.

Pratyahara Exercise: Withdrawing the Senses and Energy

This exercise withdraws the focus away from external stimuli and gradually turns attention inward. Withdrawing of attention from outer surroundings starts the process that can be achieved progressively in stages.

Begin by listening to the sounds outside. Also notice what you hear, see, or smell. As you do so, let your breathing be relaxed and allow your body to become comfortable. Then withdraw your attention from these outer stimuli to bring your attention closer, to the immediate surroundings in the room. Notice as many details as you can: the temperature, the sounds that you hear, the objects that you see around you, the texture of the area you are sitting on, and anything else that you notice. The outside stimuli fade away as the closer surroundings move into your foreground. Continue to breathe comfortably and relax as you focus attention around the room.

Now, narrow the field even more by turning your attention away from the room and toward your body sensations. You might find it easier to close your eyes now. Begin with your skin and notice if it feels warm or cool. Do you notice any other sensations? Breathe, relax, and then sense deeper in your muscles. Are some muscles tight and others loose? Moving inward, notice your heartbeat, your breathing, and any sensations in your stomach. As you turn your attention inward, the sights and sounds from the room drop away. Breathing comfortably, let your attention focus inward.

Finally, allow your attention to focus simply on being calm and quiet, without being directed to anything. Sustain this quiet, inwardly focused attention until you feel ready to stop. By withdrawing your senses stepwise from the outer environment, while simultaneously calming your energy with quiet breathing and relaxed muscles, you will develop a comfortably poised awareness. From the doing and not-doing practices of pratyahara, you are now ready to concentrate, contemplate, and meditate.

Enhancing Pratyahara Control

How do you quiet down a group of children who want to play? One way is to let them be free out on a playground. At first, they will rush around everywhere, but eventually, they become settled and play quietly. This principle can help for quieting down the run of thoughts that are continually flowing through the mind.

Sit quietly and let your thoughts run on. Allow them to jump around wherever they want to go, with one difference. Notice where each thought goes as it goes. Think about each thought as it appears. Stay aware of thoughts as they happen, without losing touch with the noticing part. At first, your thoughts will come and go very quickly, like a young child running and jumping around, but in time, just as the child becomes settled, the thoughts settle down as well. Practice this meditation regularly, and your thinking rate will slow down, becoming calmer.

Dharana Concentration

Narrowing the focus of attention is the beginning of *dharana*, concentration. Concentration is focused into a single point and kept there. One metaphor for dharana is like a method used to control a dog that wants to run wild. The owner can tie a string to the dog's collar and attach the string to a post in the ground. Now the dog can run wherever he wants within the radius of the rope, but no farther. Similarly, in performing dharana, the attention can roam freely, but it is tethered to the object of focus and nowhere else. But unlike the dog in our metaphor, the meditator *chooses* the object of focus and *deliberately* holds attention on that object. By sincerely making these decisions, a pointed, selective concentration can be trained. From the commitment, attention naturally flows toward greater discipline. Paradoxically, this willful act of deliberate attention prepares for the development of the ability to automatically allow a meditative union to happen at the later stages of meditation.

The skills of dharana can be especially helpful to people who feel driven by uncomfortable feelings or thoughts. By developing the ability to hold attention fixed on a neutral object, emotions and thoughts often become calm and steady of themselves.

Dharana on an Object

Any basic activity or thing can be used as an object of concentration, and we will offer opportunities later in the book for applying dharana in creative ways. *To begin learning this skill, pick an object that you find interesting, such as a painting, sculpture, or any object you like. Place it in clear view. Sit upright in easy pose and look at the object. Keep your attention focused on it, and notice everything you can: color, texture, shape, size, function, and meaning, if relevant. Do not think about anything else. If your attention wanders away, bring it back to the object. Gradually narrow the focus until you are just looking at one point on the object. Keep your attention focused only on the one point. Begin with just two or three minutes of concentration. Gradually increase the time as you become able to maintain your focus. Skills in concentrating improve with practice.*

Dharana on Breathing

Pranayama breathing may be used for dharana concentration. Focus all of your attention on breathing as you do it, to develop the deep, one-pointed concentration. This will also lead into deep meditation.

For this exercise, sit or lie prone in one of the postures described previously. Most important is to allow your breathing passages to be relatively relaxed. Close your eyes and turn your attention to your breathing. Breathe through your nose, not your mouth. Notice the air as it comes in through your nose, then flows down into your lungs and out again. Pay close attention to how your chest, diaphragm, stomach, and back move as you breathe. Do not interfere with the natural pattern of breathing. Just relax and breathe normally as you keep your attention focused on the process of breathing. If your attention wanders, gently bring it back to focus on breathing. These skills respond to practice, so be patient and keep trying.

Dharana on a Mantra

Another effective way to focus attention is by using a mantra. Mantras are practiced on several levels. First is the pure sound of the word; then the meaning of the word is contemplated; next comes the idea that this meaning embodies; and finally is a spiritual experience of the mantra. There are many mantras, and we will refer to several at various places in this book. The traditional mantra is OM. OM is the cosmic vibration of the universe that represents creation and the unity of all things.

Sit comfortably in easy pose or in the sitting chair pose, allowing your spine to be straight and your breathing passages to be open. Look at the OM picture here (Figure 5.7). The sound of OM is like the word "home" without the "h." Then, close your eyes and breathe gently for several moments as you relax. When you feel calm, slowly inhale, filling your lungs as in the complete breath. As you exhale, let out the sound OM. As you get close to the end of your breath, close your lips and vibrate with the "mmmmm" until the sound fades away. Then, gently inhale again and repeat the process. Continue for several minutes, keeping your attention entirely focused on the sound.

Next, imagine yourself making the sound as you breathe in and out, silently. Do this for several minutes as you breathe comfortably.

Now, look at the picture of the word again (see Figure 5.7) and then close your eyes as you visualize the word.

Contemplate the meaning and think deeply about ideas that are embodied in unity and creation. Allow the deeper spiritual feeling to rise within you. Sometimes you may want to continue chanting as you go through the steps. When you feel ready to stop, open your eyes.

Figure 5.7

Dhyana, Meditative Contemplation

As you practice fixing your attention on an idea, concept, image, sound, and so on, and holding the focus there in a meditative process, a transformation begins to happen, and the meditator is no longer pointing to something outside. The contemplating self and object join together as one flowing process. Thought, object, and thinker are one. Patanjali defined *dhyana* as "a current of unified thought" (Yoga Sutras III, 2 Patanjali, translated by Woods, 1927, p. 85). This is the moment of dhyana.

Training the intellect to hold a thought in mind allows it to be available to other thoughts in a chain of association. Connections are made. It is the play of the mind around it. This meditative contemplation can understand the object of focus so well that a more complete knowledge just happens. Yogic literature refers to this kind of knowledge as penetrating the essence of objects. Contemplation is a great mental tool for learning and a way of giving an opportunity through a trained attention to experience the unity of reality.

Contemplation Exercise With a Concept

For example, concentrate for a moment on the concept of yoga. Then think of one of the side topics in this book, such as asanas. Consider what they are and how they fit into yoga, and then return to the central concept, yoga. Do not lose the link. Then think of another topic, such as breathing with pranayama. Consider what it is, and how it relates to yoga. Then, return to the central concept of yoga. Keep the back-and-forth flow of thought. Think of each linked concept. You may want to note your thoughts down. Then come the links for contemplation/meditation, the play of thought and ideas concerning the meanings and relationships. Hold these in mind with concentration, as you contemplate each of the aspects of yoga. Next, simply allow effortless thought to continue. Trust the process you have set in motion, sitting quietly, and allowing any insights to emerge. Let your thoughts roam, as they will, perhaps becoming quiet or ranging around freely. You may find now, or later, that new ideas will occur to you that deepen your understanding of yoga.

From Contemplation to Meditation

The training that begins with withdrawing the senses, concentration, and then contemplation, readies you for deeper unity: immersion and oneness of Samadhi. Objectless and open, this form of meditation differs from rational thought, activating unconscious processes that use other areas of the brain. Refer to Figure 4.1 for a visual representation of this process from dharana and dhyana to Samadhi.

Immerse yourself in the process, permitting the whole to form, the unified pattern of interrelationship. Be one with the unified pattern. It is like shifting from a two-dimensional view to three dimensions, including all and encompassing all. The state of Samadhi develops as you forget your ego concerns, becoming fully engaged in something larger. New thoughts flow, creative and fresh.

Meditation brings higher consciousness, in harmony with the deeper spiritual nature of the world. Yoga meditation can help the therapist and client get the most out of each therapy session while discovering spiritual depth in everyday life.

Allowing Meditation

Lie down in savasana pose or sit up in one of the seated postures. Close your eyes, imagine a single point, and focus your consciousness on it. Imagine that the point gets smaller and smaller until it vanishes into nothingness. Breathe comfortably and let your body relax. Stay in this moment of focused attention, just here and now, effortless stillness, and become part of the emptiness. Let go with the process, trust, and eventually you will feel the joy of Samadhi.

CONCLUSION

Study the eight limbs carefully and get to know each one thoroughly. Then the appropriate application for your client will readily come to mind. You may also find these practices can be personally helpful.

PART III

APPLICATIONS

6

Overcoming Stress With the Eight Limbs of Therapy

Without discipline
He has no understanding or inner power
Without inner power, he has no peace
And without peace where is joy?

Bhagavad Gita (*Miller, 1986, pp. 36, 38*)

BACKGROUND AND THEORY

According to an American Psychological Association survey taken in the United States over a several-month period during 2008, 8 in 10 Americans feel stressed. Women outpace men in their stressful reactions to the economy and money matters (American Psychological Association, 2008). Stress symptoms are also a component of many common psychological disorders and are experienced as disturbing. Thus, therapists can expect that many of the clients who come for treatment are seeking relief from their stress reaction. These clients are often in the midst of a demanding, tense, or traumatic situation that cannot be avoided or immediately changed, such as from the workplace or financial concerns. However, research has clearly shown that *how* people cope with their stress can make a significant difference. Thus, therapists should understand how stress affects the mind, brain, and body and know what the best ways are to alleviate it. Yoga offers techniques that target the responses to stress in the mind-brain-body system, by altering consciousness, changing brain reactions, and easing body tensions. It builds skills that can be applied to help when discomforts from stress arise.

Stress Defined

Stress is a syndrome that is nonspecific to any one illness but is a component in them all. Canadian physiologist Hans Selye (1907–1982) was the first to recognize that there is a general pattern of stress (Selye, 1974). The pattern can be broken down into three phases. First is the alarm reaction that mobilizes internal resources to ready the body to handle the stressor. The sympathetic nervous system is activated, with an increase in heart rate and a concomitant deactivation of the parasympathetic nervous system with slowed digestion and decreased blood flow to the extremities. Second is the resistance, when the individual uses whatever resources are available to fight off the effects of stress. A cognitive component of interpretation comes into play at this stage, when people worry or think they are helpless, which may interfere with the body's natural ability to cope. By stage three, when the stressor persists, the resources become depleted, and the organism is exhausted. Symptoms may develop, such as high blood pressure, tension headaches, anxiety, depression, emotional outbursts or panic attacks, as well as disruptions to the natural sleep-wake cycle, appetite problems, and even substance abuse. This syndrome is a nonspecific reaction of the body as it adjusts to demands that are placed upon it, to try to return to balance.

Stress can be understood as the body's attempt to restore balance. The idea of balance is very old in the East, but also in the West. Hippocrates (460–360 BCE), the father of Western medicine, proposed that every illness comes when people get out of balance, and they remain sick until balance is restored. Today, we know the specific etiology of illnesses and treat them accordingly. However, the general, nonspecific imbalance in the body is still a factor, and the stress response is widely accepted as an accompanying component in most physical and psychological illnesses.

Balance was originally construed as homeostasis, that the body has one ideal internal balance point that it will always tend to strive toward no matter what has happened. But today, with a more integrative perspective, a new concept of balance has emerged, known as *allostasis*. Environment and past circumstances must be included as part of a dynamic balance between the organism and environment that is continually adjusting and adapting. Allostasis takes into account an ongoing updating of the body's balance point, depending on what has been experienced over time. So, for example, when clients have been stressed for an extended period, their brain-mind-body system will form an adjusted, allostatic equilibrium at a more activated level to meet the stressful needs of the situation (Ganzel, Morris, & Wethington, 2010).

Neurobiology of Stress

Several brain systems with a strong link to cognitions and emotions are involved in the stress reaction. When facing a perceived threat or danger, the brain sends messages to the endocrine system as part of a reaction pathway that links the hypothalamus, pituitary, and adrenal glands together, known as the HPA (hypothalamus-pituitary-adrenal) pathway (refer to Figure A.10). Generally, the hypothalamus is important in maintaining the allostasis between the body and the environment, and it does so through the HPA pathway. The hypothalamus also helps regulate many basic functions, such as sleeping, eating, and sex: thus, stress's disruptive affects. The hypothalamus receives excitatory and inhibitory inputs from the autonomic nervous system along with inputs from the senses that are related to what is being experienced within the body and input coming in from the environment. The hypothalamus then releases neurotransmitters and hormones that are routed quickly into the circulatory system for a fast response.

Several hormones are produced and released when people are under stress: corticotropin-releasing hormone (CRH) from the hypothalamus, adrenocorticotropic hormone (ACTH) from the pituitary, and cortisol from the adrenal glands. Production and release of another hormone, glucocorticoids, is fed back into the brain and pituitary to slow down the synthesis of CRH and ACTH. This circular process of activation and deactivation is usually kept in balance, but when a stressor is present, the system responds rapidly with a large increase in activity along the HPA pathway. Any increases are quickly brought back into balance when the person is healthy. An allostatic load from long-standing psychological factors, illnesses, or difficult external circumstances can create a balance that keeps the HPA pathway continuously activated. The more activated balance is experienced as stress.

Thus, the generalized stress reaction adds a higher level of activation to the brain-mind-body system. The positive side is that these processes are dynamic, always changing and responding, and so they can be deactivated at any point. By lessening the stress response, a more comfortable balance is found. The generalized, overall rebalancing of the brain's stress reaction can be a powerful force for psychological health. Research clearly shows that people can have an effect on stress. Even though the cause of a stress may be beyond their control, handling stress is within their control when they are armed with the mental and physical tools to combat it.

Why Some People Cope with Stress Better Than Others

Life is fraught with difficulties, and no one is immune from problems. Researchers have wondered for a long time why some people cope well with the stressors of life while others who have a similar situation do poorly. Stressful situations can even have a positive effect, spurring some individuals on to do better than they did before they encountered the stressor. For example, victims who were exposed to trauma during World War II sometimes had surprising effects. Many soldiers and concentration camp survivors had illnesses such as ulcers, migraines, and colitis disappear, whereas others who underwent the same circumstances came back from these experiences with emotional breakdowns and other serious illnesses (Whitehorn, 1956).

A great deal of research was done, with helpful answers found about the question of why some people deal with stress better than others. In general, successful coping strategies modify whether a situation or stimulus becomes helpful harmful to the individual (Lazarus, 1977). People cope better when a situation is appraised as a challenge rather than a threat. Thus, expectations about the stressfulness of an event can influence the effects of stress (B. P. Dohrenwend & Dohrenwend, 1981).

Irving Janis (1971) refined the understanding of expectancy when he followed the outcome of patients undergoing major surgery. Those who coped well had accurate perceptions and preparation, with realistic expectations based on being properly informed and prepared for the surgery. Those with unrealistically high expectations were disappointed and tended to be upset from the inevitable discomfort during recovery. Those who had low expectations also were uncomfortable and coped poorly. Clearly, with regards to anxiety about potentially stressful events, realistic concern—not too much or too little—leads to adequate preparation for challenges and less difficulty subsequently coping or adjusting.

Different kinds of stress require different strategies for coping. Lazarus distinguished between problem-focused coping and emotion-focused coping (Lazarus, 1991; Lazarus & Folkman, 1984). Personality factors can also affect how stress is endured, whether it is experienced as an overwhelming threat or as a challenging opportunity. According to prominent researcher Suzanne Kobasa (1979), the personality trait of "hardiness" gives a person the ability to endure stress by finding meaning and challenge in difficult life situations.

A Yoga Interpretation

The eight limbs of yoga can be used as eight limbs of therapy. Based in yoga theory, we can draw a new interpretation that adds another dimension for better handling of stress. Those who do well with stress often approach it like a form of yoga. They bring every resource into their coping with single-minded devotion. A mother cares around the clock for her feverish child, and in so doing, her breathing rate is held steady, and her body is ready for whatever action is required, such as staying alert throughout the night to hear if her child cries out in need. The mother who copes best keeps calm in order to be a positive source for support. So, even though her attention is fully focused on the needs of the situation, she has the detachment to do what her child needs without allowing herself to give in to worry, frustration, or anger. She approaches the stressful situation with attentive focus, absorbed in the process. All of her capacities are engaged—intellect, emotions, and body—without being distracted. Then, when the crisis has passed, she relaxes with a long night's sleep, in tune with a less demanding situation.

This ability to rise to a challenge, sustain attention, respond appropriately, and then relax again is one of yoga's greatest teachings. Through training in its methods, people learn the yoga of action, forged as habits that engage automatically to guide healthy responses no matter how difficult the situation. The Bhagavad Gita offers this paradigm for a philosophy of action, and the exercises given here present methods for bringing these teachings into practice.

TAKING YOGA FROM THEORY TO PRACTICE

Marta came to see us because she felt under tremendous stress. She had two teenagers, a daughter and a son. Her husband had left the family six months ago to live with his secretary. Marta and her children felt hurt and betrayed. Although he sent them child support, he was critical, hostile, and pressured Marta to get a job. Marta spent much of her time focused on her husband. She complained bitterly about how cruel he was for leaving her and the children. She felt unable to think about anything else. Marta was trying to find work, but she felt inadequate. She had stopped pursuing her career goals, working in higher education, after she got pregnant with their first child, and she had been a full-time mom ever since. Now she stayed up late at night, going online looking for jobs. She had trouble sleeping and often was awake until 4 AM. When she got up to make breakfast for the family, she was exhausted all day. She felt trapped and did not know how to escape.

Early in the treatment, we taught Marta how to relax using pranayama breathing methods and pratyahara withdrawal to give her some temporary relief. She learned techniques of meditation to narrow as well as to broaden the focus of her attention. She began practicing regularly.

We discussed the observance in the yamas concerning lying. At first, she was offended at the idea that *she*, the one who had been wronged, could be lying. We helped her to see that even though it was true that her husband had lied to her, it was not true that he was completely ruthless, since he was supporting the family financially. As she sorted out truth from falseness, her responses to the situation became truer. She took responsibility for the part she played in the breakup of their marriage, facing the problems that were there.

We also discussed opening herself to new learning, one of the niyamas. She was already familiar with the Internet, so why not use her time online more productively to read articles about modern theories of education? Gradually, she became less angry and her body rhythms normalized. As she started to feel better, she was able to go to sleep earlier and found herself able to spend more time with her children, which helped them be more comfortable. And as the family felt less stressed, her husband seemed to respond by being less critical. When we followed up on her some time later, she said that she was happier now than she had been for a long time during the marriage. She was working at an interesting job for an online university and enjoying her relationship with her children. Therapy helped her recognize that her stressful situation had challenged her to grow, and she was pleased to report that she had met the challenge well.

Yoga offers many ways to intervene in a stress reaction. People appreciate having tools they can bring into their everyday situation to help them. Yoga can be applied to approach stressful situations more adequately, thereby improving the situation as best as possible. The yamas and niyamas present an opportunity to reassess the situation through a helpful lens that promotes more adaptive and healthy interpretations and habits. For situations that are not possible to change, a different focus of attention may be needed. The use of yogic meditational approaches can help narrow the scope for better concentration. They also can help broaden the scope when clients are magnifying the problem by losing sight of the larger picture. Relaxation that calms the HPA pathway is also usually helpful. In addition, yoga can be applied to help clients perform therapeutic exercises, such as for posttraumatic stress disorder (PTSD), learning to shift focus away from the trauma and refocus on healthy, daily activities.

USING THE YAMAS AND NIYAMAS

The yamas and niyamas can act like a rudder to help people steer through difficult times. Similar to how cognitive behavior therapy helps people examine and then alter their irrational thought processes that may be leading to emotional discomforts, the yamas and niyamas offer guidelines for examining and then altering irrational thinking and destructive personal habits that may be adding to the difficulties of the stressful situation. We offer here some typical issues that arise under stress and some ways to think about and deal with them differently, using the yamas and niyamas to guide the process. These can be readily worked into the therapy, with variations suited to the person and the situation.

Often when people are in the midst of stress, they neglect their own health, in a sense harming themselves. Here you can draw from several of the yamas and niyamas together. Finding the time to be sure to take care of fundamental needs, such as bathing, eating, and getting adequate sleep, provides the nervous system with what it needs so that the HPA pathway is not overactivated from deprivation of basic needs. Clients may not realize how much caring for the brain and body can help them to feel better! Keeping physically fit, even if simply performing a few gentle stretches and breathing exercises each day, will help clients function better as well. Addressing the needs of the body can alleviate part of the discomfort of a stress reaction.

Cultivating moderation is another part of healthy functioning, and even though stressful situations often place extreme demands on people, finding a middle way to respond will help them maintain balance. For example, John was working excessively hard, traveling most of the time for business. He was an executive who was involved in large financial transactions, which carried a heavy weight of pressure and responsibility. He had to work late into the night in the hotel to prepare for the next day's work. His only relief from the stress was to treat himself to eating at expensive restaurants. At first, he felt justified in indulging himself, because he was working so hard, and the company was paying, so he reasoned that he was getting some compensation. But now he was overweight, uncomfortable, and having difficulty keeping up with the pace. His doctor warned him that he was at risk for a heart attack and should lose weight immediately.

John rediscovered his balance through meditation and self-awareness. He learned to focus his attention on the food as he ate it, and he realized that he did not need as much food as he thought to feel rewarded. He found enjoyment in the taste, not the quantity. And he discovered even greater satisfaction in moderation and self-control: eating less and enjoying it more. He also found that by meditating regularly, he felt less stressed with the pressures at work, handling them better. Much to his surprise, some of his coworkers turned to him for support as "the steady one."

The yama of not lying can also be interpreted as facing the truth about a situation, as with our client Marta. When people are stressed, they often exaggerate or distort their perspective, and in this sense, they are lying to themselves. Research has clearly shown that a realistic appraisal will make a difference in how well stress is handled, so therapy should help clients address the truth about their stressful situation. When facing difficulties, it is also helpful to be open to learning, the fourth niyama. Many stressful situations can be handled better when the true nature of the situation is understood with an open attitude and willingness to learn.

The third yama can be cultivated to help in developing restraint and control, by the deliberate practice of pranayama, postures, and meditation. People who are stressed often feel that they have no extra time to devote to such practices, but even 5 or 10 minutes each day will make a difference. For those who feel they have no free time, invite them to meditate for 1 minute at several different times each day. They will be surprised how much better they feel and how easy it is to do.

The yamas and niyamas encourage people to act according to values, such as not being greedy or stealing. When people can handle difficulties without violating their ethical principles, they come out of it stronger, with inner confidence. Therapy can show people how to draw from the strength of standing firm with values and having faith in better times to come. The belief in a higher power, as encouraged in the fifth niyama, fosters positive expectancies that can serve as a guiding light through even the darkest of times.

PRATYAHARA: WITHDRAWING

Pratyahara can help clients become aware and let go by withdrawing from habits that prevent, perpetuate, or intensify a stress response. For example, when people are stressed, they often carry unnecessary tension without realizing it. Here is an example of using pratyahara to let go of extra tension, thereby clearing the way to lower the stress reaction naturally:

Turn your attention away from the outer world toward the inner, the experience of your body. Notice what sensations you have in that area. Begin at your head. Pay attention to your face or neck. How are you holding the muscles? Are you tightening them unnecessarily? If possible, relax any unnecessary tightness that you notice. Then direct your attention down toward your shoulders. Pay close attention to them. Mentally trace out how wide your shoulders are. Notice whether you are holding the muscles tight, and let go if possible. Continue down through your body, first paying close attention and then trying to relax any extra tension. You may be surprised to notice areas that are tightly tensed but don't need to be. If your attention wanders away from your body to outer concerns, bring it back. But do not force relaxation; simply notice where you can or cannot relax, and gently keep trying to release unnecessary tension, which will naturally increase your relaxation.

Pratyahara Exercise: Withdrawing the Senses

This exercise will help direct the focus away from too many thoughts at once. Calm awareness develops with practice.

Lie down in savasana pose. Withdraw your attention from your outer sur-roundings as much as possible. Do not, for example, listen to the sound of traffic outside. Instead, turn your attention to your thoughts. Try to relax your thoughts just as you relaxed your body. Without forcing your thoughts to relax, simply let any irrelevant thoughts go and stay with this peaceful, relaxed moment. You do not need to think about anything in particular. If your thoughts wander away, gently bring them back to this calm moment as soon as you can.

Dealing With Resistance to Pratyahara

Clients who have difficulty doing pratyahara exercises may be engaging in attentional habits that interfere. For example, some people are distracted by subvocal planning of what they will do next, continually rehearsing their next steps. Others find their attention drawn to remembering past events, situations, or people. Help clients to understand what patterns may be in-terfering by turning their focus to their present experience.

Do you have hidden assumptions that might be preventing you from focus-ing attention inward now? Notice what you are doing instead. Are you thinking of the past or worrying about the future? Sometimes people believe they must be busy to be happy and that relaxation is just laziness. Are you feeling like pratyahara is doing nothing? Delve deeply and question any possible hidden assumptions.

Once you become aware of a habitual tendency or an assumption misdirect-ing your attention, make a small change during your pratyahara practice. For example, if you notice yourself planning, thinking about what you will be do-ing after your pratyahara session, notice this, and then try to stop planning and gently bring your attention back to the moment. Or if you are recalling what you were doing earlier, let go of the memories, for now. Whenever you notice that your thoughts are not on your practice during pratyahara, gently bring them back, and eventually, extraneous thinking will stop.

DHARANA: NARROWING THE FOCUS

People who are under stress often find it difficult to concentrate, are easily distracted, and cope poorly, adding to their stress. Correctly directing the focus helps narrow the attention. Attention can then be concentrated to a single point and kept there, leading to deep absorption. When the concentrated mind is absorbed in something, alterations of the body and mind take place naturally. Breathing calms, heart rate steadies, and the body relaxes. In addition, by eliminating extraneous details, the inner meaning of that thing may be revealed. Like an fMRI that can penetrate through the skull to show inner brain activations, so focused concentration can cut through to important details that might have been overlooked. Focus, cultivated and developed by this practice, becomes a great resource for accurate perception and clearer thinking.

Focusing attention has been taught since the early days of yoga, as this ancient story illustrates. Archery was offered to the youth of the warrior class in India to train their focus and acuity. Arjuna was a young warrior in training, later to become the main character in the Bhagavad Gita. Arjuna's class was instructed to draw their bows and aim for a bird perched in a distant tree to see who was the best. While the students held their bows taut, the teacher asked, "What do you see?"

The first student answered, "I see a field, some trees, and a bird in one of the trees."

The second student said, "I only see the tree that has the bird in it."

Arjuna's response was, "All I see is the eye of the bird." The teacher declared Arjuna the winner.

The exercises given here will guide in how to utilize the theory to develop a useful skill that will help tolerate stress better. With this new information, the stressful situation may be understood differently and thereby transformed. All of these qualities work together to help face adversity well.

Archer Pose

The legend of Arjuna can inspire focus of attention. Sometimes it is easiest to begin with a body posture that offers an accessible object of focus. The archer pose simulates holding and pulling a large bow, as in archery. It teaches clients to focus attention on posture and balance while gently twisting the upper body. It offers a good upper-body stretch while helping improve concentration.

Begin with your left foot directly in front of your right, toes pointing straight ahead, as though standing on a narrow balance beam. If you are a beginner, you may want to allow your stance to be a bit wider, with feet shoulder width apart, until you get accustomed to the posture. Pretend that you are holding a large bow. Extend your right arm out straight ahead with the fist closed as if holding the bow. Place the back of your left hand on your forehead as if you are resting the string across your hand. Look straight ahead at your extended right hand and inhale (Figure 6.1). Then slowly begin exhaling while turning toward the right, keeping your arms positioned, gazing at your extended thumb. Twist your upper body back as far as you comfortably can, and hold this position for a few seconds (Figure 6.2). Inhale as you gently untwist to face front again. Switch position by placing the right foot forward with the left arm holding the imaginary bow extended in front and the right arm bent. Now repeat the movement, twisting to the other side.

Figure 6.1

Figure 6.2

Focus on One Thing

Any object, picture, or piece of art can be used as the object of focus. Pick an object that is personally interesting, such as a painting or sculpture, or focus on the picture provided here (Figure 6.3) of Anahata, the heart chakra. Anahata is located in the chest (see Figure 3.1), and focus on this area is thought to bring about equilibrium when stressed.

Place the image in clear view. Sit upright cross-legged on the floor, on a small pillow, or on a straight-backed chair and look at the object. Keep the attention absorbed in the chakra and notice as many aspects of that object as can be thought of: its color (green), shapes, and balance. Think about how the balance of the form suggests equilibrium, being centered, and calm.

Now focus on the process of absorption. Notice the quality of your attention. If your attention is focused, intense, and fully engaged, continue to use it to explore the form and meaning of this chakra. If your attention is unfocused, vague, and undifferentiated, explore this quality of attention. For example, when attending to the picture: Are there any points of interest? Do you have difficulty thinking about the picture? Or did you have difficulty sensing the area in your chest? If your attention wanders away, where does it wander? Gently bring your

Figure 6.3

attention back to the object originally selected, noticing the process of doing so. Perhaps an unselected object of attention distracts you. Retrace the links back to the object of focus. Begin with just 2 or 3 minutes of concentration. Gradually increase the time as you become able to maintain focus. Skills in focusing of attention improve with practice.

Absorption in an Inner Image

After focusing on the picture (or object) with eyes open, close the eyes and imagine the chakra within your chest area, as a glowing green color or a sensation of tingling or warmth in the chest. People who are naturally able to form visual pictures will see a vivid image of the chakra. For others, body sensations might be more vivid. Keep your attention focused on the image or sensation, even if the picture is vague. Notice all of the details that you saw when looking at the object, such as its patterns and meanings. Stay relaxed in the sitting position with eyes lightly closed. If you notice your eyes tightening up as you concentrate, try to relax them. Keep focused on your eyes for several minutes, and then go back to focus on the inner image using the same methods first in the previous exercise and then in this exercise.

Narrowing the Focus to Develop One-Pointed Awareness

Pick a small area of the image and direct attention there. For example, if you are imagining the picture provided, focus attention on the star in the circle or on the lotus petals around the circle. Look carefully for a moment. When you have a clear sense of the part of the chakra you have chosen, close your eyes and imagine it vividly. Then, narrow your focus even more, perhaps to one point of the star or one lotus petal, and then to a single point. Keep the attention focused on this single point. Relax as you observe, inwardly. Let your breathing be calm and steady. If your thoughts drift away from the one-pointed awareness, gently bring them back as soon as you notice, and without criticizing yourself for losing focus, return to one-pointed awareness.

DHYANA: OPENING THE FOCUS

Sometimes people handle stress poorly because they are overly focused. They pick out one detail or aspect of the situation to notice, and then react to that as if it were the whole. For example, our client Marta was only focusing on her husband's leaving and ignoring the positive qualities the separation offered her. Yoga methods also teach clients the ability to expand their perspective in dhyana meditation.

Using the object of focus in the previous exercise, return to focus for several minutes, bringing the object of focus down to a pinpoint. Can you let the pinpoint become so small that it vanishes? Now, focused on nothing, allow yourself to simply be here in the moment, quiet, with nothing in mind. Let the sense of nothing spread outward, a quiet, vast, empty space, as you sit calmly. Stay with the flow of the quiet emptiness. If a thought or image occurs, simply let it go and return to this moment of quiet emptiness. Stay with the experience for at least several minutes, up to 15 minutes or longer if you can. You may be surprised that after performing this meditation, new options may occur to you about your situation as your thought processes open up, allowing in a broader perspective.

FOSTERING RELAXATION

The stress response is an activated state of readiness in the mind, body, and brain. A certain amount of alertness is helpful for handling demanding situations, but often the response is exaggerated and more than what is needed. Taking steps to restrain thinking and work through negative cognitions helps to lower activation. Now, the way is cleared for allowing relaxation. The following series of exercises brings relaxation through breathing, body poses, and visualizations. Practice these exercises regularly while in the midst of handling stress or for winding down following a stressful experience. Any of the relaxation exercises found elsewhere in this book could also be used.

Relaxed Breathing

The breath is a direct link to the emotions and the nervous system, so it can be used as a resource for calming. This classic yoga breathing exercise helps gently slow the breathing pattern, thereby setting in motion a calmer mind and body. Perform this exercise at different times throughout the day and evening when in the midst of stress to offer an oasis of relaxation and calm. The body eventually responds with a shift toward a more comfortable level of activation.

Sit in easy pose with your legs crossed. For those who prefer a chair, sit in an upright chair with feet flat on the floor. In either position, let the back be relatively straight, so that your breathing passages are unobstructed. Take a few minutes to focus on breathing, either listening to the breath or counting the breaths. Then, when your attention is fairly well focused on breathing, count 4 counts as you slowly breathe in, hold for 2 counts, and then breathe out for 4 counts. Make sure that the counting keeps your breathing at a comfortable pace. If 4 counts are too long or too short, adjust the speed of your counts until you can breathe comfortably and a little slower than before you started the exercise. As the exercise becomes easier for you, extend the count to 6 in, 3 hold, and 6 out. Use the instructions for a complete breath to make each breath fill your lungs, lifting your rib cage, as you breathe in. With each exhale, let your rib cage drop down as the air leaves your lungs and travels out through your nose. Also, keep in mind that you should not be breathing hard. Breathe naturally and lightly, but slightly slower. Keep your attention focused on the breathing process and sustain this for several minutes, working up to 10 to 15 minutes.

Savasana or Crocodile Relaxation

Take a periodic break to lie down either in savasana (on your back) or crocodile (on your front) pose. Refer to the instructions in Chapter 5 for the positioning. As you lie comfortably, allow your breathing to be soft and steady. Notice the surface you are lying on and how your body meets this surface. If you notice you are holding your body away from the surface, try to let go as if sinking into it or floating lightly over it. You may notice tension in your neck, back, shoulders, or perhaps arms or legs. If so, can you let the muscle relax?

Visualizing Beyond Thought

In this exercise, use a peaceful visualization to reduce and slow the continual flow of thoughts and thereby offer some relief from a difficult situation. Several visualizations are offered, but you may prefer to use something that is personally meaningful for the client.

Sit or lie down comfortably. Close your eyes. Think of the mind as a vast river and thoughts as small leaves or branches floating along. Watch from the banks of the river and allow the leaves and branches of thoughts to simply float past, with little notice except to observe that they do move past. Keep applying the same procedure: Notice the thought, think about it briefly, but disengage from it and return to concentration as soon as possible. The task is to stay focused. Eventually the stream of consciousness clears, and no new leaves of branches appear as thoughts clear. Remain in meditation, watching the quiet stream. If a thought intrudes into consciousness, notice it, think about it for a moment, and then let it go. Return to focused attention: poised, observing the stream, until you are ready to stop.

Another image that many people find helpful is a vista of grassy hills, rolling as far as the eye can see. *The clear blue sky meets the green hillside. All is quiet and still. In fact, it is so quiet that you can almost hear your own heartbeat. The muscles relax a bit, without effort. The colors are soothing; the breeze is soft. Just looking at this peaceful scene, your thoughts tend to slow, leaving an experience of calm and stillness. Do not do anything; simply enjoy the scene.*

A pond can also be an apt metaphor. *Sit quietly with your eyes closed. Imagine sitting on the shore of a pond. The pond is alive with activity. Frogs croak; crickets sing; birds fly overhead; a fish jumps out of the water, feeding on insects, splashes back, and jumps again after a bit, in another spot. Wind whips over the water, stirring up the muddy bottom. All is movement. Then gradually as the day passes, the conditions begin to shift. The wind dies down. The frogs settle in for a nap, the crickets are silent, the birds perch in the trees, the fish stops jumping and waits. The pond is quiet. The murky rippled surface calms as the mud sinks to the bottom, and the water is again crystal clear, reflecting the natural surroundings. All is stillness. Imagine this scene vividly. Stay with the quiet, crystal-clear water.*

CONCLUSION

Practice regularly. As skills build, clients will find it helpful to practice even in the midst of stress. The exercises can be performed briefly, for a few minutes, during the day or night, gradually and naturally increasing the time spent meditating. Eventually, a subtle change takes place. The automatic stress response can be moderated both physiologically and psychologically, bringing greater comfort and calm. And with this comfort comes a new element of calm for others who are also involved in the situation. This calm may become stillness in motion, to transform the larger interpersonal system.

7

Transcending Anxiety

The cause of suffering, which can be escaped, is the connection between the observer and the phenomenal world.

(*Patanjali in Miller, 1998, p. 49*)

THE ANXIOUS MIND, BRAIN, BODY, AND SPIRIT

Any yoga approach to mental disorders includes physical and mental dimensions and their interaction with the environment. The problem will be better understood by drawing from theories of mind, brain, and body in their context. Then, interventions can be multidimensional and multileveled, to work with the problematical connections from many different points of entry. Each theory of anxiety offers a dimension and a perspective. Through their integration come solutions for treatments.

The Brain-Body Anxiety Response

Anxiety involves several brain systems that have a strong influence on the brain and body. The autonomic nervous system gets involved through the stress pathway described in Chapter 6 (refer to Figure A.10), but in addition, the limbic system (refer to Figure A.6) plays an additional role. The thalamus acts as the gateway for signals received from the senses and then sent on to other parts of the brain for processing. A signal is relayed to the hypothalamus, which is the coordinator of internal functions, to put the system on high alert. The amygdala, which registers the quality and intensity of all our emotions, sends a signal to the hypothalamus that there is something to fear. This leads to the stress response. The hippocampus, where short-term memory is processed for long-term storage, monitors and adds to the signal from its experience. And the basal ganglia, involved in motivation and movement, act to coordinate emotions with movements (refer to Figure A.7). Finally, the cortex is activated, accompanied by more thoughts and ruminations about the anxious or fearful situation (refer to Figure A.8).

Several neurotransmitters play a key role in anxiety. Glutamate, the excitatory neurotransmitter, and GABA (gamma-aminobutyric acid), the inhibitory one, provide excitation and inhibition throughout the brain. Serotonin regulates moods, norepinephrine enhances alertness, and dopamine is involved in reward. When the system is overactive and tense, there is an imbalance of neurotransmitters, such as not enough GABA. Drug therapies for anxiety often increase the amount of GABA in the system, to reduce the overexcitation that people feel when they are anxious. But drugs are not the only way to alter the balance of neurotransmitters. Meditation, hypnosis, and psychotherapy can also be used to calm the system, thereby creating a more comfortable balance.

All of the anxiety patterns, even an entrenched anxiety reaction, can be changed. The methods presented in this chapter help shift the balance back to a calmer center.

The Psychological Response to Anxiety

Psychological theories describe the etiology of anxiety from an emotional, cognitive, or behavioral perspective. Emotional models consider that fear and anxiety derive from an emotionally traumatic event. The link may be direct. For example, a victim of near drowning sometimes retains a fear of water. Or the link may be indirect, as in a sexual conflict represented symbolically in a fear of snakes or a fear of intimacy. These links can be broken when the roots of the trauma are faced and courageously felt through in psychotherapy.

Behavioral theories are compatible with the emotional model. Anxieties and fears develop from some initial stimulus combined with an unconditioned response. When the two become paired, a conditioned response forms. In behavioral approaches, fear and anxiety can be unlearned or extinguished. In general, face the feared situation with a competent trusted therapist, and in time, the conditioned anxious response is not elicited.

Cognitive factors add another dimension by including the way people interpret themselves and events as playing a critical role in the etiology of anxiety (Barlow, Chorpita, & Turovsky, 1996). Perceptions and interpretations of the self, other people, and the situation can intensify or diminish the response. Learning to think more realistically can dramatically alter anxious responses.

All of these dimensions are perspectives of the personal experience of anxiety. Emotional, cognitive, and behavioral responses influence the biological system. Therapy can intervene by working with any or all of these components to bring about change. Yet, anxiety has another dimension.

Integration

From the perspective of how we exist in this world as human beings, we all must face death, tragedy, vulnerability, and the unpredictable contingencies of life. The inescapable conditions of life, with much that is unknown and beyond control, can lead to existential anxiety, a feeling known as angst. Yoga philosophy offers an answer to this condition. As a part of the greater cosmos, each individual human spirit merges with the greater universe, and in this sense, we all exist as part of the larger community. People can gain strength by drawing on their sense of being part of something beyond the confines of the individual self. By seeking higher values, people can expand their potential and transcend limits.

CATEGORIES OF ANXIETY

Intense anxiety afflicts many people and can be alleviated with proper treatment. Included here are the main types of anxiety disorders. The exercises in this chapter address these problems.

Generalized anxiety disorder (GAD) involves a broad, general feeling of anxiety that can inhibit people from doing things and going places. *Social anxiety disorder* (SAD) is felt in social situations with other people.

Sometimes it is specific, such as feeling uncomfortable doing public speaking. People with social anxiety feel as if others are judging them negatively. *Panic disorder* is often experienced as having a severe physical crisis, such as a heart attack, when there is no real physical danger. These individuals feel an intense panicky feeling, which usually lasts from 1 to 10 minutes.

Specific phobias are fears of one thing, such as a fear of dogs, heights, spiders, elevators, or open spaces (agoraphobia). These fears are often initiated by a traumatic event, but not always. *Posttraumatic stress disorder* (PTSD) may occur after someone has gone through a very traumatic experience, such as rape, war, or torture. Not all people who undergo such experiences have an anxiety reaction, but for those who do, it can be very debilitating. *Obsessive compulsive disorder* (OCD) is also categorized as an anxiety problem. Sufferers have intrusive thoughts that bring about feelings of anxiety, which leads them to engage in behavioral rituals to try to reduce the anxiety.

YOGA TREATMENTS

Anxiety can be viewed as a unified and balanced system of interactions from the body, brain, and mind, as we have described. Interventions can be made at one point or another. By making a change in one part, the whole system feels the effects. With continued input, the client readjusts to find a better balance, one without anxiety.

Clients who suffer from anxiety feel that the symptoms are beyond their control. Therapy intervenes, with ways to help them master these experiences, often through cognitive methods that alter the thinking processes. Yoga methods provide additional tools that give clients mastery over their mental processes. The control they gain from the practices can bring a reduction or even cessation of the anxiety reaction. The exercises provided here help clients enhance the skills they need to overcome problems with anxiety.

Calming the System

Slow, relaxed breathing soothes the sympathetic nervous system while activating the parasympathetic nervous system. This shift leads to lower cortisol levels, relaxed muscles, and a decrease in blood pressure. Here is one exercise to help calm the system, but you can also use any of the breathing exercises for calming that are given in this book.

Sit on a chair or on the floor in pelvic pose, whichever is most comfortable. Place your hands on your knees. As you breathe in, arch your back and head as you move slightly forward. You will feel a gentle stretch of your whole spine all the way up through your neck. As you exhale, gently round your back in the opposite direction, tucking your head slightly. Breathe fully but keep the breaths soft, slow, and flowing as you gently arch and round with each breath. Repeat this pattern up to five times. Then return to a centered position and breathe comfortably, meditating on the breath as you allow relaxation and calm to spread throughout your whole body.

Grounding the System

When people feel anxious, they feel a sense of threat coming from the environment and ignore any support that might actually be available. This exercise can help the anxious person find his or her grounding, by literally attuning to sitting and taking strength from the support of the ground or chair.

This exercise can have a powerful impact if performed outdoors sitting on the ground, but it can also be adapted to sitting on the floor indoors or sitting on a chair. Sit in easy pose for several minutes with your eyes closed and follow your breathing. Then, place your hands, palms down, on the ground at your sides. Feel the mass of the ground beneath your palms. Notice how the ground supports your body. Are you pushing down on the ground or holding yourself away from it? Allow your body to take the support from the ground (or the floor or the chair) by letting your sitting muscles relax. The ground (floor or chair) can provide support for you, and you can allow yourself to accept that support gratefully, feeling a sense of comfort and reassurance. Allow yourself to feel part of the greater universe and participating in the support that is given.

Visualizing the Muladhara Chakra

Another way to find support and grounding comes from within. The Muladhara is the root chakra (refer to Figure 3.1 and Figure 3.2), located at the base of the spine, which is often visualized as the seat of the energy channel. Attuning to this area can encourage a firm foundation, helping clients to feel grounded and balanced.

Sit in easy pose and close your eyes as you breathe comfortably, in and out with the complete breath. Turn your attention to the Muladhara chakra and imagine breathing into and out of this area. Picture the energy from the flowing breath as red in color, circling around in the Muladhara, perhaps bringing a warm or tingling sensation. Feel the sense of stability and balance as your seat becomes stabilized and centered.

Balancing the System

People who feel anxiety have an imbalance in their nervous system, with overactivation in some areas and underactivation in others. These physiological imbalances can be addressed through postures and breathing. As the nervous system readjusts, the accompanying thought patterns tend to ease, making them easier to address and work with in therapy.

Balance Through Posture

Finding your center when sitting and standing can be a helpful tool to use when you are feeling anxious. It will help you to return balance. *Begin with sitting. Sit on the floor in easy pose, with or without a supportive pillow, or sit in an upright chair. Allow your spine to straighten as you gently lift your head up, keeping eyes facing straight ahead. You will feel a slight lengthening of the spine and neck. Close your eyes and turn your attention to your body. Now, gently rock forward and back, keeping your head and spine relatively straight. Feel how your muscles relax as you sway, noting what muscles become tighter. When you move through the center you will notice a point where muscles relax, and breathing is easier. This is your balance point. Stay there for a moment and allow breathing to relax even more. Now try swaying from side to side, noting the change in muscle tone as you move farther away from center on either side. Once again, take note of that middle point where your muscles seem most comfortable and breathing is easiest. Here is your balanced center. Stay in this position for several minutes, enjoying the effortless feeling of sitting, aligned with gravity and in tune with the greater whole.*

To find your balance in standing, follow the instructions given in Chapter 5 for mountain pose, where you gently sway from side to side and from front to back until the center point is found.

Balance Through Alternate Nostril Breath

This exercise balances the energy currents on both sides of the body. It can also enhance concentration. *Curl the fingers of your left hand and rest your thumb against the left side of your nose to open up the right nostril (Figure 7.1).*

Figure 7.1

Breathe in, out, and in again, allowing the air to flow fully as in the Complete Breath (instructions given in Chapter 5). Next, cover your right nostril with the edge of your curled fingers and exhale, inhale, and exhale with the left nostril open. Alternate back and forth in this way for 5 to 10 breath cycles (Figure 7.2).

OVERCOMING ANXIETY ACTIVELY

Some clients who are experiencing anxiety may have difficulty sitting quietly in meditation. They find that when they try to meditate, their thoughts race, their heart rate increases, and they feel more anxious. Facing the problem is part of the cure, yet when they try to think about the problem, they may also become more anxious.

Figure 7.2

Action is a helpful alternative way to work with clients who have diffi-culty sitting quietly. Paradoxically, through activity, lessening of the overacti-vated nervous system and constant flow of inner thoughts comes about. But activity alone does not necessarily bring lasting relief. Many anxious clients engage in sports like jogging, which offer them only temporary relief. But activity performed meditatively will start a healing process that moves the client toward facing the traumatic experience. These techniques can change cognitions, calm emotions, alter the nervous system, and offer a spiritual connection to the greater whole.

Mantras, breathing exercises, and asana postures can become the vehicle for activity. Meditation on these activities will help attention to focus. Once the process is begun, anxious clients will be able to benefit from relaxation methods presented in other chapters to help them maintain their shift to a calmer adjustment.

Asana Series

People with anxiety often feel out of control of their thoughts and feelings. Clients can be given a simple series of asanas to practice regularly between sessions. Asana practice is a straightforward way to begin a process that allows attention to be focused deliberately and voluntarily. These asanas are a balanced, simple, and easy-to-perform set of exercises that allow the client to concentrate attention more readily than sitting in meditation. Eventually, meditation skills become possible. We offer this set of postures to open the breath by improving flexibility in the rib cage. Many postures tend to relax the body and open the breathing passages. Some postures with symbolic meaning can elicit archetypal experiences, becoming a resource for self-soothing and comfort.

Perform each posture slowly, with your mind fully focused during every movement. Pay attention to the subtle differences in tension and relaxation of various muscles. Observe sensations and positioning. Notice how your breathing affects the posture. Stay fully attuned at all times and you will derive deep benefit: From the simple comes the profound.

Backward and Forward Bend

Stand with feet together and arms down at your side in mountain pose. Hold your hands together, palms touching, and breathe comfortably for several minutes (Figure 7.3). When you feel calm and ready to begin, exhale completely. Then, begin inhaling as you circle your arms out and above your head until your palms touch each other, extended above your head. Bend backward as you look up and complete a slow inhalation. Hold for a moment and then breathe out and in (Figure 7.4).

Breathe out slowly as you bend forward from the waist. Try to keep your back straight for as long as possible as you lower your body all the way down (Figure 7.5). Tuck your head between your arms as you exhale. Your arms hang down at your sides (Figure 7.6). Go only as far as you can. If your legs are too tight at the backs of the knees, you may at first bend them a little for comfort. Later, you should be able to have them straight. Hold this position and breathe comfortably in and out several times. Now slowly return to the standing position. Stand in mountain pose for a moment, relaxing as much as possible. Breathe comfortably.

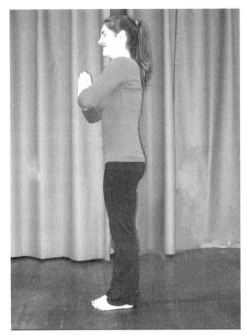

Figure 7.3

Figure 7.4

Figure 7.5

Figure 7.6

Triangle Pose

Place your legs approximately 2 feet apart, raise your arms out sideways to shoulder height, and inhale. Slowly bend to the left, keeping your arms stretched out, and begin exhaling. Rotate your left hand down to lightly grasp your left leg as the right arm comes overhead and until it is pointing straight up as you continue to bend sideways (Figure 7.7). From this position, relax your neck muscles and any other muscles that are not involved in this stretch and breathe comfortably. Slowly straighten as you inhale again and return to the starting position. Repeat the same motion on the other side.

Figure 7.7

Twisting Triangle Pose

The triangle posture can be varied to add a twisting stretch (Figure 7.8). *To perform the twisting triangle, place yourself in the opening part of the Triangle Pose with feet wide apart. Inhale as you raise and extend your arms straight out from your sides so that they are parallel to the floor, palms facing down. Exhale as you bend forward toward your left leg, placing your palm on the inside of your left ankle with your right hand. You may need to hold higher up on your leg if you cannot reach your ankle. Let your open left hand point straight up, with fingers loosely extended. Look at your raised hand gently with your right hand to increase the stretch, keeping your knees straight. Hold for a few seconds and then return to the standing position as you slowly inhale. Repeat on the right side, exhaling slowly as you go down, and inhaling as you stand up.*

Figure 7.8

Cat's Breath

The cat's breath helps to relax and stretch the back and midsection, coordinating breathing with movement. Begin on your hands and knees. Inhale as you gently and slowly arch your back and raise your head to look straight in front of you (Figure 7.9). Feel the movement. Do not push to the point of pain. Let the air fill your lungs completely. You should get a full stretch along your entire back. Then exhale slowly and round your back carefully as you pull your stomach gently in and tuck your head down (Figure 7.10). Again, do not push to the point of pain. Repeat the entire sequence several times, moving and breathing slowly. Keep the rest of your body relaxed, such as your jaw, face, and neck, as well as your arms and legs. This requires focused attention and slow, aware movements.

Figure 7.9

Figure 7.10

Child Pose

The Child pose is a good, relaxing posture to perform after stretching or curving the back. It can give a feeling of reassurance and comfort, a resource when feeling anxious.

Sit on your feet in the pelvic pose, kneeling position. Bend forward slowly until your head touches the floor. Allow your arms to rest comfortably at your sides, with your elbows bent so that they can rest on the floor (refer to Figure 10.6). *You may need to shift or move slightly to find the most comfortable position. Adjust your breathing to a calm rhythm, and rest in this position.*

Meditation

End this routine in savasana (corpse pose), for a deep and relaxing meditation. Begin by tightening your feet and legs. Hold them tightly for about 30 seconds, but keep the rest of your body relaxed. After the 30 seconds has passed, let your legs and feet relax completely for one minute. Next, tense and relax each part of your body, one by one, gradually moving up. Finally, tighten all over and hold for one minute. Then, let go of tension as completely as you can. As you perform this exercise, keep your attention focused on each muscle group as you scan through your body. If your attention wanders, gently bring it back to what you are doing. If you notice that you lost your concentration as you worked on an area, repeat the effort again with more awareness. Now that you are fully relaxed, rest your mind and body together. Do not do anything; just enjoy the feeling of absolute calm. You may feel sensations of release, a spiritual experience of being detached from the everyday worries and concerns, completely at peace.

DYNAMIC WORK ON THE ANXIOUS MIND-BODY-BRAIN SYSTEM

When people are anxious, they take on a certain posture, breathe in a particular patterned way, and focus thoughts on certain redundant patterns. This pattern of breathing, body positioning, and thoughts can become an object for meditation, similar to meditating on a yoga pose. Focusing attention on the posture helps to face the anxiety and gain insight into the anxious memories, thoughts, and emotions as they are expressed in the body. These exercises should be practiced during the therapy session, with your therapeutic expertise to guide clients in working through corresponding thoughts and feelings as they come up.

Meditating on Posture and Breathing

Begin by thinking about something that brings on anxiety. Let the feeling begin to develop. Let your body move as you feel the emotion. Notice the body positioning that goes with it. Pay attention to your pattern of breathing. Sit in this position for several minutes. Notice accompanying thoughts, and then shift back to paying attention to breathing in the body position. If the experience becomes uncomfortable, stop and relax for a few moments, and then try again, when you feel ready. Talk with your therapist about what you are feeling in this posture, if appropriate.

Working With Complementary Opposites

In general, yoga is concerned with contraction and extension: bending forward and bending backward, action and reaction. So, if you are anxious and bent forward, do the opposite, bending backward. If your breathing is tight and short, try breathing loose and long. Explore the opposite, and notice what you are feeling as you stay with this new posture for several minutes. Scan through your body to notice what muscles are tight and what muscles are loose. Do your thoughts and feelings change somewhat? Notice how they do. Once again, discuss what is experienced now. Compare it to what you were feeling in the opposite position.

Centering

Now find a posture that is centered. You might find yourself in a straighter position, perhaps with your breathing rate steady. Find what feels natural and comfortable. Notice your breathing and let it find its natural rhythm. Allow your attention to focus on your body and breathing, and sit comfortably for several minutes. Talk about what you are feeling now. Often people will experience a calm, steady emotional state along with a relaxed body position.

WORKING WITH PANIC DISORDER

Anxiety sometimes involves linking uncomfortable body sensations in the chest to beliefs about what such physical symptoms usually signify, such as worry about having a heart attack. A real and existing pattern emerges from associating these components together, although not originally from an actual heart condition. Even if a medical checkup determines that no underlying physical cause exists, the sufferer must truly accept that there is no physical problem to become free from the anxiety. Yoga meditation combined with cognitive behavior therapy (CBT) can help bring about this change.

Deconstructing Anxiety

The first step is to contemplate the idea that sensation and cognition are actually distinct and separate. A pure sensation and the thoughts about the sensation can be distinguished using meditation, and this begins a process that helps deconstruct the anxiety reaction.

Dharana Focus on Sensations

Start by meditating on the sensations of anxiety. Notice the qualities of your breathing. Next, zoom in to focus on the sensory details, such as the air coming into your nose, its temperature, and its sound. Notice that each breath has its own group of sensations. Turn your attention to the feelings in your chest. Notice how your rib cage lifts and drops with each breath. Pay attention to any other sensations, such as the temperature of the skin.

Dharana Focus on Thoughts

Turn your attention to your thoughts. Notice how your thought processes distract your attention from focusing on sensations. Recognize that the thoughts are not what you are feeling either. Thoughts are interpretations, abstractions from the pure experience. The idea of an anxiety attack is a group of thought patterns about sensations and emotions. Your thinking builds up a repetitive pattern of cognition. Just as each breath is a combination of several sensations, so each anxiety attack is a collection of sensations combined with an interpretation added to it, probably a negative interpretation. Can you recognize how sensations and thoughts are two different things?

Dhyana Contemplation

Contemplate the validity of the thoughts. Knowing as you do that there is nothing medically wrong, can you question the truth of those thoughts? The idea that anxiety is a sign of something physically wrong is an illusion. Yoga meditation has shown you how to perceive what is truly there and let go of anything that you have added. Can you recognize now how you are adding an interpretation to the pure sensations and then feeling frightened by your thoughts about those sensations?

People often compress all of their anxious experiences together into one dreaded experience, but as you break it down into its elements, you can contemplate the truth of the matter. Mentally break down the anxiety into its component parts. Anxiety can be thought of as a conglomerate of moments, during which a frightening interpretation is added to describe an uncomfortable sensation. This process tends to increase the intensity of the sensation, leading to a further interpretation, such as "It's getting worse." Each successive moment includes an interpretation followed by an even stronger sensation in reaction. First, observe this spiraling process as it unfolds. Then as soon as possible, notice the separate parts: sensations, interpretations, and emotions. Try to recognize that the interpretations are separate from and are not the same as the sensations or the emotions.

Now extend the meditation. Notice how the components influence and are inseparably part of each other: Worrying interpretations provoke more worry, and the worry brings on more discomfort, in a self-perpetuating cycle. Question the realistic certainty of this reaction with inwardly focused reassurance, such as "I know that my worry may not necessarily be what the sensation will bring; I have checked out my condition, and I know that there is no physical problem."

Be patient with the process. Keep returning to the actual sensations and experiences and question any illusions that take you away from what is actually perceived. Allow breathing to find a natural rhythm appropriate to the moment. Question your interpretations. Keep attention focused on sensations, and note the periods of time that the feeling diminishes. Anxiety in general tends to become easier to handle and eventually diminishes in intensity.

TREATMENTS FOR PTSD

James had suffered a traumatic experience during his military service in Iraq. He came from a poor family and was raised by his hard-working mother. He realized that there would be little opportunity for him, so he joined the military. He planned to attend college after his service, counting on his tuition being provided by a military scholarship.

He had risen to the challenge of daily life in the army and had become close friends with the people in his unit. One day he was riding in the back of a truck with several of his friends to transport supplies. Suddenly, a deafening sound filled his ears, and then he was flying through the air, feeling a searing pain as he hit the sand and rolled. He struggled to his feet, unaware that blood was streaming from a cut on his forehead and nose. What he saw shocked him. Amidst the flames were the dead bodies of his friends.

James had suffered several injuries that required he be sent back to the United States to recover. Now, some time later, his body had healed, but he could not completely overcome the shock and loss from his traumatic experience. He had gone through CBT. Feeling somewhat better, he enrolled in college, but whenever the workload from his courses mounted, he was flooded with terrible images and found himself unable to concentrate.

We helped him to take up where his CBT had left off and go one step further. He learned meditation, using a mantra and breathing techniques to help him regain control of himself, even when he faced stress and challenge. In time, he was able to successfully pursue his education and go on to a fulfilling career that made his mother proud.

The Role of the Hippocampus in PTSD

Research has found that people suffering from PTSD have a smaller hippocampus, which makes them less capable of drawing on memories to evaluate the nature of the stressor. But if the correct learning experiences are given, the hippocampus can increase in size (McEwen, 1998). For example, cab drivers tend to be continually engaged in spatial orientation tasks, also a function of the hippocampus. Researchers found that cab drivers had larger hippocampi than noncab drivers of the same age (McGuire et al., 2000). So, the hippocampus may grow as well as shrink, depending on stimuli. Correct learning experiences are likely to stimulate its growth. Given the research that meditation reduces anxiety, combined with the capacity of the hippocampus to grow, meditation is likely to help the impaired hippocampus to regenerate (Piver, 2008).

The methods included here offer tools that work on several levels. Clients learn how to deliberately focus attention and build skills they need to shift attention away from the trauma. In addition, those who have undergone a traumatic experience have faced some of life's most difficult challenges: tragedy and loss, in life-and-death situations. Having endured, they have gained recognition of forces acting beyond the self. Therapy can help draw on positive forces for inner strength to meet life's challenges well.

People suffering from PTSD can benefit from practicing dharana meditation, to direct attention and pinpoint it. Use exercises from Chapter 5 and elsewhere in the book to help build these mental skills. The mantra meditation that follows helps clients build mental focus, while also drawing spiritual strength from their faith.

Mantra Meditation

The use of mantra meditation has been tested with veterans and found to be helpful (Williams et al., 2005), as reported in Chapter 1. People who are suffering from PTSD need to be able to refocus their attention away from the problem to encourage the nervous system to return to a more comfortable balance. Over time, the allostatic balance shifts from an overactivated state to a calmer balance. Then the anxiety feelings begin to subside as the brain-mind-body system finds a more comfortable balance.

Here is a list of mantras from different spiritual traditions that were used in the Williams (2005) study. Choose one that is meaningful to you to recite. Recite the mantra in its original form, rather than reciting the translated words, because the syllables are significant for their vibration of tones in combination, not just for their meaning. We provide some possible choices, but please feel free to choose something else if you have a mantra that you prefer to use.

Buddhist: Om Mani Padme Hum (Aum Mah-nee Pod-may Hum): An invocation to the jewel (self) in the lotus of the heart.
Christian: Kyrie Eleison (Kir-ee-ay Ee-lay-ee-sone): Lord have mercy, or the Lord is risen.
Hindu: Rama (Rah-mah): Eternal joy within.
Jewish: Shalom: Peace.
Muslim: Bismallah Ir-rahman Ir-rahim (Beesemah-lah ir-rah-mun ir-rah-heem): In the name of Allah, the merciful, the compassionate.
Native American: O Wakan Tanka: Oh, Great Spirit.

Once you have chosen one mantra, sit down in easy pose. Speak the mantra, beginning with 6 minutes and working up to 30 minutes each day. Begin with 2 minutes devoted to each part of the practice, and work up to 10 minutes for each segment. Repeat the practice a second time each day for even stronger results.

Begin by speaking the words aloud slowly, repeatedly, as you relax your chest to allow the words to flow. Focus your attention on the sound of the words and the vibration in your chest and voice box as you speak. Next whisper the words slowly, aloud, keeping your attention focused on the sound and the vibrations.

Now, close your eyes and imagine speaking the mantra for 5 minutes. Keep your attention focused only on the imagined speaking of the words. Finally, with attention focused, just sit quietly for several minutes as you allow the calm, centered, quiet experience to be. When you feel ready, open your eyes and stretch gently as you stand up.

TREATMENT FOR OCD: TRADING RITUALS

Clients with obsessive compulsive disorder (OCD) use rituals in an attempt to allay their anxiety, but these rituals are ultimately emotionally unfulfilling, and the anxiety reaction continues. Yoga includes many rituals to move toward health in body and mind. You can introduce a yoga ritual that gives the client something healthy to do instead of the symptomatic ritual, and at the same time yoga practice will address the underlying anxiety.

The first niyama, Shaucha, refers to purity, cleansing, and neatness of body, mind, and spirit. People who suffer from OCD are often concerned with cleanliness. Therapy can gently direct their interest in a healthier direction by the introduction of cleansing meditations. These meditation traditions offer a visualization of replacing stale air with fresh air. The fresh air brings a feeling of energy and renewal. These meditations can be substituted for the usual ritual, thereby building control, fostering calm, and facilitating change.

Cleansing Breath 1

This meditation alters the rhythm of breathing, clearing out impurities and making room for clean, fresh air. You may like performing this exercise outdoors in fresh air, such as at the beach, in the woods, or in a garden. Sit comfortably and breathe consciously for a few moments, to center yourself in your breathing. When you feel ready, inhale for a count of 3, with a complete breath in. Hold the breath for a comfortable count of 1 or 2. Then exhale for 4 counts with a complete breath out. Finally, hold for 1 or 2 counts. Practice this gently and softly, letting your breathing be as relaxed as possible. Over time, you may be able to increase the length of each part of the breath, but keep the ratios the same. Controlling the timing of breathing is a more advanced skill that develops very slowly with practice. Be patient, because these skills take time to master.

Cleansing Breath 2

This exercise uses the abdominal area to push out stale air that can accumulate from shallow, incomplete breathing. Modify it in accord with your experience and response. Stand or sit upright, allowing your spine to be straight. Breathe comfortably and naturally for about a minute. When you feel relatively calm, exercise your diaphragm by exhaling quickly through your nose with a quick, short burst as you pull your abdominal muscles in until all your air is expelled. Beginners start with one round of a few quick breaths out. Each short exhalation should make an audible sound from air pushing out. Once the air is expelled, relax your abdomen and breathe normally for close to 1 minute.

If you feel ready, take another breath in and perform a few quick bursts, followed with normal breathing. Do three rounds, with each round lasting for about 30 seconds, and include rest time between. Gradually work up to a number of breaths as you gain skill in the repetitions, over a period of at least a month. Be patient and do not push yourself. If you feel discomfort or dizziness, stop doing this exercise and rest for a few minutes. Increase the number of quick breaths only as you are able. Practice this exercise for several minutes, regularly at daily intervals. Many people find that this meditation clears away troublesome emotions, leaving calm and comfort.

CONCLUSION

Combine the exercises from this chapter with methods in the stress chapter. Anxiety disorders usually bring additional stress. When people are suffering, practice should be every day, twice daily for stronger results. Even a few minutes spread throughout the day will start the process. Confidence builds with practice, and so do the beneficial results!

8

Freedom From Depression's Grip

Yoga is known as the disconnection (viyoga) of the connection (samyoga) with suffering.

(Bhagavad Gita *(6.23) in Feuerstein, 2003, p. 31*)

THEORIES OF DEPRESSION AND THEIR INTEGRATION

The prominent theories of depression address how it is manifested in the brain, the mind, and the environment. The neurochemical views describe how the brain's neurotransmitters influence the way people feel; the cognitive theories account for how cognition impacts feelings and moods; and the sociological perspectives explain how interpersonal relationships and actions in the world shape whether people become depressed or not. Taken together, these theories can all be incorporated into therapy to help people comprehensively change. Yoga provides techniques to work on depression at all these levels, and in their union, to transcend the disturbance and find freedom from suffering through liberation.

Neurochemical Theories of Depression

At the neurochemical level, depression is a disruption in norepinephrine and serotonin, two neurotransmitters that are important for arousal, attention (norepinephrine), and mood, pain, aggression, and sleep (serotonin). Norepinephrine travels throughout the entire brain. Serotonin is made from an amino acid in the diet, tryptophan, making it one of the few neurotransmitters that can be controlled by the right diet. Drug therapy uses selective serotonin reuptake inhibitors (SSRIs) to block the reuptake of serotonin in the limbic system. Bipolar disorder has been treated successfully with lithium carbonate to even out the mood swings. Lithium acts on the neurotransmitters serotonin and norepinephrine as well as dopamine, which is involved in feelings of reward.

Another factor is genetics. Twin studies have shown that depression and bipolar disorders have strong genetic components. Katz and McGuffin (1993) found that 52% of depression variance and 80% of bipolar variance was a result of genetics.

Cognitive Theory of Depression

There is a neurological component to depression; however, which comes first, the neurological state or the experience of feeling depressed? Cognitive theories of depression credit a negative view of the self and dysfunctional attitudes as the underlying cause that sets the symptoms and neurological reactions in motion (Abela & D'Alessandro, 2002). Recent studies showing that drug treatment is no more effective than psychotherapy are evidence for cognitive processes playing an important role in depression. A meta-study reviewed a wide range of comparative studies and found that there was no difference between pharmacological treatments and psychotherapy, even when depression was severe. They also found that psychotherapy was more effective in developing social skills and in relapse prevention over time (Antonuccio, Danton, & DeNelsky, 1995).

In light of research findings, working with cognitions and behaviors can be helpful for altering the symptoms of depression. Cognitive behavior therapy (CBT) and rational emotive therapy (RET) are two well-tested methods for helping people overcome depression. The underlying principle is that what we think can influence emotion and behavior. By challenging the client's typical forms of cognition that accompany depression, such as perfectionism and self-doubt, depression will subside.

Learned Helplessness

Seligman's theory of learned helplessness (1992; 2002) adds another dimension to cognitive theories. His idea is based on research he did in 1965 with dogs. The dogs were conditioned to salivate to a tone as Pavlov had done, and then they were given a shock when the tone sounded. The researchers expected the dogs would feel fear when they heard the tone and would run away. Instead, the dogs just lay passively, having learned to be helpless. This theory was extended to people suffering from depression. Similar to the dogs, depressed people have learned that their efforts are futile, they have no control, and they are bound to fail. People can overcome depression by undergoing cognitive therapy that challenges the false beliefs that have led to feeling helpless, and instead develop beliefs that lead to "learned optimism" (Seligman, 1990).

The learned helplessness theory correlates with neurochemical views. In one experiment, Weiss and Simson (1985) found that rats exhibiting learned helplessness behavior also had decreases in norepinephrine. The mind and brain function together in a bidirectional system of interactions. Therefore, brain reactions can be influenced by cognitive methods.

Sociological Theories of Depression

There are several sociological theories of depression. How people think, feel, and relate to others has a strong influence. According to Yapko, depression is contagious (2009). Depression arises within an emotionally toxic interpersonal relationship. By using an emotionally focused form of therapy (EFT), this toxic quality of relationships can be significantly reduced (Johnson, 2008). Johnson has developed a well-researched system for couples to stop hurting each other and rediscover the natural, loving bond that becomes hidden behind the hostility and fighting. By strengthening the loving bond that is natural to our neurobiology, people feel secure, happy, and fulfilled and overcome depression.

Integration of Theories

Each of these theories offers a different perspective of depression. Like seeing a house from varying perspectives, we can gain true knowledge of the phenomenon by viewing it from the outside as well as the inside, even seeing the blueprints that include the internal plumbing and electricity. All of these theories offer important understandings that can contribute to an effective therapeutic program to help with depression. Because the mind, body, and brain function together in a bidirectional way, thoughts influence neurological reactions in the brain, body movements affect emotion, and environment has an ongoing interaction as well. Thus, the wise therapist incorporates yoga.

Yoga offers clear-cut methods to intervene at many levels, to help with depression. Gradual development of a sense of control is one of the byproducts from practicing yoga meditation, breathing, and postures. Through voluntary efforts, the mind and body are brought under conscious control in tangible ways. A feeling of mastery emerges from gaining control, providing a way to combat the learned helplessness the client may be experiencing psychologically. And on this more comfortable foundation, opportunities to express caring and warmth in a relationship can develop, leading to love. With love, relief from depression becomes possible. "It is only when there is love that all our problems can be solved and then we shall know its bliss and its happiness" (Krishnamurti, 1968, p. 284).

WORKING WITH DEPRESSION INTEGRATIVELY

Depression is a pervasive component of many problems. People suffering from anxiety, stress, or addiction are also often depressed. We encourage incorporating exercises from other chapters to individualize treatments. Think in terms of addressing the problem on many levels at once, and clients will find changes begin to happen naturally.

Barbara was depressed and resentful. She was 16 years old and could not wait to leave her family. Her parents were well-educated professionals, her mother a college professor and her father a successful engineer. Barbara did not restrict the expression of her hostility to her home. She liked to hang out at the beach, sitting on the boardwalk drinking beer. One day, a police officer walked by and asked for her identification. When she could not prove that she was old enough to drink, he decided to give her a warning and a little kindly advice. Instead of being grateful and even considering altering her behavior, Barbara hurled curse words toward him and then threw the beer can in his direction. As one would expect, Barbara ended up in juvenile hall, which prompted her mother to bring her in for therapy.

Barbara felt unhappy with her life now and her future. She knew her parents expected her to go to college to become a professional like them, but she had no interest in these things. She felt hopeless and helpless to do anything about her situation. She was dissatisfied and unmotivated. The only thing she did enjoy was spending time with her friends. As far as she was concerned, society seemed to be against her, because whenever she did what she wanted, she ended up in trouble.

Therapy began by teaching her to distinguish between pleasures: having enjoyment from within versus getting enjoyment from something outside of herself, such as provoking a reaction in someone else. She did not realize that she had lost her self-control by getting authorities to restrict her, in essence being controlled by forces outside of herself. But she felt unable to do anything else, because she was unhappy, helpless, and out of control in her personal life. Getting into trouble seemed to be her only way to enjoy herself. Through the therapeutic process, we taught her how to have a good time without getting in trouble.

Barbara learned meditation, beginning with dharana focus on an object. At first, she had difficulty focusing on one thing, finding her thoughts roaming to her dissatisfactions and annoyances. But with practice and time, she began to be able to hold her attention steady. She was surprised when she noticed that she had moments of feeling comfortable. We encouraged her to practice at home between sessions. As she did so, she began to feel more in control of her mental processes. She added some of the postures described in this chapter, directing her one-pointed awareness to body positioning and breathing. Her sense of personal control grew.

We talked about her enjoyment of social interactions. What did she actually like about it? She realized that what she found satisfying was talking to people. She especially liked to hang out in places where she would encounter people who felt rebellious and alienated as she did. She had a strong interest in them as unique individuals. As she became more confident in her own mental abilities, she learned to enjoy herself without coming into conflict with the system. In fact, she found ways to work with the system and wanted to help others develop a lifestyle that would allow them to live creatively as individuals within the system as well. She began to consider a different future from the dismal one of rebellion and self-sabotage she had been following and decided to become a social worker. She told us that although it was not what her parents wanted, they were gradually accepting that she had her own interests and her own life to live.

ALTERING THE NEUROCHEMICAL BALANCE

The symptoms of depression often include feeling sluggish and fatigued. Introducing some gentle movement will help the sympathetic nervous system to rebalance, at a higher energy level, activating and revitalizing the client's slowed-down system.

Offered here is a modified sun salutation that anyone who is capable of standing, sitting, and kneeling can easily perform. Clients can follow these instructions themselves and perform this modified version of the sun salutation at home between sessions. For those who are less mobile, use the chair-sitting asanas in Chapter 9. These gentle asanas will help to get clients moving in a safe and gentle way. Therapists who practice yoga may want to instruct clients who are physically capable in performing a full sun salutation. These clients may also benefit from joining a Hatha yoga class where the sun salutation and other classic yoga routines are taught. We also recommend our book, *Yoga Basics* (C. A. Simpkins & Simpkins, 2003), which includes the complete sun salutation along with longer asana routines to enhance functioning.

The sun salutation limbers the whole body by carefully applying the pose-counterpose principle: For every bend forward, there is a bend backward. In this way, the sun salutation brings about greater flexibility, strength, tone, and vitality. The exercise also has a symbolic significance. The sun gives and sustains life. The sun salutation symbolizes gratitude and respect for the wonders of the universe of which we are a small yet significant part. Just as the sun gives its energy to the world, the sun salutation is believed to energize the entire body. The dynamic movements reach from head to toe. Another benefit is that by deliberately coordinating breathing with each move, lung capacity gradually increases, which will help rebalance the autonomic nervous system.

Modified Sun Salutation

The sun salutation is performed in slow, continuous motion, gently and slowly. Do not push beyond what is comfortable for your body. Breathing combined with movements helps develop control as it expands breathing capabilities. Keep your mind focused on your movements and your breathing. Do not force yourself to take deep breaths, just breathe normally, inhaling and exhaling as instructed, with each part of the movement. Relax any unnecessary tensions to allow the energy to flow freely, without obstruction. With breath and movement united, you will maximize the flow of energy, invigorating your entire body!

Breathing should be coordinated with each move in the following way: Breathe in when you stretch back or arch. Breathe out when you bend forward or contract inward. Breathe and move slowly and continuously. After you learn to keep attention on what you are doing and your breathing synchronized with your movements, you will experience a union of mind and body that can be uplifting. Allow yourself to enjoy this experience with a brief meditation following the practice. You can repeat the entire series several times, up to 10 times each day, but 2 to 3 times can be helpful. Be patient and persistent for the best results.

Opening Position

Begin by standing straight, with your feet together, chest lifted, shoulders square, and neck lengthened (Figure 8.1). *Bend your elbows and hold the palms of your hands together, thumbs touching, at the center of your chest. Keep your weight evenly distributed between your two feet. Close your eyes and breathe in and out several times, centering yourself in your body experience in the moment.*

Upright Arch

Open your eyes and inhale as you stretch your arms up over your head, palms facing each other (Figure 8.2). *Arch back as you push your hips out, keeping your legs straight. Gently relax your neck back. Form the arch with your upper back rather than your lower back. Arch slowly and carefully.*

Forward Bend

Next exhale as you slowly bend forward, keeping your arms extended (Figure 8.3). *Move your arms and upper body downward, bending at the waist, toward the floor. Keep your back straight for as long as possible as you go down* (Figure 8.4). *Let your neck relax and your head hang down. Bring your fingertips down to*

Figure 8.1

Figure 8.2

Figure 8.3

Figure 8.4

your toes and bend your knees slightly if needed. Hold briefly as you relax fully into the forward stretch.

Kneeling Arch

For this modified version, inhale and exhale as you kneel on both knees and place your hands on the floor to steady yourself (Figure 8.5). *Then raise your hands overhead and inhale as you arch back slightly toward the sun* (Figure 8.6). *If you feel shaky in your balance, place your hands back down on the floor at your sides as you arch. Hold briefly, allowing your upper body to stretch backward as much as is comfortable.*

Figure 8.5

Figure 8.6

Modified Dog Pose

From the kneeling position, place your hands down on the floor as you exhale and inhale. Then, while exhaling, move your hands, palms down on the floor, to extend out in front of you as you lift your hips up as high as you can. Expand your chest as you relax your neck and look down between your hands; exhale and feel a gentle stretch (Figure 8.7).

Cobra Stretch

Next lower yourself face down to the floor in crocodile pose and inhale as you perform the cobra pose, placing your two hands on either side of your head near your shoulders, palms flat on the floor (Figure 8.8). Arch as you draw your upper body up slowly, vertebrae by vertebrae, beginning at your lower back and moving upward. When you get to the neck area, allow your head to arch back slowly until you achieve a full upper body stretch. Slowly lower as you exhale and then inhale.

Figure 8.7

Figure 8.8

Now you are halfway around the series of movements. For the second half of the sun salutation, repeat all of the same motions in reverse on the opposite side. Following the cobra pose, perform the modified dog pose as you exhale. Then from kneeling as you inhale, smoothly arch back with your upper body. Exhale as you stand up as you bend your upper body down, bringing your head toward your knees. Straighten your upper body up, and lift your arms overhead to stretch backward as you inhale. End as you began, with your arms returning to the position at your chest, palms and thumbs touching. Pause, close your eyes, and pay attention to your feelings as you sense the effects of the sun salutation. Meditate for a moment in this position, and then begin again.

Breathing Exercises for Vitalizing

Lie down in savasana pose on your back. Raise your knees and place your feet flat on the floor so that your lower back rests flat on the floor. As you inhale through your nose, raise your rib cage and arch your back slightly as you allow the air to move down through your nose and into your lungs (Figure 8.9). *Then, as you exhale gently, press your back slightly in the opposite direction against the floor. Repeat the gentle movements coordinated with your breathing for several minutes. Remember not to force the movements or the breathing. Keep both relaxed and gradual. This pranayama exercise will vitalize you gently while also relaxing tensions in the back.*

One of the best breathing exercises for vitalizing is the regular practice of the complete breath.

Start with some complete breaths in a standing position. When you perform the complete breath, remember to remain relaxed throughout. Breathe in through

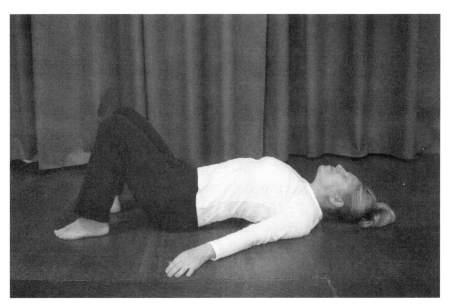

Figure 8.9

your nose and let the air move all the way down, expanding your abdomen, then contract and let it out again. Detailed instructions for the complete breath are found in Chapter 5.

Raising the Kundalini

Perform the Activate the Kundalini exercise in Chapter 5, breathing through both nostrils together. Pay close attention to your body. Imagine and feel energy flowing through you while you breathe with relaxed, normal breaths. Visualize your energy invigorating you all over.

Once you can visualize the energy flowing around, beginning from the root chakra, visualize the energy flowing up and into each chakra (refer to Figure 3.1). *Focus attention on each area, one at a time, as you breathe comfortably. Imagine the energy flowing around in the area as you breathe, and then picture it moving up to the next chakra. If you notice any areas where the flow of your energy seems blocked, perhaps you are unnecessarily tensing. Can you let go of the tension in that area and then allow the energy that gets released to continue to flow freely up to the next chakra? Follow the chain up through your body until you visualize the energy entering the highest chakra at the top of the head. Feel the energy flowing at the crown of your head. According to yoga tradition, this phase of the meditation brings a feeling of great happiness and peace. Enjoy the experience!*

FOSTERING COGNITIVE CHANGE

Clients often compare themselves to an ideal and assess that they fall short. This traps them in repetitive thought patterns comparing how they think they should be with how they think they actually are. The impulse to be better, to strive toward an ideal self, is not the crux of the problem. Rather the means of achieving an ideal self is flawed. Inwardly criticizing faults will not bring about change, as all therapists know. Typically, cognitive approaches help clients to become aware of their ruminations and form realistic expectations. Yoga encourages healthy striving for the highest of human goals: knowledge and wisdom. The practices include many active solutions to help reframe the human tendency to ruminate.

Focused immersion in the methods of yoga can help the client bridge the gap between the actual and ideal self. Indeed, the yoga practitioner merges the two together through the process of performing the techniques.

Awareness of breathing, narrowing or broadening the focus of attention, meditating on an asana, or chanting a mantra all offer ways to bring striving toward an ideal self into the actual present moment. The gap can be bridged here and now by practicing in these ways. Replace destructive patterns of rumination and self-criticism with constructive processes that elevate and strengthen. By pointing correctly toward the ideal, the client can merge the ideal with the actual, in the here-and-now moment of practice.

Find and facilitate clients' impulse for self-improvement, often expressed in hidden ways, to help them begin improving right here and now. So, when clients are ruminating with negative judgments of themselves and they feel helpless to do anything about it, you can point out that they are right and they are wrong! They are right that they are imperfect, like all of us, but they are wrong, because they can do something about it. Perfection begins with the actions they take. They can put their body into postures, breathe in patterned ways, and guide their attention with classic meditation methods to help bring perfection about, or at least move in that direction. The methods are accessible, doable, and rewarding.

From Learned Helplessness to Mastery

Once there was a man who made an error and was imprisoned in a tower. He wanted to escape and told his wife what to do. His instructions puzzled her, but she loved him, so she followed his instructions exactly. He told her to get a beetle, which she did. Then he asked her to find a thick rope and tie this thick rope to a thin string. Then he instructed her to tie the thin string to a thread. Next, she should tie that thread to the thinnest gossamer silk she could find. Finally, he told her to tie that thin piece of silk to the beetle. Once all this was done, she should release the beetle at the bottom of the tower. She found these instructions strange, but she did exactly as she was told. At the top of the tower, the man put out sweet honey. The beetle, smelling the sweetness and wanting it, climbed up the tower, pulling the gossamer silk, that pulled the thread, that pulled the string, that pulled the thick rope up to the top of the tower. Now, the man could use the rope to escape (Vivekananda, 1953).

This traditional story illustrates how yoga works. We are imprisoned in a state of suffering from which we cannot easily escape. But yoga techniques, linked together from the smallest to the greatest, can be applied to bring relief. You start with the smallest practice, for example, simply noticing a breath in and out for 10 seconds. Who would imagine that just turning your attention to an object or simply observing your breathing could free you from discomfort? What could be easier or simpler? But this practice leads to a stronger effect, from making a complete breath, relaxing the entire body to bring about feelings of well-being, leading to relief. By aligning practice with the laws of inner nature, much like the beetle's drive for honey, the links will unfold, setting us free.

When people feel helpless, they perpetuate it in even the smallest act. Frustration may be symbolically expressed, even when attempting a simple breathing exercise. But with sensitive gentle guidance, resistance can be overcome. Concentration through meditation from dharana to dhyana begins with the link to the specific experience and ranges around to look at the situation from every side. The next few exercises offer a paradigm for working with resistance by focusing on it in a variety of different ways. Gradually, understanding comes, and then, the wisdom to change. Here we use an exercise to follow the flow of thought, but you can choose any of the meditations offered in the book, such as attention to breathing, noticing posture, or focusing on a memory as the place to begin. For the purposes of working on resistance, the yoga technique can be a nonthreatening starting point for deeper work. Use what fits the client's needs.

Start Small

Begin with 1 minute or less for meditation. Even people with disturbances can focus briefly, and so can you. As soon as attention drifts, stop the meditation. Open your eyes, relax by taking several comfortable breaths, and then when you feel ready, try again. Keep working in this way, in small increments. We have seen people who begin by focusing for only 10 seconds, but with this careful practice, they eventually built up to focusing for as long as they wanted. Each step forward, no matter how small, adds up over time. There is an old meditation saying that if a snail sets off for Mount Fuji, eventually he will get there.

Becoming Aware of Resistance to Focus

As you are trying to pay attention to your breathing now, what prevents you from focusing? Do you have a feeling that you cannot do it? Or perhaps intruding thoughts about something that bothers you are distracting you. Notice whatever is intruding. Look at it, as if you are standing on the side of a road and watching cars drive by. Stay by the side of the road with your thoughts, simply noticing whatever intrusions are occurring. As soon as possible, go back to just noticing any other intrusive thoughts or feelings as you make a mental note of each one.

Working Through Resistance for Cognitive Focus

Once you know what thoughts or feelings are interfering with your focus, you can work on them, one at a time. Here is one example of a way to work with resistance. Undoubtedly, other ideas that are specifically related will emerge.

Suppose you noticed that you were thinking "I can't do this." Instead of accepting it as a fact, challenge the assumption. Implicit in this statement is an assertion about the future: "I can't do this now, and I won't be able to do this in the future." Why are you so convinced? You are making a prediction about the future, and yet, do you actually have compelling evidence for your prediction? You probably have not done this form of yoga focusing before, so you do not have evidence that you will not be able to ever learn how to do it. When learning a new skill, no one begins by already knowing it. Given this line of thought, can you entertain the rational possibility that you could learn if given enough time, careful instruction, and above all, practice?

Working Through Emotional Resistance

Resistance also has a personally meaningful emotional component that may be irrational. The inability to do a simple breathing meditation often draws from the same kinds of feelings and thoughts that occur when trying to accomplish anything that seems to be challenging.

Using our example, "I can't do this," you can work on the emotions involved. How does this statement make you feel? Perhaps it reminds you of other times when you tried to do something and failed. If a particular incident comes to mind, what happened? Did you stop trying because someone punished you? Did you feel uncomfortable succeeding when someone you loved failed? There are many ways that people feel unable to succeed in their efforts, and these feelings can be explored carefully in therapy.

Stay with the emotion, which may have intensified. Notice how you feel and any associated thoughts. Perhaps you realize that there were many repeated incidences where you felt criticized. Notice how your emotion alters as you recall these events.

Taking the Other Side of Resistance

As you become aware of having felt criticized, try for a moment to take the other side by being the critical one. How do you feel now as the criticizer? How do you view the person who is feeling criticized? Are you trying to help, intending your statements as constructive criticism? Maybe you think that these remarks will be motivating.

Shift back to the other side and answer that possibility. You might ask, if the criticism was intended to be helpful, why was it so harsh and negative? Back again to the other side, you might answer that the stronger the statement, the more realistically it would prepare someone for the harsh realities of life.

This might lead you to think about your overarching philosophy of life. Do you feel like life is somehow negative, or perhaps you are inherently unlucky? Now you have the opportunity to work on fundamental, deeply seated beliefs in limitations that could be holding you back from trying. And then, you are free to try.

IMPROVING SOCIAL INTERACTIONS

The actions we take are often for the sake of something else. Aristotle cogently distinguished between an action and the goal of that action. So, for example, we might work for the sake of earning money or exercise for the sake of becoming fit. All such actions can bring rewards, but the rewards are not intrinsic to the act itself. Are any actions done not for the sake of something else? Aristotle said yes, and this form of action is the highest good that brings true happiness. Karma yoga also places action done for itself and not for the fruits of action as the highest form of activity that will lead to freedom from suffering and ultimate happiness. This form of activity can be achieved, as Krishna instructed Arjuna in the Bhagavad Gita, by the practice of yoga.

When people are depressed, they often do many of their actions for the sake of something else. They put more stake in how other people perceive their actions, seeking approval or recognition, and lose touch with the doing of the act. Yoga can help practitioners to turn back to the action. Therein, people will find true satisfaction and happiness in what they do.

In the classic Greek myth of Sisyphus, Sisyphus was doomed to perpetually roll a boulder up the side of a mountain to the top, only to have the Gods cause it to roll back down, forcing him to toil again. If Sisyphus had been a practitioner of Karma yoga, he might have freed himself by learning to take pleasure in the act of pushing the boulder. Right there in the act of pushing, he would have found satisfaction that no God or outside force could ever take away from him. Krishna instructed Arjuna in the Bhagavad Gita to handle life's challenging tasks by performing each action for its own sake, not for the sake of something else—or in classical terms, not for the fruits of the action. Similarly, clients can take control of their own moods when they learn to take pleasure in the doing, rather than trying to find enjoyment from what their actions may bring.

Action for Its Own Sake Exercise

You can experience this by performing a simple act, such as washing dishes or washing the car. Prepare before you start by getting everything that you will need ready. Then, just before beginning, sit down for five minutes to meditate. Perform a pratyahara meditation to center yourself in the present moment, quietly turning attention from the outer stimuli to your inner experiencing. Breathe comfortably until you feel ready. Then begin the task, paying close attention to all of your sensations. Notice the temperature of the water, the texture of the suds, and the surface of what you are washing. Proceed carefully and patiently without hurrying. Note how the surface of the dish shines after rinsing. When you are finished, clean up completely. Then, sit again in meditation and look back on the experience, taking pleasure in the act.

If you find that you cannot stop thinking about the goal, such as the clean car or dishes, give yourself a goal-less task such as digging a hole in the yard and then refilling it, or moving papers into one pile and then restacking them into another pile. Separate out the goal and simply perform the action for itself with mindful awareness as you do it.

Distinguishing Actions From Their Fruits

Often the results of actions are so intertwined that people cannot immediately separate them. Certainly, many of the rewards of actions are worthwhile, such as getting a college degree to facilitate better earning and a more interesting profession. However, even such an ideal result can interfere with enjoyment of the act for itself. Education is a good example of an act that can be a reward in itself. The student may develop a lifelong love of learning through the process, which is an invaluable treasure.

Think about an action that you feel uncomfortable about. For example, a student might feel depressed about school, ruminating about grades, whether they are high enough, whether they are representative, whether intelligent responses were made on tests, and so on. Challenge this by questioning: What is the true goal, besides just getting a degree? Perhaps you are just trying to please your parents or attempting to prove that you are worthy or intelligent. Sometimes people compete or compare their performance with someone else. These sorts of motivations are not intrinsic to the action but are added to it. External to the action, these motivations may be like Sisyphus's goal, impossible to attain.

Question your goals and ask whether they are really part of the action or something you have added. Then, using dharana meditation as performed earlier in this chapter, work on how this goal came about, what you feel about it, what beliefs may be driving it, and how it might be interfering with your full experience of the act just as it is, for itself. There are many facets to the experience of school, which often seem to have little to do with the degree itself. Yet, from a larger perspective, these facets are a meaningful part of the experience.

Selfless Love

You can enhance the process of helping yourself by helping others. Performing acts of selfless love can have a healing effect. You might be surprised how reaching out to help another person in need will lift your depression. Doing action for no other reason than for good brings happiness. Getting involved in volunteer work for a cause or institution that you find meaningful can be an important adjunct to your therapy and will add a new dimension to your functioning.

Improving the Interpersonal Aspect of Depression

Troubled relationships trap partners in a web of resentments and hostilities. The love that once was there may now seem to be lost, but as yoga theory proposes, the layer of illusion is what separates individuals from each other, as well as the larger world. Clarifying perception cuts through illusion to illuminate the deeper truth that is there, just waiting to be seen. This clarity applies to the perception of others as well. Yoga meditation methods described earlier in this chapter and throughout the book can be used to help resolve interpersonal problems that influence feelings of depression. Couples will discover a more direct and realistic way of relating, which then allows the deeper feelings that first brought them together to emerge.

John and Mary were the archetype of a hostile, depressed couple. She thought that he was slovenly and lazy. He considered her obsessive and controlling. As they worked on applying meditation, their angry feelings subsided temporarily to allow them to work on their problems. They both learned to distinguish their actions from the fruits of their actions. At first, they both thought their actions were noble: He wanted to enjoy life as it went along, and she hoped to have a beautiful home and raise their children well. With further probing, they discovered hidden motivations: John realized that he could express his anger by inaction. His passivity was really a refusal to do what she asked, a form of action against her. She found that her way of running the household had a hidden agenda of controlling the contingencies of life she found threatening.

As they probed deeper, they both saw a positive side as well. She recognized that he was expressing his anger without yelling or losing his temper, and he could see that she had the best interest of their family in mind. With some of these issues cleared away, the love they had for each other resurfaced. Built on clarity of perception, they both made changes that led to enjoying daily life more while also incorporating ways to keep the household in order and foster the children's growth. They added a weekly family fun day to just be together that satisfied John's wish to have some fun. John helped more around the house, which helped Mary to feel less out of control as she saw some of her needs being met.

Turning Outward to the World

As shown in the diagram (Figure 4.1), yoga meditation, pratyahara, begins with attention pointing outward and moving inward to dharana and dhyana. The process clears away illusory thinking and clarifies perception. Once the process is complete, whether you point outward toward the world or inward to internal processing, perception is clear and direct. At the highest levels of dhyana, object and self become one. These meditative steps can be applied with couples. Apply the methods used throughout the book to help them, working as a couple, to follow the meditative course together. As they go through the process, they will strengthen their bond, found in the shared yoga experience. They can explore ways that they have become stuck in illusions, and clear them away to rekindle their love and lift the depression one or both partners may be feeling.

Shining the Light of Meditation on Relationship

Couples who meditate together will find that a bond begins to form from the quiet seat of the shared experience. Sit together on a couch or on the floor and quiet the thoughts for a few minutes. Then, sense your body position, wherever you are seated. Feel the sensations of sitting on the chair. Pay attention to the relationship with the seat. Note how you push down as the chair pushes back with an equal and opposite force to keep you supported. Let awareness range out further to notice your partner. Can you hear his or her breathing? Can you sense how the temperature might be warmer on the side from your partner? Allow yourself to sense the sharing in this moment, to be present with your partner here and now. Recognize how both of you are participating together in this shared experience, and enjoy a moment of sharing. Allow your feelings of goodwill, perhaps even love to extend outward to your partner.

Extending Love and Compassion

As you develop your awareness of this shared moment with your partner, move out to other family members, friends, housemates, and so on. Feel the presence of the others with feelings of love and compassion for them. Next, range out further to people in the neighborhood. Sense their being, and feel the connection to them. Search for feelings of compassion for others by caring about their concerns and their struggles. Intend goodwill and kindness toward them as in the natural instinct to care about a child in distress. Keep extending outward, with feelings of goodwill to the city, the state, the country, and the world. Become aware of the many ways of interdependence. As you allow your own feelings of goodwill to develop, you will feel your mood lift.

CONCLUSION

Depression is a multidimensional problem that is best improved by working at several levels at once. The balance for each client is different. As the change process begins to take form, other aspects can be addressed. Through the practice, mind and brain, body and spirit are transformed as a happier future unfolds for the client.

9

Addiction: Five Steps to Lasting Release

From right-living results pleasure; from wrong living, pain.
(*Patanjali in Woods, 1927, p. 314*)

Addiction is a mind-brain-body problem. The mind becomes one-pointedly focused on the substance, the brain's reward pathway rewires, and the body is racked with pain if the substance is withdrawn. One of the reasons that addiction is so difficult to change is that it is heavily reinforced, both positively from the pleasure the substance brings and negatively from the pain withdrawal causes. Yoga is a well-suited intervention that can change the mind's focus, rewire the brain, and help soothe and strengthen the body.

Another crucial issue in treatment of addiction is motivation. Many clients who seek treatment do not really want to give up the habit, or at best are only partially committed to change. Often they have been sent for treatment by a family member or ordered by the court. Thus, the early steps of therapy need to build sincere motivation. The eight limbs of yoga have clear guidelines in the yamas and niyamas that will help clients make that positive choice on a deep level, to truly change.

Drawing from the mind, brain, and body techniques, therapists can facilitate what is needed to rebalance and find unity. Using yoga for treatment of addiction has been well researched, with some key studies covered in Chapter 1. The techniques provided here will give you tangible means for dealing with the client's dependence, both mentally and physically. Liberated from the pattern, the client can explore life beyond substance use and find new meaningful fulfillment in the world.

DEFINITIONS

The American Psychological Association defines addiction on its public website as "a condition in which the body must have a drug to avoid physical and psychological withdrawal symptoms" (American Psychological Association, 2010). It occurs in stages, with dependence at the first stage where obtaining the drug tends to dominate the individual's life. The second stage, tolerance, is the loss of the drug's effect with continued use. Building up a tolerance occurs sometimes, but not always. The course of dependence is usually accompanied by corresponding feelings of depression, anxiety, and irritability when access to the drug is prevented. *The Diagnostic and Statistical Manual of Mental Disorders* (American Psychiatric Association, 2000) has two different sets of criteria: Abuse and Dependence. Abuse is voluntary and conscious, whereas dependence is pathological and involuntary.

Impulse control disorders share similar tendencies with substance abuse and dependence. Impulse control disorders are characterized by a repetitive behavior and impaired inhibition (Grant, 2008). People with impulse control problems have an urge to engage in a behavior with negative consequences, just as those with substance dependence do. They experience increasing tension unless the action is taken, and they tend to repeat the process after a short time (hours, days, or weeks). The negative syndrome is strengthened by positive reinforcement at the early stages and later, by negative reinforcement from the discomfort of stopping. These features are shared with addiction and have led some to propose that impulse control disorders are a form of behavioral addiction (Grant, 2008). Others believe that addictions are a form of compulsion (Koob, 2003). Thus, the therapist may find that similar methods, with appropriate adaptations, are helpful for both addictions and compulsive disorders.

NEUROBIOLOGY OF ADDICTION

In general, drug-taking behavior involves three physiological processes in the nervous system: the blood-brain barrier, drug tolerance, and the reward pathway of the brain. Normally, the blood-brain barrier prevents the passage of molecules into the brain, keeping the nervous system stable. But many drugs, including pharmacological medications, penetrate the blood-brain barrier, altering the balance of neurotransmitters. Nicotine, alcohol, cocaine, barbiturates, and opiates such as heroin can easily pass through the blood-brain barrier, which is how these drugs have such a powerful effect on the nervous system.

There are different kinds of addictive drugs that have varied specific actions and effects, but they all share in the same general impact they have on the brain through the reward pathway. The use of an addictive substance brings about a strong sense of pleasure as the substance enters the bloodstream and brain, resulting in an intense craving to repeat the experience. The powerful experience of pleasure results from how drugs activate the reward pathway.

The reward pathway begins in the midbrain, projects to the forebrain, and then goes back to the midbrain (Figure A.9). This pathway is involved in the normal feelings of pleasure for behaviors that are necessary for survival, such as eating, drinking, and sex. When the cortex receives and processes a rewarding sensory stimulus, such as a favorite food, it sends a signal activating the ventral tegmental area (VTA) in the midbrain. The VTA then releases dopamine to the nucleus accumbens (NA), the septum, the amygdala, and the prefrontal cortex. The NA activates the motor functions, while the prefrontal cortex focuses the attention. Dopamine transmits the sensation of pleasure, the reward for eating the tasty food. The endocrine and the autonomic nervous systems interact via the hypothalamus and the pituitary to modulate the reward pathway, and so the body tends to self-regulate (Squire et al., 2003).

But when an addict abuses a drug, he or she expends all of the pleasure at once. The drug inhibits the release of the inhibitory neurotransmitter GABA, which is like taking the foot off the brakes, thereby releasing more dopamine. Thus, the drug reward pathway involves the natural reward pathway, but in a compromised way. The midbrain, forebrain, and neurotransmitter systems activate positive sensations from taking the drug. The drug dramatically alters the brain's activity all the way down to the synapses between neurons, altering the reward pathway to become intertwined with the drug effect.

Tolerance is involved in how the brain adapts to the continued used of the drug. At first, the brain becomes sensitized to the drug. The presence of the drug becomes part of the body's attempt to normalize toward an allostatic balance. More quantities of the drug are required for a similar effect and tolerance builds (Squire et al., 2003). The allostatic balance of addiction is stable and becomes a rigid system. Thus, addicts often find little joy in anything but their drug.

Withdrawal feelings occur when the user has been away from the drug, to give an opposite experience, including negative affect, anxiety, and strong physical discomfort. The marked and long-lasting change in dopamine and serotonin (5-HT) levels is opposite to the effect when the drug is taken, leaving the addict feeling depleted. Anxiety and stress are common elements of dependence and withdrawal. The individual's normal body, mind, and brain balance has been altered to activate a stress response. The user feels a strong desire to use the drug for relief, thereby perpetuating the dependence cycle. Impulse control problems follow a similar pattern, in which carrying out the impulsive behavior seems to offer relief, but actually perpetuates the cycle.

A FIVE-STEP METHOD FOR TREATING ADDICTION

Treatment for addiction is often understood as taking place in steps, such as the 12-step methods widely used for working with alcohol and drug dependence. Having tangible steps helps clients build the courage they need to stay the course. Yoga also provides an achievable set of steps to follow.

A recent study with 872 smokers found that five steps were involved in bringing about lasting change in their habit. The steps in this Transtheoretical Model of Change are precontemplation, contemplation, preparation, action, and maintenance (Prochaska, DiClemente, & Norcross, 1992; Prochaska, DeClemente, Velicer, & Rossi, 1993). Reinterpreting these steps in terms of a yoga intervention may help to frame the protocol clearly to the client. These steps are used here in the yoga treatment for addiction.

Rene seemed to be a successful executive, but she was dependent on alcohol. From the very first meeting, we saw an untapped core of higher potential in Rene. As therapy unfolded, she disclosed that she worked for the family business, but during the time we were seeing her, both of her parents were sent to jail for illegal business activities. Rene thought that she felt comfortable with what they were doing and had no compunction about "bending the rules," as she put it. The family philosophy was that if someone was lax in protecting their discoveries, they were indirectly offering them to be taken. This approach seemed to work well for the family business until the law intervened.

We helped Rene overcome her dependence using the five-step yoga method presented here. When she was ready, we continued to see her regularly while she went through a detoxification program that monitored her withdrawal process. She examined her addiction beginning with precontemplation, using the yamas and niyamas. Deep down she had always felt that what she was doing was somehow wrong, but she had pushed these feelings aside. She contemplated what alcohol did for her. She had to face the difficult recognition that she had developed a hidden sense of self-loathing and tried to obliterate the feeling with alcohol. She began to feel something else emerge: her sense of values. She developed strong feelings of conscience for all the people the family business had cheated. She felt regret as she took responsibility for what she had done. Now she was motivated and prepared to take action.

Through the therapeutic process, she became completely clean and sober. Now she had to work on her feelings of anger toward her parents. Using meditation, she felt compassion for them in their unrelenting commitment to a dishonest lifestyle. She learned that carrying anger for them would only poison her own life, and so she forgave them as she moved on to a healthy and happy life of her own. She got involved with a man who had nothing to do with crime. They married and had a family. When we heard from her again several years later, she told us that she was a manager at a large company and was enjoying moving up the corporate ladder in the honest way. She was able to find some positive lessons about business she had learned from working with her family, and she developed her talent for management that had always been there. Now she lived happily with integrity, knowing as she did where the dark path of greed and dishonesty led.

Ed, another client, told us he was a former hippie. He was middle-aged when we saw him. He had gone to the Haight-Ashbury area of San Francisco during the peak of the 1960s and had experienced the infamous Summer of Love in 1967. He participated in the utopian lifestyle and was moved by the higher ideals of the community. He recalled how residents had reached out to him when he first arrived and the many ways the community shared a vision of happy, peaceful, and creative living. He took LSD as a sacrament regularly, and he had vivid experiences that he felt opened his consciousness psychedelically in meaningful ways. He committed himself to a new lifestyle in accord, to be an artist and live with compassion.

He returned to the East coast in the early 1970s and then moved to a major city, where he began to live with some friends, hoping to continue to share this vision. In search of a reliable source for sensations of enjoyment, they had found hard drugs, mainly heroin. Ed joined in at first, but as the embrace of drugs reached out to him, he recognized the potential strength of its grip. The values he had formerly committed himself to could not be lived in this way. Drugs could become a constant pattern of activity, not art. He felt disillusioned. He abruptly moved out.

Over the years, he worked as an artist, barely getting by financially. He took hallucinogens and smoked marijuana regularly. He had a string of casual relationships that never lasted, and he felt unsatisfied. Two things brought him to therapy. First, he met a woman whom he thought he truly loved. He wanted to make the relationship last, but he feared he did not know how. Secondly, he had developed a strong fear of flashbacks. He thought perhaps his drug use was a problem, but he had no idea how he could do anything differently after all these years.

Through therapy, he trained his attention so that he could focus as he chose to and experience more deeply. He was surprised to discover that he had the ability to perceive in creative ways without drugs! He avidly explored the reaches of his own mind and found it fascinating. He stopped using drugs, recognizing how limiting they were for him.

Later in the therapy, he told us he had believed that the spirit of the 60s was lost, but he now felt a renewed feeling for the positive intentions behind its values. And he could express higher values again, in how he lived day by day. As Ed evolved, living his life with values and without drugs became his source of happiness, wisdom, and fulfillment. And his artwork evolved in new and unexpected directions, expressing his inner vision.

Applying yoga philosophy to therapy can help clients who are struggling with deeper issues. Often people turn to something outside of themselves, such as drugs or alcohol, because they unconsciously sense that something is missing or wrong. Therapy involves precontemplation and contemplation, moving the client to become motivated on a deep level to make a change. As you work with clients using these methods, the important issues will emerge and can be dealt with using your therapeutic methods in conjunction with these yoga techniques. Yoga practices provide ways to help clients take the necessary actions to overcome their dependence and then maintain a sober lifestyle.

Precontemplation

Making the decision to stop taking drugs is not an easy one. The client will inevitably have to go through a period of pain and discomfort. Here the yamas and niyamas can be enlisted to build inner resilience. By holding to values, people gain a source for strength. These values can be relied on throughout the entire treatment process, adding resolve to each step along the way.

*People have been drawing inner strength for thousands of years from the yamas and niyamas, and you can too. As a review, here are the yamas, the things one should **not** do: violence (ahimsa), lying (satya), stealing (asteya), excess (brahmacharya), and possessiveness (aparigraha). Substance dependence might drive you to do wrong, even though a part of you knows it is wrong. Think about the ways that you have lost control of your own destiny and felt forced to act in ways that go against your values.*

*Now consider the niyamas, those things that you **should** do: purity (saucha), contentment (santosha), self-discipline (tapas), self-study (pranitara), and dedication to a higher power or principle (ishvara pranidana). Living your life in accord with these principles can help you to overcome your dependence.*

Saucha applied to addiction at the level of the body means ultimately to become free of artificial substances. The lifestyle of drugs includes many negative aspects that you probably will not miss. Once you have gotten through withdrawal, your body and brain will return to normal, allowing you to function well. On the spiritual level, saucha implies purifying your life, to live with integrity, without the aid of drugs.

Santosha entails learning to find satisfaction in what you are and in your endeavors. You learn how to make needed changes that will bring contentment, instead of seeking satisfaction from outside oneself. This can help not only to get past drug use, but also to embark on meaningful projects and have the strength of mind to follow through. The self-study of tapas encourages knowing yourself, honestly facing who and what you are, and using your meditation skills to develop sharpened perception of yourself and of the world around you. Then you enhance your mental capacities so you learn whatever you need in order to succeed in your endeavors.

Finally, with ishvara pranidana comes recognizing and living in accord with higher principles, greater than just you, which can help with resisting the powerful influence of the drug. Trust in the greater wisdom of the universe, in God, an absolute ethical standard, or whatever source of higher power speaks to you. Your life takes on a larger significance, a source for greater strength and wisdom. Consider your own situation in light of the yamas and niyamas, and make a vow, your deep commitment to change.

Contemplation

Yoga methods commit practitioners to a process of cutting through illusions in order to recognize deeper truth. The contemplation phase of recovery involves questioning illusions about substance abuse in order to see the truth about how it is hurting the body and interfering with realistic perception. Addicts believe that the drug makes them happy, but they are often basing this belief on the memory of how good the drug made them feel when they first started. They chase after an impossible goal, because the neurotransmitters in their own brains build up a tolerance for the drug and prevent them from ever feeling that way again. They become trapped in a losing battle for normalcy, trying desperately to achieve a pleasurable feeling they can never regain.

Educate yourself about how the drug you are taking alters your brain chemistry. Each type of drug has a different effect, but generally, all rewire the brain's dopamine reward pathway as described earlier. Review the information included in this chapter until you understand how your reward pathway has become hijacked. You can strengthen your resolve as you begin to understand why you are not finding pleasure in normal rewards, and thereby losing your enjoyment of life.

Seek Higher Values

Now delve deeper. What do you worship? Are you really willing to live and die for your drug? In giving your will over to the drug, you ultimately surrender your life. As you cut through your illusions, you may see that continuing on the course of abuse will destroy your body and brain and shorten your life.

By clarifying your perception of value, you can see that your consciousness does not have to be directed outside of yourself. Drug addiction involves yearning for something external to your being. Overcoming the craving for a substance involves more than control of an impulse. Your entire motivation changes as you learn to find enjoyment just in being. Life itself can be bliss, and when you discover contentment in your life as you live it, you can be free from the desire to seek contentment in drugs. The exercises in this chapter can set you on the path to discover the joy you are missing.

Preparation for Withdrawal

Yoga builds confidence from many opportunities to master skills. By holding the body in a posture, staying attuned to breathing, or keeping attention fixed on a single object, clients build hardiness. Clients gain a sense of being able to endure, and this experience can generalize to enduring discomfort. In addition, you can use the information and exercises found in the Pain Control section in Chapter 11, if the client is also fearful about the pain he or she might be experiencing. Understanding how pain sensations are processed in the brain and gaining tools to deal with them (covered in this section on pain) help clients rise to the challenges and face them well.

Begin preparation by teaching methods that can help clients to better tolerate the discomforts of withdrawal. This alone may encourage many people to try withdrawing from the substance. Whenever clients undergo withdrawal from an addictive drug, they should be monitored medically. Work in conjunction with a hospital or drug treatment center where the client can be under medical care throughout the process.

Pratyahara From the Senses Using Sound

One of the classic ways to perform pratyahara is to withdraw from sensory experience. Withdrawing from the senses does not mean trying not to feel. The law of reversed effort from hypnosis literature shows that the more we try not to do something, the more compelled we feel (C. A. Simpkins & Simpkins, 2010). We set up an internal argument that says, "Don't do this, but I want to." Pratyahara involves a subtler use of your attention that bypasses this problem. This exercise prepares for pratyahara to cope with discomfort.

Begin with the use of sound. Sit down as comfortably as possible, close your eyes, and meditate on the sounds around you and notice everything that you hear. Then focus attention on the subtler sounds, perhaps the wind outside, a repetitive sound from an air conditioner or heating system, or street sounds coming from another room or outside. Finally, focus on the silence between sounds, those moments when all is quiet.

Dharana Meditation to Transform Discomfort

Discomfort is often felt as an overwhelming experience, something that hurts you, but in truth, pain is a combination of sensations and cognitive appraisal. By learning to separate out the parts and distinguish them, the sensations become manageable and the interpretation can alter.

Try this exercise when you are feeling only a slight discomfort. As your skills improve, you will be able to apply this meditation to strong cravings or pains. Notice the sensory component of a discomfort you are feeling. Focus on its qualities: Is it hot or cold, sharp or dull? Notice any other qualities that you can sense. Do you feel the discomfort as an intermittent pulse with spaces between, or is it a continuous wave?

Pay particularly close attention to the spaces between, the times when the sensation is not there. What are the qualities of these moments, when there is no discomfort or less intensity? Do not pass judgment on the sensation as good or bad, pleasant or unpleasant. Simply attend to it, like data to be observed. When you have been able to sustain attention to the sensations, move on to the next exercise.

Withdrawing from Discomfort

Now that you have noticed the elements of the uncomfortable sensation, apply pratyahara to withdraw from these sensations. Begin by noticing the strongest sensations, but then turn your attention to the subtler ones, then to the spaces between, and eventually to moments without any sensation. Can you allow the relief from lulls in pain to spill over into the moments of intense sensations, softening them a bit? Let the feeling of calm that you develop spread. As it becomes deeper and stronger, the sensations may become milder and easier to handle. Keep breathing comfortably, and allow as much relaxation as possible.

Overcoming Negative Thoughts

Discomfort is a sensation, but it does not have to hurt you. The negative thoughts you have about the sensation make the experience far more uncomfortable than

it needs to be. What are the thoughts you typically have about your pain? Typi-
cal thoughts are "This is awful." Or "I cannot stand it!" If you are having such
thoughts, notice them and then recognize that these thoughts may be about the
pain, but they are not the pain sensation itself. You may not be able to change the
actual sensations, but you can stop evaluating them. Challenge predictions you
are making about them, anticipating how bad you will feel in the future, because
the future has not been written yet. Reassure yourself that the sensations are what
they are, but you are developing new and better tools to lessen their intensity. The
therapeutic process may involve challenging the tendency to think negatively in
general. So, when negative thoughts occur, keep working on letting each thought
go as it occurs, and gradually, they will begin to subside. Then, painful discom-
fort can become easier to endure.

Meditation on Something Else

Learning how to withdraw from pain is one method to use, but concentrating attention on something else is another effective way to lessen the effect
from experiencing pain and discomfort. Everyone has moments when they
become spontaneously absorbed in something interesting. It might be great
music, a fascinating book, an intriguing movie, or being deeply involved in
interacting with others. Although this exercise guides in focusing attention
fully on music, another object of attention can be chosen.

Pick something that you can enjoy easily. Play a piece of instrumental music
you find soothing. Listen carefully to the melody one time through. Play the
music again and listen to the background sounds, perhaps a subtle rhythm, or
a secondary thread that runs through the music. Play it a third time and listen
only to the pauses between notes, the quietest sounds, the empty moments be-
tween. Play it one more time and listen to everything together. In the union of
melody, background sounds, and spaces between, you can find the full enjoyment
of the music. Finally, simply sit quietly and allow listening, open and absorbed
in the experience. You may hear the music as you never have before and enjoy
it fully. With practice, you can learn to be absorbed in whatever you choose to
attend to.

Try applying this exercise to other sensory experiences, such as the sweet aroma
of a rose, the taste of a ripe piece of fruit, or the enjoyment of viewing a beautiful
art object. Keep your attention focused on it. Seek enjoyment in the experience
itself. You may be pleased to find that the discomfort vanishes.

Action for Building Strength

The action phase is the process of building inner and outer strength to take action and endure through the process. We create ourselves through every action, for better or for worse. Yoga postures direct the body into a set position. To follow these patterns exactly requires action with discipline. Unifying mind and body in action with discipline generalizes to daily life. Meditation and breathing combined with asanas will build strength that is both mental and physical. This practice will permit thoughtful, deliberate control of action that can be directed to bring about positive results.

Whenever you do a posture, focus your attention fully on the area you intend to strengthen. For example, when building strength in the legs, shoulders, or arms, direct your attention there. Feel the sensations in the muscles. Notice it gets warmer as blood flows to the area. Pay attention to other sensations. Directing and focusing attention begins to unify thought and action. Use the meditations at the end of this routine to help enhance the links.

Strengthening Warm-Ups

Begin with some simple warm-ups (see Appendix I). You should always begin your routine with moving stretches to ready your body. Make certain that you stretch each area gently and carefully. Warm-up exercises help to prevent injury, loosening muscles and tendons, moving fluids around in the joints, while enhancing circulation in general throughout the body to help promote a healing process.

Strengthening the Breath

Sit in pelvic pose of easy pose, with your back held relatively straight. Perform several relaxed, complete breaths. Next, inhale naturally, hold for 3 counts, and then exhale completely. When you get to the bottom of your exhale, gently draw in your stomach muscles and hold for 3 counts. Inhale slowly, letting the air completely fill your lungs and expand your stomach muscles. Perform the pattern 3 times and then perform 3 comfortable complete breaths. Repeat the pattern for several minutes. When you are ready, sit quietly, relaxing your breathing.

Breathing Exercises to Accompany Asanas

Breathing can help build strength as you work out. Imagine that your breathing is sending prana to the area you are exercising. As you breathe in, imagine that the air carries prana to that part of your body, bringing vitality to help this area develop. As you exhale, imagine that you are expelling toxins from the area. Contemplate this image during asana practice. Concentrate attention on your posture while breathing, to link them.

Building Strength with a Warrior Sequence

Recovery requires inner strength and self-discipline, and so asanas that build strength may help. This warrior sequence develops strength in the feet, arches, calves, and thighs. It also works the abdomen and shoulders. The second and third parts of the sequence lengthen and firm the muscles of the waist and rib cage, as well as the abdominal areas. The position is symbolic of taking a strong stand, and you will feel your strength build as you embody this posture. This pose can be performed by most people, but be sure to coordinate with the client's medical doctor who is managing the withdrawal process. Clients who enjoy this series may want to try other yoga strengthening postures. We include a more extensive strengthening routine in our book (C. A. Simpkins & Simpkins, 2003), and many yoga classes will build strength as well.

Begin by stepping out approximately 3 feet (Figure 9.1). *Bend your right front knee, keeping the lower leg perpendicular, and the thigh parallel to the floor so*

Figure 9.1

that the bent leg forms as close to a 90-degree angle as possible. Keep your hips level. As you move into the foot position, bring your arms up overhead. Then spread your arms out from your sides, directly over your legs, parallel to the floor with fingers held together and pointing straight out. Turn your head to face the forward bent leg, keeping your neck and back straight. Lift your chest and stretch out through your arms and fingers. Hold the position as you breathe in and out for as long as you can without discomfort.

Next, face your chest and torso toward the right so that your whole body faces squarely right (Figure 9.2). You may let the back foot pivot diagonally to take strain off the knees. Then raise your arms straight over your head with palms facing forward and arch back gently with the inhale. Hold for several seconds as you breathe comfortably in and out several times. Then lower your arms back to the first warrior position as you exhale.

Exhale as you lean to the right, resting the elbow of your right arm on your right knee (Figure 9.3). Extend your left hand overhead and toward the right

Figure 9.2

Figure 9.3

as you lean your upper body to the right. Feel a stretch through your right arm, waist, and left leg.

Move slowly in and out of each position, keeping your motions smooth. Hold each position as long as you can, breathing in and out, and then move slowly into the next position. Repeat all three positions on the other side. Perform the whole sequence two times.

Maintenance

Maintaining the process involves daily practice. Clients should practice the meditations and breathing exercises included in this chapter and in the stress, anxiety, and depression chapters depending on the symptoms. The more frequent the practice, the easier the recovery. The meditation that follows may be difficult to sustain at first, so begin with only a few minutes. In time, all skills improve, and the experience of mastery is rewarding.

Meditation

After having performed the warrior pose, or at the end of the therapy session, lie down in savasana pose. Close your eyes and completely relax your body. Let your muscles sink into the couch or floor where you are lying prone. Breathe lightly and comfortably, allowing the air to circulate through your entire body. Let your thoughts drift without attaching to any one thought. Simply return to this quiet moment. As you deepen your relaxation, can you allow a calm feeling to spread through your body? Keep returning to this meditation at different times between sessions, allowing relaxation to develop. In time, you will experience a deep sense of calm and contentment.

Calm Confidence Within

Embodying a strong pose, focusing the mind and body, breathing with the movement, and meditating, you will feel a new experience develop, a sense of inner confidence in your own mind and body. As you begin to take care of yourself through the practice of asanas, regular relaxation, and mental exercises, you have initiated a process of self-care. By taking charge of your own destiny, you transcend some of the circumstances that are beyond your control. Let yourself feel the pleasure in your achievements, however small they may be. Remember that even the smallest steps, continually taken, will get you to your destination. This quote from Gandhi may be inspirational in your journey:

> *But with proper discipline, we can make ourselves into beings only a "little below the angels." He who has mastered his senses is first and foremost among men [and women!].*
>
> (**Gandhi 1960, 143**)

CONCLUSION

The five steps given in this chapter are not hierarchical. Although you may start with the precontemplation stage, often people need to loop back and forth, as they make discoveries and changes along the way. Apply the steps flexibly, to fit the individual client's needs.

10

Adapting Yoga for Children

To educate a child is to help him to understand freedom and integration.

(*Krishnamurti, 1953, p. 45*)

Childhood is a wonderful period of life, filled with impulses to be curious and playful. The challenge is in being able to freely express all of these positive impulses in a way that enhances the child's development for the best fulfillment of his or her potential. So, therapy must work from two directions: to free the healthy, natural impulses, and to develop executive control of their expression. Then, healthy impulses can help the child grow to maturity.

Children are naturally flexible and will enthusiastically embrace yoga techniques. The practice is gentle, natural, accessible, and fun! Increased awareness of body, thoughts, and emotions from yoga practice as part of the therapy session can promote healthy prefrontal cortex functioning in children. Clinicians will find that these mind-body methods offer additional ways to work with children who are suffering from a broad range of problems. And as children master the skills, they gain confidence that ripples through every aspect of their lives.

Children are going through a process of prefrontal cortex development as they learn to utilize executive control over their behavior, emotions, and thoughts. During the developmental growth period, there is a marked increase in grey and white matter, and distributed neural networks form to facilitate higher cognitive functions. Thus, early childhood years are foundational for the development of executive cognitive functioning (Tsujimoto, 2008). Education is one way that this development is fostered, along with correct nurturing from the home environment. Children who come in for therapy are often having problems that bear some relationship to poor executive implementation. Yoga offers interventions that facilitate the healthy development of several key executive functions while also promoting relaxation, inner calm, and affect regulation. ADHD, stress, anxiety, and aggressive behavior can be improved by enhancing executive control using yoga methods. For other problems not covered here, apply the methods from other chapters, such as Chapter 8 on depression and Chapter 9 on addiction, adapting the methods by presenting them in the spirit of yoga for children shown here.

Many of the most successful treatments for children offer active methods. Yoga can be presented to children as an active method, giving them tangible things to do, both in the office and at home between sessions. Children can be taught asanas, breathing techniques, and meditation methods. All of these techniques can be integrated with the therapeutic methods you are already using.

ADHD: DISCOVERING STEADY ATTENTION

Attention deficit hyperactivity disorder (ADHD) is characterized as a problem of attention and concentration. Executive control skills to inhibit, modulate, focus, select, and sustain are lacking in ADHD sufferers (McCloskey et al., 2009). Introduced correctly, yoga can be a powerful intervention that addresses these problems directly. Yoga techniques, applied in conjunction with other appropriate therapeutic methods, can help restore the nervous system to a healthier balance. When yoga improves specific executive control brain functions, better self-regulation results. Then, children can improve their ability to direct attention, keep it concentrated, and hold it at will. This section offers methods for working with attention and concentration through postures. The next two sections (anxiety and aggression) present methods to improve attention and concentration using breathing and executive control exercises. All of these exercises are helpful for overcoming ADHD.

Jerry was a thin third grader, short for his age. He was light and quick in his speech and movements. His father brought him in for therapy to help with ADHD. Jerry was on medication, but he continued to be unable to sit still and pay attention in school. As a result, he was falling behind in his work. He often got into fights, which alienated him from his classmates, so he had no close friends.

We began teaching him meditation at the first session, beginning with a focus on his favorite color. Jerry was unable to hold a steady image of a color for even 10 seconds. So, we encouraged him to let his color change. He said his favorite color was black. His color changed dramatically, from black to blood red, and then shifted to a television showing cartoon ninjas kicking and punching, and all of this in 10 seconds! After each trial, we asked him to share what he had experienced. Normally inhibited in his speech, Jerry enjoyed talking about his inner imagery. We praised him for his creativity and vivid imagination. He was surprised by the positive feedback and wanted to keep trying. With each mini-meditation, he was able to increase the time.

As he became more comfortable with the exercise, we asked him, "Are you up for a challenge?" Avidly, he said, "Yes!" While he performed the meditation, he was squeezing his eyes tightly shut and moving his legs and arms. Could he sit absolutely still for 20 seconds? We explained how to sit in easy pose, with his breathing relaxed and just thinking about his color. He could close his eyes gently without squeezing. He met the challenge by remaining motionless for 30 seconds!

As we continued in this way, he developed a feeling of pride in his achievements. He began to recognize that he was imaginative and that this ability had positive potential for shared entertainment. We encouraged him to follow this interest by drawing a picture with the crayons in the office, and he set to work. He created a picture of characters fighting. Without realizing it, he had stayed focused on this effort for 5 minutes. Soon, he began to spend time drawing in each session.

We talked about his pictures, helping him turn his attention deliberately to his thoughts and feelings and disclose them. He had been disconnected from his emotions and used continual motion to avoid feeling anything. He began talking about his mother leaving the family, and how he thought it was his fault. Jerry lived with his father, who had been trying to control him with punishment. Eventually, we brought the father in for several sessions. We taught him how to find the positive in Jerry's behavior and encourage that. Now Jerry was rewarded when he succeeded instead of just being punished when he failed. Father and son talked about the divorce. Jerry began to understand that he was not the cause of his parents' divorce. They meditated together during the sessions, as well as meditating regularly between sessions, which initiated a trend to share positive experiences together.

Eventually, through the combination of yoga, behavior modification, and consistent support from his father, Jerry was able to lower the dose of his medication. He performed better in school and became less provocative. Soon he was making more friends than enemies. He even excelled in art, winning a prize for his work, and having it displayed in a community exhibit.

Developing Body Awareness to Foster Self-Awareness

Children who suffer from ADHD are often out of touch with their bodies, thoughts, and emotions. One easy place to begin developing awareness is through asanas. Attention focused on postures fosters children's ability to know what they are doing while they do it. Asanas are also helpful for children who cannot stay still, because they present an opportunity for stillness while refining motion and control. Being flexible, children are naturally able to perform simple postures. These postures can be applied to help with the other problems children face, such as depression, learning problems, and anxiety.

Yoga practice cultivates listening to body signals, an essential part of body awareness and self-awareness. Judging how far to stretch from the sensations of moving into, holding, and moving out of poses will help children develop a sense of body awareness they can bring into other situations. Children will be better equipped to stay in tune with what they are doing while they are doing it, a useful tool to help change impulsive behavior.

You will find large differences in coordination and ability among children, but this is not crucial for the therapeutic application of asanas. Give positive feedback for the effort made and the coordination of attention with movement. Gently correct mistakes, but keep in mind that the real goals are therapeutic ones, such as integration of mind and body, awareness, calming, self-regulation, and confidence.

Yoga uses both dynamic and static stretching. Dynamic stretching takes place during movement into and out of postures. Static stretching takes place when a posture is held without moving. Children often instinctively perform the asanas quickly, but they can learn to slow down as they become aware. Although you will guide them into the correct pace combined with attention, be supportive of each small step they take. Keep in mind that speed of reaction time is a positive measure of intelligence. Properly channeled, young clients' quickness can become an asset. Asana practice can teach how to be simultaneously quick and aware or slow and controlled when needed.

We have chosen a group of asanas that represent concrete things children like, drawn from nature and animals. Engage them in taking on the quality of the animal. They may want to bark while doing downward dog or roar like a lion in lion pose. Encourage an atmosphere of playful fun. You can also use any of the other poses provided in this book.

General Instructions for Asanas

The beginning phase of dynamic stretching will set the body correctly for the posture. Movements should be slow and smooth, without jerks or bounces. Once in position, the posture is held while breathing normally. Then come out of the posture smoothly, returning to standing in mountain pose.

Tree Pose

When presenting the tree pose (Figure 10.1), engage young clients' ability with imagery. Talk about trees, how they grow tall, reaching into the sky and down low with roots deep down into the ground. Trees are stable and grounded from the roots and trunk, but flexible and responsive from their leaves and branches. Invite them to think about trees they particularly like and what they can learn from trees. Ask them what kind of tree they are. You will often get clues about deeper dynamics as you would from a projective test.

To perform this position, pick a spot directly in front of you to look at that allows you to keep your head straight. Raise your right leg and place your right foot, toes pointing down, as high on the inside of your left leg as possible. Press

Figure 10.1

the foot inward against the left thigh. When you find your stability, exhale completely. Then raise your arms straight overhead, bring your palms together, and balance. Bring your leg down and return to the mountain pose. If you have trouble staying balanced, hold on to a chair or table with one hand as you raise the other one.

Downward Dog Pose

The dog pose (Figure 10.2) gives a releasing stretch that leads into relaxation. Begin from a kneeling position. Breathe comfortably to prepare. Then, inhale as you go up on the balls of your feet and raise your lower body and hips backward, high in the air. Bend over forward at the hips and place your hands on the floor with your head pointing downward. Straighten your arms, with fingers spread

Figure 10.2

on the floor, and arch your back slightly as you stretch forward. Your entire back will elongate naturally from this position. Hold for several breaths, in and out, and try to stretch comfortably. Do not stretch beyond what is comfortable. As you continue to breathe and relax, you will probably be able to stretch a little more. Then, exhale as you slowly return to the kneeling starting position.

Camel Pose

Begin by kneeling with your legs separated shoulder width apart (Figure 10.3). *Bend back, and grasp your left heel with your left hand and your right heel with your right hand. Push your hips forward as much as possible and allow your head to tip backward. Hold this pose for several seconds as you breathe normally. Then remove your hands from your heels as you sit up straight and relax.*

Figure 10.3

Lion Pose

The lion pose helps release emotional tension (Figure 10.4). It appeals to children to be invited to stick out their tongue and widen their eyes! Some children will love this pose, whereas others will feel shy about doing it. The lion is performed in the pelvic pose, kneeling position.

Place your hands on your knees and inhale completely. Then exhale sharply as you learn forward. At the same time, tense and separate your fingers, tense all the muscles in your face and neck, open your eyes and mouth wide, and stick out your tongue. Hold for approximately 15 seconds and then slowly withdraw your tongue, relax your eyes, face, and neck, relax your fingers, and settle back into the pelvic posture.

Figure 10.4

OVERCOMING ANXIETY AND STRESS

Children may be exposed to chronic stress, especially when there is divorce or poverty in the family. These stressful situations can lead to the symptoms of stress and anxiety described in Chapters 6 and 7. Yoga methods help to alter the mind-body balance by offering techniques that bring relaxation. Practice fosters new habits that help children to respond more effectively, thereby lessening the stress response.

Children with generalized anxiety disorder show more activity in the amygdala. Therapy activates executive control from the orbitofrontal cortex, which is the area of the prefrontal cortex that helps evaluate how rewarding an emotional stimulus is. Better executive control can regulate anxiety and calm an overactive amygdala (Rolls, 2004). The process of executive control can be initiated by teaching children how to direct their attention deliberately and keep it focused over time. Breathing, meditation, and asanas can all be used to develop executive control. A primary symptom of anxiety is uncomfortable sensations, and this is usually linked to breathing. People who feel anxious often develop tightness in the chest area. Yoga techniques can help to correct breathing patterns by fostering relaxed, comfortable breathing that will diminish anxious feelings. Through meditation, children develop skills for discriminating between accurate and inaccurate perceptions. And turning attention to asana practice is another way to increase executive control, as attention is linked to placement of the body as it moves in space. These methods will have a ripple effect that builds confidence in the child's personal ability to make a change.

Kathy suffered from severe anxiety that disturbed her falling asleep. She regularly practiced the techniques included here and found that if she meditated at bedtime, she was able to fall asleep and sleep comfortably through the night. As she became more rested, she was better able to address the problems that were involved in her anxiety.

Josh was a socially awkward adolescent who used meditation to help him with test anxiety. He learned how to meditate during his sessions and practiced between sessions. As he became more skilled, he tried using it at school. Just before an exam, he would spend several minutes meditating. He told us that when his classmates saw him meditating, they wanted him to teach them how, which he did. As Josh progressed in his academic performance, he improved his interpersonal relationships.

The cat's breath posture combines pranayama with an asana to initiate a change by loosening the muscles around the lungs. Attention to breathing builds meditative skills. By moving with breathing, children start to make the link between attention and breathing. Then the meditations that simply focus on breathing become easier to perform.

Cat's Breath

Sit on your knees and bring your hands down to the floor so that you are on all fours. Inhale as you smoothly, slowly, and carefully arch your back and raise your head to look straight in front of you (Figure 10. 5). *Remember: Never push*

Figure 10.5

to the point of pain, and always move slowly and smoothly, without tension. Stretch sensitively, along your entire spine. Then exhale and smoothly round your back up, not to the point of pain, as you pull your stomach in and tuck your head down (Figure 10.6). *Repeat the entire sequence several times, moving and breathing gently and slowly.*

Meditative Breathing Methods

Children are surprisingly adept at learning to meditate. Their minds are agile and quick; their imaginations are vivid and immediate. Once they overcome any reluctance or fear, they like meditating. They will find the skill useful at

Figure 10.6

school, to clear the mind before a test or performance, and may apply their skills at home to help them fall asleep or calm down when they are feeling anxious. We encourage practice between sessions, as the skills will improve when practiced.

Introduce the skills gradually. Begin with as little as a few seconds. When first teaching children to meditate, we begin with 30 seconds or 1 minute. Make it something fun to do. As skills build, offer more challenge. Children with problems such as anxiety and ADHD like to keep moving. You can utilize this impulse as a motivation. Keep increasing the difficulty incrementally as each skill is mastered. So, you might begin with only 10 seconds of meditation, as we did with Jerry, and increase stepwise, to 2 minutes. In this way, children feel like they are moving forward and doing something new each time.

Focus on Breathing

The place to start in pranayama meditation for children is usually with counting the breaths and listening to the breath (instructions given in Chapter 5). Sometimes children will try to breathe deeper or louder at first, but explain that breathing should be natural and normal. When they are able to stay relaxed in their breathing and count comfortably for several minutes, you can introduce awareness of breathing (Chapter 5). Children will also enjoy a variation that engages the imagination, breathing in one color and out another.

Close your eyes and breathe comfortably. Imagine that the air you breathe in is one color, and the air you breathe out is another color. You might like to breathe in a light color and breathe out a darker color. Be imaginative and stay focused on your breathing. Your colors might be sparkly or bright or shiny. After several minutes of breathing comfortably in this way, open your eyes and stretch. What did you imagine?

AGGRESSIVE BEHAVIOR

Aggressive behavior is a problem often seen in young clients. Children who are aggressive show damage to their orbitofrontal and ventromedial prefrontal cortex, reflected in their aggressive reactions (Blair, 2004). Normally, these areas help modulate aggression as a result of their close mapping with the limbic system. One theory is that when these links are lacking, children misperceive and misjudge situations, leading to aggressive responses (Feifer, 2009). Another possible factor is low levels of cortisol, also found in stress reactions (refer to Figure A-10), which have been linked to antisocial behavior and aggression (Susman, 2006). Developing cognitive strategies for improved concentration, tolerance of discomfort, and renunciation of harming will help modulate aggression. Give the nervous system opportunities to respond differently, fostering new neural connections to be formed where they are lacking. In time, the child will feel differently, reflected literally in brain and mind changes.

Clearly, developing executive control is especially helpful for children who express their problems in aggressive acting-out behavior. Meditation is a gentle way to teach children how to stop and think before acting. One client often found himself in the midst of a fight without even knowing how it happened. Meditation helped him to become aware of what he was doing to get him there. Through regular meditation, he developed self-awareness to help him regulate his reactions before they escalated into violence.

Self-control begins by learning how to focus attention. The instructions from Chapter 5 for dharana focus can be adapted for children. Use an object of focus that appeals to the clients, such as a fantasy figure they like or an interesting object in the office. We often begin with focus on a color meditation when working with children, because it is accessible, and children usually have a favorite. Adults like to do this as well, because it offers something tangible and manageable.

Focus on a Color

Close your eyes as you sit comfortably in easy pose. Picture your favorite color. Imagine your color and only your color. You can think of a vast expanse of the color everywhere. If you have difficulty thinking of just a color, picture an object that is one color, such as a blue sky, a blackboard, or a brown animal.

Focus on One Thing

Next, imagine your color in the shape of a square. Visualize the square getting bigger and bigger. Stay with this image, contemplating it, breathing comfortably. Then let the square become gradually smaller until it is just a tiny dot of color. Stay focused on the dot and only the dot. When you are ready to stop, open your eyes and stretch.

Dhyana Open Meditation

Once the child has developed the ability to focus comfortably for several minutes, teach about clearing the mind of all thought. Children will ponder the idea of thinking about nothing and enjoy the process. When this skill is mastered, children will have a resource for relief from some of their discomforts.

Think of nothing (represented by a vast empty sky, large whiteness, or perhaps an expanse of darkness). Concentrate and hold your attention there, without thinking about it as directed toward an object. If a thought comes into your mind, let it go and return to thinking of nothing.

Transitioning to Focus on Feelings

Children are often out of touch with what they are thinking and feeling, and they may lack the skills they need to recognize their emotions, thoughts, and behaviors. Once children learn how to direct their attention to breathing, an image, or an object of focus, you can introduce a focus on feelings. Yoga meditation teaches mental skills that make it possible to recognize the sensations associated with emotions, the thoughts that occur, and the affect involved.

Use meditative focus and turn it toward an emotion. Once children have gained some ability to focus attention at will, they find it easier to attend to a feeling or a thought. Begin with attention to sensations, such as butterflies in the stomach, warmth in the face, or whatever the child notices. Then gently move to thoughts and emotions. Use the skills from other chapters, such as depression and anxiety, to work on troubling emotions and thoughts.

Child Pose

The child pose is a posture for self-soothing. It offers a feeling of self-support that can be reassuring, especially after dealing with disturbing emotions. Some clients may prefer savasana or crocodile, described in Chapter 5, but child pose has a special quality that many people, children and adults alike, will find comforting. The variation offered may feel better for some clients, so you may want to present both ways to let clients chose their preferred way.

Sit on your feet in the pelvic pose, kneeling position. Bend forward slowly until your head touches the floor. Allow your arms to rest comfortably at your sides with your elbows bent so that they can rest on the floor (Figure 10.7). *You may need to shift or move slightly to find the most comfortable position. Adjust your breathing to a calm rhythm, and rest in this position. An alternative child pose is to extend the arms out in front* (Figure 10.8).

Figure 10.7

Figure 10.8

SOME SPECIAL VARIATIONS FOR CHILDREN

Here are some variations we have used in working with meditation for children. They enjoy them and usually respond by feeling motivated for further and deeper practice.

Meditation Contest

In group therapy, we occasionally offer a meditation contest to see who can be the quietest and go the deepest. We say occasionally, because you do not want to take meditation outside of its context of doing it for its own sake, not for another purpose such as winning. However, some children will be motivated to try harder with a competition, and these efforts will help them get to a more advanced level in their practice. We have had young elementary-age children successfully sustain a deep meditation for more than 30 minutes during such competitions.

Judge these competitions by watching carefully. A deeper meditative state is reflected in the body and face. There will be complete stillness, even breathing, and lightly closed eyes. You can use any of the meditations that the child is familiar with using, or let them choose their favorite, "meditation of choice."

Meditation With Distractions

Children love this meditation! Begin with several minutes of quietly meditating, using focus on a color, focus on one thing, focus on breathing, or clearing the mind of all thoughts. Then the therapist makes noises such as clapping, stomping, humming, or silly scraping sounds that would usually make a child laugh. They will try extremely hard to stay focused. This humorous exercise helps children of all ages learn how to maintain awareness even in the midst of imperfect circumstances.

Engaging the Family

Often the family system is involved. We include some sessions with the family to guide parents in working with their child at home. Sharing meditation (Figure 10.9), pranayama, and even postures (Figure 10.10) is a helpful way to get a family sharing some positive experiences and working together (Figure 10.11).

LEARNING AND MEMORY: USING WISDOM TO GAIN KNOWLEDGE

To common sense, nothing is more obvious than the fact that learning requires concentration, effort, sustained attention, or absorbing interest. If these conditions are present in sufficient degree, we can learn almost anything.

(*Allport, 1961, p. 105*)

Figure 10.9

Figure 10.10

One of the main occupations for children is learning. Problems at school often come about because the client is having psychological problems, but learning problems can exacerbate the situation, adding another dimension

Figure 10.11

to the disturbance. Thus, addressing learning ability directly by developing mental skills will improve scholastic performance. A byproduct is that clients' confidence and skills increase generally, making it easier to tackle psychological problems.

Learning ability can be enhanced by meditation and yoga, as the many studies cited in Chapter 1 have shown. Approaching learning with mental skills makes any lesson easier to master. Meditation helps attune mental tools for greater success. All of the meditations already presented will help develop skills in focus that will improve attention to learning. The meditations that follow are helpful for older elementary school through college-age clients.

Listening in Class

Learning comes more readily when the student fully absorbs material that is presented in the classroom. Taking notes and listening carefully are the customary tools and are good skills to develop, but sometimes attention drifts when the teacher is talking, and the student misses the important points.

Dhyana Listening

This exercise is helpful for adolescents, to learn how to listen openly. *Before you enter the classroom, relax your body and mind with a brief meditation. Open your senses to the moment and notice your skin, the sounds around you, and your breathing. When you get to class, sit up straight but as comfortably as possible. Breathe gently. Pay attention to the sound of the teacher's voice. Notice when he or she seems to give special emphasis, and write this down in your notes.*

Do not concentrate on each detail as an isolated unit, but listen more deeply to the organization and sense of what is being communicated. Allow yourself to receive the material for what it is, not for what it can do for you or whether you like it or not.

Reading Comprehension

Reading comprehension, one of the functional applications of intelligence, can be improved by searching for and perceiving the significant relationships among ideas and concepts. Many tutoring and learning programs are founded on this belief. The interrelationship of all things is a fundamental enlightened construct of yoga: the oneness. Mental focus on interrelationships stimulates associations of ideas, leading to concepts in one frame of reference, to theory in another. There are partial unities, subcategories that have their place in the universal oneness. Unity is within an interrelationship, not outside it.

If reading comprehension depends on grasping the interrelationships of concepts as well as understanding the intended meanings, then tools that apply the mind to noticing these relationships will help develop the ability to read well. This approach is also the basis of mnemonic memory systems.

This meditation is best done sitting comfortably, with eyes closed. Take a few moments to become attuned to your body and mind as you sit. Feel your presence within. Then notice your skin and how you meet the floor or chair. Now, expand your awareness to include the space around you. Notice the details, and experience yourself within it, as part of it. Consider how the air you breathe has been a part of this space and how it now enters your lungs to be cycled through your body. Expand your awareness outward to include the building, the other people in it, then the entire area, the city and all its inhabitants, the country, the planet, and out to the farthest reaches of your imagination of our universe.

Now that you have meditated on your interrelationship with the greater whole, apply this meditation to the subject you are trying to comprehend. For example, if you are studying chemistry, begin with the subatomic units and expand outward to contemplate the chemical structure of the universe and how intricately objects are interrelated. If you are studying a literary work, contemplate the plot, style, and so on, of the particular work. Meditate on the period in which it was written; then generalize to writings of this type, perhaps even to the meaning of literature in general. In all these applications, take the time to search for subtle interrelationships.

Freedom From Redundant Patterns

When children have learning problems, they often keep repeating the same inadequate strategies. Clearing away illusions can remove faulty strategies that create obstacles to learning and open the possibility for a new approach to emerge. Teachers will often tell students what to do, but until the student truly thinks about the instructions personally, change may not happen. Free from such problems as excessive analysis or narrow classifications that interfere with the process, spontaneous discovery can occur. Spontaneity and personal discovery are key elements.

Sit for at least 5 minutes using your favorite meditation to relax and ready yourself. Then think about how you usually approach studying for a test. You can also perform this exercise to consider how you write a paper or approach a school project. Concentrate on it: Surround yourself with it imaginatively as if you are doing it now. Do you gather all of the materials together and go through them one at a time? Do you move back and forth between books and notes? How do you memorize? What methods do you use? Concentrate all of your attention on the process of studying. Observe your reactions and insights. Tell your ideas to your therapist, write them down, or draw them. Find a way to record them until you run out of ideas and insights.

Now, with no more ideas in mind, clear your mind again and contemplate this nothingness. You will find it easier to think of nothing after running out of ideas. Wait. A spontaneous image or symbol may occur to you. Note it down somehow. You may have a useful insight and understandings of perhaps what is missing, what could be improved, or something entirely new. Do not analyze the image or idea at first. Let your reaction be. Concentrate and allow, staying in the center, and your creative understanding will take form.

For example, one teenage client saw an image of a big broom, sweeping leaves. She realized that she often began studying with many thoughts rumbling through her mind. After this exercise, she decided that she needed to sweep away the distractions first, and then her mind would be clear to study. She found that she had a much easier time studying for tests after she cleared her mind in meditation.

Creative Learning

The key quality of creativity is the ability to detach from habitual, established patterns of thought and apply new variations. Through meditation, we learn to let go of set constructs, to recognize that things are not what they seem. Transformation into other forms is basic to creative thinking.

Use your meditative skills to transform something into another form. The ability to take the situation apart analytically and put it back together again brings about a greater depth of understanding. Train your mind by deconstructing an object into its different parts and then reproducing the pattern as a whole.

Find a simple household object, such as a table, a potted plant, or a fan. Look at it closely, noticing all the parts and how it is put together. Close your eyes. Picture the object. Then imagine taking it apart. When you can picture it in several pieces, try to put the pieces back together again in a new way. Some people may want to draw the pieces on paper and then draw the new configuration. Others may prefer to do the entire meditation imaginatively. Finally, reassemble it as it was originally. Open your eyes and look at the real object. Do you see it differently now?

Using additional senses can be helpful. Touch the object. Notice the textures, the temperature of the object. Look at its colors. Does it have a perfume or scent? The added dimension of other senses gives you more detail for your imagery.

CONCLUSION

Using yoga methods to work with children can be creative and playful, leading young clients toward new and useful skills that may set them on a lifelong path of healthy habits, both mentally and physically. You may find, as the therapist, that the process is enjoyable and rewarding for you as well, especially if you participate in some of these techniques at times along with your clients to model the methods. We often meditate with clients, and we all gain in the sharing together.

11

Healthy Aging

The future has yet to be made. Our present choices give a new form even to the past so that what it means depends on what we do now.
(*Radhakrishnan in Schilpp, 1952, p. 42*)

People age differently. Some suffer sharp declines and loss of cognitive functions in aging, whereas others live extremely well in their later years. Normal aging has a wide range of variations. For example, Grandma Moses (Anna Roberts, 1860–1961) began painting later in life. When she could no longer do embroidery because of arthritis, she turned to painting. She continued to be prolific and even created 25 new paintings in the last year of her life. Her final work was painted shortly before she died at age 101. She created nostalgic scenes of Americana that portrayed happy people busily engaged in a simple farming life. She drew from her memories of her childhood on a farm. Her life demonstrates that people can remain optimistic and productive even into advanced age. She also exemplifies how we can learn new skills later in life, and even excel at them.

THE AGING MIND, BRAIN, AND BODY

Most of us know people who continue to work well and live happily into their later years with competence and wisdom. This may be helped by what is called crystallized intelligence: the accumulation of skills and knowledge built up over time and usually related to work or profession. This form of intelligence tends to remain stable with age (Kaufman, Reynolds, & McLean, 1989).

The mental decline that occurs with aging is closely related to changes in the brain. For example, the mild impairment of memory that often accompanies aging is related to reduction in size of the hippocampal formation (Golomb et al., 1994). Generally, the type of cognitive function that seems to decline the most is what is known as fluid intelligence. Fluid intelligence involves mental flexibility, processing speed, abstract and complex problem solving, memory, and new learning. Digit span and block design, two subtests of the well-known WAIS-R (Wechsler Adult Intelligence Scale Revised), are tests of fluid intelligence (Zillmer, Spiers, & Culbertson, 2008). And corresponding to the drop in fluid intelligence resulting from aging, we find the nervous system and the body becoming less flexible.

Brain Changes

Brain changes vary greatly from person to person (Johansson, 1991), but there are some structural trends. The size of the brain in terms of its weight and volume diminish with time. One myth is that as we age, large numbers of neurons die, but with the newer imaging methods, researchers now believe that in normal aging the number of neurons remains relatively constant. What accounts for the smaller brain size is that individual cells become smaller. Thus, cortical thinning could simply be caused by the shrinking of cells, not cell loss (Haug, 1985). The prefrontal cortex is an important area for higher-level cognitive processing that suffers with age and may account for some of the loss in fluid intelligence (Esiri, 1994). However, recent studies of meditation have found that regular meditators do not experience a cortical thinning as they age; instead, they retain thickness in the attentional areas of the cortex comparable to younger people (Lazar et al., 2005).

Although some parts of the brain alter with age, other parts remain robust. Positron emission tomography (PET) scans of elderly people showed that the cerebral metabolism stays relatively constant (Breedlove, Rosenzweig, & Watson, 2007).

Environmental factors can affect the brain, leading to more or less aging. Long-term stress has been shown to age the brain significantly

(Epel et al., 2004) and shrink the hippocampus (Lupien et al., 1998), but exercise enhances performance on cognitive tasks and increases brain density (Colcombe et al., 2003). As mentioned previously, meditation has also been found to slow cortical thinning in the attentional areas as well as lower stress (Lazar et al., 2005).

Cognitive Changes

Two general theories are used to explain why we find so much variability in cognitive function as people age. These models are known as *the cognitive reserve theory* and *the differential preservation hypothesis* (Salthouse, Babcock, Skovornek, Mitchell, & Palmon, 1990). The cognitive reserve theory is based on the idea that studies have shown a strong link between early intelligence and less cognitive decline. For example, a long-term project, known as the Nun Study (Snowdon et al., 1999), followed 678 Roman Catholic nuns who took regular cognitive and medical tests and agreed to donate their brains following their death. The research found that those who had higher "idea density," complexity and sophistication of concepts, when they first entered the convent continued to have higher mental ability in later years compared to those who were less linguistically sophisticated at that time of life, between 18 and 32 years old. Those with higher idea density early in life showed less cognitive decline in later years.

The differential preservation hypothesis (Salthouse et al., 1990) is that normally aging adults can maintain stable cognitive functioning by continuing to be mentally active. Just as we should keep physically fit, it is important to remain mentally fit. Challenging oneself mentally can keep mental functioning working well.

Integration

Clearly, the mind, body, and brain are interrelated. When working with aging, all three components show effects, and a change in any one will influence the others. All of the theories about aging provide springboards for techniques to help enhance functioning as people age. The research described in Chapter 1 also shows many ways that yoga can be applied to help seniors. Therefore, we have little to lose in using the techniques of yoga with older clients.

Disorders of Aging

Normal aging, although it has some of the symptoms and brain changes we have described, is not considered a disorder. A healthy lifestyle with exercise and mental challenge can help a person maintain a normal quality of life even when some slowing down and memory loss is evident.

Seniors have certain therapeutic issues along with typical problems that are characteristic of long living, such as dealing with loss of a significant other, coping with declining faculties, both physical and mental, and handling the completion of career and child-rearing, along with entry into new phases such as being a grandparent, having more time, and financial changes. These issues can be addressed well with yoga, through meditative practices of detachment and union, enhancement of mental and physical faculties, and the experience of Samadhi, which brings happiness and fulfillment.

Therapy treats the problems of seniors, similarly to those of younger patients, so long as there are no specific aging disorders involved. If there are disorders requiring specific treatment, yoga can help, when appropriate, as an adjunct to treatment specific to the condition.

Prolonged Stress

Exposure to stress may prematurely age the immune system and brain cells. For example, in a group of women who were under an extended period of severe stress from caring for a seriously ill child, the end cap on their chromosomes, known as *telomeres*, was shorter. The length of the telomeres is a measure of the life of the cell. The telomeres on these caregiving mothers were equivalent to 10 more years of aging (Epel et al., 2004). Stress can have a strong influence on aging and should therefore be addressed right away. The stress-reduction methods offered in Chapter 6 should be introduced in treatment of seniors who are experiencing any kind of stress.

Mild Cognitive Impairment

Mild cognitive impairment (MCI) is one of the most common complaints of aging. The disorder is considered a transitional stage between normal aging and problems of dementia. The diagnosis is somewhat controversial, because it can be overused as a catchall term for any cognitive change that an elderly client is experiencing (Zillmer, Spiers, & Culbertson, 2008). MCI usually involves memory-related problems, similar to Alzheimer's disease but less severe. Research has found that people diagnosed with MCI show more pronounced atrophy in the hippocampus and brain size than is found in normal aging (Jack et al., 2000, 2005). Exercises that promote learning and new experiences may stimulate new growth in these areas, thereby helping to improve functioning.

Dementias

Dementia is the term used to describe a group of behavioral symptoms that involve a wide range of impairments to memory, cognition including executive function and language, decline in social skills and work abilities, along with clouded consciousness. Dementias are also classified in terms of the part of the brain that is affected. Two broad classifications are made: cortical and subcortical dementias. Knowing which classification a client has can reveal a great deal about the nature of the behavioral, cognitive, and emotional changes that will occur.

Alzheimer's disease (AD) is a cortical dementia, because it shrinks major areas of the cerebral cortex. As one would expect with loss to these brain areas, memory becomes severely impaired, with a breakdown of semantic knowledge and long-term declarative memory. Interestingly, short-term memory is relatively spared, along with language skills. AD also attacks some subcortical structures such as the hippocampus and amygdala. Most of the subcortical damage occurs in the pathways connected to the association areas in cortex. The subcortical damage is reflected in loss of visual-spatial functioning. AD patients often become lost or disoriented, even when traveling through familiar areas. AD also influences many of the neurotransmitter systems. Widely distributed neurotransmitters such as acetylcholine, catecholamines, glutamate, and neuropeptides are reduced in numbers. The brain losses and neurotransmitter reductions account for the general decline of intelligence that takes place. AD sufferers have difficulty with executive functioning, directing attention, and regulating moods. Often the personality style becomes exaggerated.

Subcortical dementias include Parkinson's disease (PD) and Huntington's disease (HD). Parkinson's disease is the result of a severe loss of dopamine in the substantia nigra of the basal ganglia. Because the basal ganglia control movement, both PD and HD sufferers have problems with motor movement. Normal aging tends to bring some decrease in dopamine, so PD symptoms get worse with age. However, if dopamine levels drop below 50%, patients exhibit PD symptoms, regardless of age. The symptoms include developing a resting tremor as small, uncontrolled movements that gradually worsen over time. PD sufferers also become rigid in the muscles and joints. PD brings problems with visual-spatial tasks as well, especially when motor movement is involved. PD patients have some difficulty with executive functioning that is tied to their premotor areas and the parts of the basal ganglia that project to the frontal lobes. PD patients have difficulty being mentally flexible and have trouble with temporal organization of events. They also tend to suffer more depression than other chronic problems (Raskin et al., 1990).

UNCOVERING THE VALUE OF AGING

Larry was in his early seventies. He came to see us because he was feeling depressed, hopeless, and uncomfortable. He was planning to retire in a year because he felt too tired and uncomfortable to continue working and did not really see the point anymore. He felt like there was nothing to look forward to, only memories to look back on, and most of the significant people he remembered were now dead. He felt discomfort in his body, had trouble sleeping, and had found little enjoyment in work during recent years.

He had undergone analytical therapy before, and so had a great deal of insight about his problems. He was well-read, dignified, and eloquent, with refined manners. He cogently told us about his relationships and his past battle with drugs that he had won many years ago. He was not married and had decided early on to commit himself to his gay lifestyle. He had been content with his longtime partner, socializing regularly with a close group of friends. Things began to change when his partner began a difficult battle with AIDS and slowly died. Larry cared for him throughout the entire illness. Now, several years later, he still deeply missed his partner.

We asked him if he might like to learn how to meditate. He told us that he had never been able to focus very well, because he was always thinking, but he was willing to try it. We began with meditation on breathing, starting with counting the breaths and listening to breathing. Much to his surprise, Larry could sustain both of these meditations for several minutes. He quickly moved on to focus his attention on breathing, the complete breath, and relaxing his breathing. Within several sessions, he was able to develop a deep, comfortable state of meditation. He reported each week that he felt better right after the sessions and when he did meditation at home, but that the effects always "wore off."

We discussed the yogic idea of having goals directed to a higher purpose. At first he hesitated and said, "I've done my life, and now it's time to do nothing." We guided him toward searching for the meaningful moments he recalled in his life. Gradually, he began to realize that his most meaningful times had been the most painful ones. He felt that he mattered when he helped his partner to cope with AIDS; he recalled feeling that what he did had meaning. He liked the yoga principle of living in relationship to value. He began to feel a wish to regain meaning again in his life by volunteering to help others with AIDS.

Seniors often have misconceptions about retirement and aging, believing that the best part of life has passed. But in the ancient Indian culture, the elders were the spiritually evolved ones. The elderly have the potential to seek higher wisdom now that their responsibilities of career and raising a family are behind them. With all the experience of age, seniors can find meaning. The source of meaning may be found in unexpected places, even coming from past tragedy, as Larry discovered.

ENHANCING VITALITY, FLEXIBILITY, AND STRENGTH: CHAIR-SITTING YOGA

Seniors may question the idea of doing more with their lives because they feel fatigued and uncomfortable. Here is where the therapist can guide the client toward gentle yoga asanas. Everyone can benefit from some exercise. These asanas are accessible even to those who are bedridden or restricted to a wheelchair. So long as there is no medical reason interfering with performing light movements, even the most uncomfortable and inactive person can probably raise an arm or move the head, and these simple movements offer an accessible way for clients to begin. Chair-sitting yoga is a gentle and easy way to introduce simple exercises that will help raise energy, increase strength, and produce flexibility. An additional benefit is that these exercises, when practiced regularly, enhance clients' confidence that is grounded in a sense of physical confidence.

These exercises can also be performed in the office with clients of any age who are having difficulty focusing, to quiet the mind and body and direct attention. Clients can be encouraged to perform these exercises in your office, but they can also do them between sessions in a chair at work and at home. These exercises can also be recommended for clients who are healing from an injury. A further application is for depression, or when people are having difficulty with motivation. Chair yoga can be an easy way to set a more active adjustment in motion.

Note: Whenever recommending exercise, ensure that clients have the approval of their medical doctor. Encourage them to ask someone else nearby to monitor if they perform these exercises at home between sessions.

Begin With Sitting Awareness Meditation

Sit in the upright pose on the chair and close your eyes. Focus your attention on sitting. Notice how your legs meet the chair, how your spine feels, your neck, and head. Feel your feet, sitting flat on the floor. Take several minutes, breathing comfortably, to feel your body, here and now, sitting in the chair. Relax any unnecessary tensions as much as possible.

Chair-Sitting Arm Reach

Begin sitting with hands placed on your knees, palms down (Figure 11.1). *Close your eyes and take several comfortable breaths. Then, raise your arms out from your side and around above your head with palms touching as you inhale and look up toward your hands* (Figure 11.2). *Then exhale as you lower your arms around slowly and gaze straight ahead. Repeat 3 times, breathing in as your arms circle up overhead, and then exhaling as you circle back around to place your hands back on your knees.*

Chair-Sitting Arm Swing

Extend your arms straight out in front of you with palms touching as you exhale (Figure 11.3), *then arc your arms out, keeping the sweep of the circle parallel to the floor as you inhale. Go as far back as you can safely—without feeling any strain—to get a gentle stretch in your rib cage and chest* (Figure 11.4). *Then, slowly bring your arms back around to the front as you exhale. Repeat 3 times.*

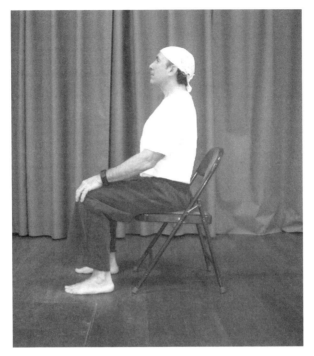

Figure 11.1

Figure 11.2

Figure 11.3

Figure 11.4

Chair-Sitting Triangle

Lift one arm up overhead as you place your other hand on the edge of the seat of the chair, take hold, and inhale. Then gently exhale as you lean slightly from the waist, keeping your back straight (Figure 11.5). You will feel a gentle stretch in your waist and side. Now return to upright with your arm extended straight up and inhale. Exhale as you bring your arm down, place your hand on the side of the chair, and take hold. Now repeat on the other side, raising your other arm up as you inhale, bending sideways as you exhale, coming back to upright as you inhale, and lower your arm again while you exhale. Repeat again on each side.

Chair-Sitting Sun Salutation

Begin sitting on the chair with palms together at chest level, similar to the standing sun position in Figures 7.3 and Figure 8.1, and breathe comfortably for one

Figure 11.5

minute. When you feel ready, slowly look up toward the ceiling as you lift your arms overhead and gently stretch backward, letting your shoulders move back slightly and allowing your back to arch a bit (Figure 11.6). If you feel unsteady, keep your hands holding onto the lower back of the chair as you perform this stretch. Next, exhale as you lean forward over your knees and let your arms move down to hang down near your head. Let your head drop forward as well and go as low as is comfortable (Figure 11.7). If you feel unsteady, keep your hands holding onto the sides of the chair as you stretch forward. Then gradually lift up, returning to a straight position, replacing your hands at your sides on the chair as you inhale. Then, exhale again as you return to sitting upright. Repeat the palms-together hand position, followed by the backward bend, and forward stretch once more.

Figure 11.6

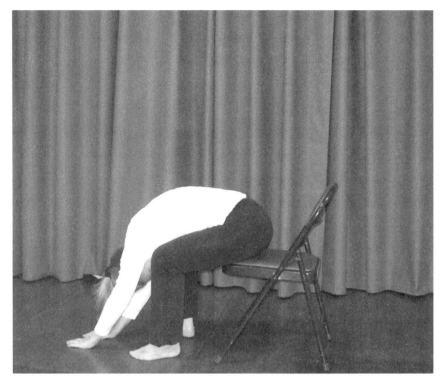

Figure 11.7

Wrists, Ankles, Knees, and Hip Joint Rotations

These exercises are particularly helpful for those who spend long hours typing at the computer, to revitalize the joints. Sitting upright, extend your arms in front with fingers extended out in front and palms facing down as you inhale (Figure 11.8). Now, rotate your hands around in a complete circle at the wrist as you exhale. Inhale, keeping your hands still, and then rotate again as you exhale (Figure 11.9). Repeat several times. Drop your arms back down to your sides as you inhale and exhale.

Now, raise one leg, holding it up under your knee as needed and inhale (Figure 11.10). Then, rotate your ankle as you exhale. Inhale as you hold your leg still, then rotate your ankle again as you exhale. Repeat the pattern of inhaling and exhaling several times, and when you are finished, gently lower your leg as you inhale and exhale. Now lift the other leg and perform the same pattern.

If you are able, do a similar rotation of your knee and of your hip joint, always slowly and combined with breathing. Use your hands to support your leg if necessary. You should not feel strain.

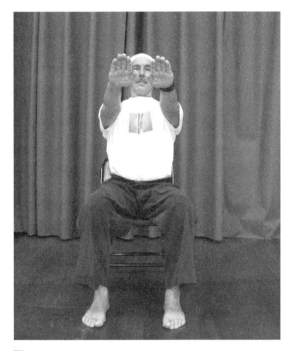

Figure 11.8

Figure 11.9

Figure 11.10

WORKING WITH MEMORY

Most people over the age of 40 begin to notice some changes in their memory. Much can be done to improve memory, drawing on training of attention to facilitate brain encoding to start the memory process. Knowing that the hippocampus can grow at any age lends confidence to the idea of training the memory to help foster brain plasticity.

Attention is one of the components of memory, and so the highly refined yoga techniques for training attention can enhance memory skills. Attention can be either conscious or unconscious, as described in Chapter 2. Yoga works with both conscious and unconscious attention. Dharana uses the declarative parts of attention, purposely directed and consciously performed. Dhyana turns the process over to the unconscious, nondeliberate attention, which can also intelligently learn. Both forms of meditation can be used to enhance memory.

Working With Attention Consciously and Unconsciously

Paying attention is one of the key components of memory, as one might expect. But as we discussed in Chapter 5 in the section on pratyahara, attention is two-sided, involving doing (focusing) and not-doing (screening out everything else). As people age, their ability to ignore distractions becomes impaired. A recent fMRI study of older adults found that their difficulties with memory were more a result of interference from irrelevant information than from their inability to focus on relevant information (Gazzaley, Cooney, Rissman, & D'Esposito, 2005). When people cannot block out distracting information, they cannot focus on what they need to, interfering with getting information into memory. Furthermore, they are also distracted when trying to remember, making the retrieval phase of memory from long-term storage difficult to do as well. The exercises that follow can sharpen the ability to tune out distractions, narrow the focus, and enhance it, so that information can get more easily encoded into memory to be more readily retrieved.

Pratyahara to Narrow the Field

Choose a place where distractions are minimal. A body position that will help is to lie prone comfortably or to sit in a comfortable chair. The body can be relatively relaxed, and so concerns about discomfort do not intrude. Remember, when lying down or sitting in a comfortable chair for the purposes of meditation, stay alert. At first, thoughts may wander around and little things could seem distracting, but be patient and eventually, attention will become easier to hold in focus.

Begin by noticing all of the objects in the room. Make note of the furniture, the decorations on the wall, and what might be sitting on the table or on the floor. Listen to the sounds, perhaps from a heater, an air conditioner, or a clock. Then pick one object and focus your attention on it. Notice all of the details you can about it: its color, shape, and texture. Notice the areas of light and shadow and anything else you perceive.

Pick the object you noticed in the room before, and look at it once again. When you have it clearly in mind, close your eyes, and if possible, visualize the object, noticing the details you observed, such as color, size, texture, shape, scent, etc. Then try to put them together, to think about the object as a whole. After 30 seconds, open your eyes to look at the object again, noting the details. Then close your eyes again and visualize the object. It may take several times of opening and closing your eyes to gain a clear inner sense of the object. Some people will have a vivid picture, whereas others have a vague sense. Keep thinking about this particular object and nothing else. If another thought intrudes, gently bring your attention back to the object as soon as possible. Gradually increase the time for focusing to several minutes.

Mindful Attention

When you have contemplated the object thoroughly, withdraw further by deliberately turning attention away from the surroundings toward what is closest: Notice what you are experiencing right now. So, for example, if you are thinking about trying to focus on thinking, notice all the details of how you are focusing your attention. Or you might notice whether your muscles are tight or loose, how the chair supports you, etc. Pay attention to anything you are experiencing right now. But if a thought pops up, such as, "I wonder what I will have for dinner," notice that your thinking has moved away from the present moment and gently bring your thoughts back to your present experiencing, of sitting or lying down now. Keep following along with what you experience moment by moment. Keep your thoughts narrowed to focusing on this present moment as you lie quietly, bringing your attention back if it drifts away. When you feel ready to stop, sit up and stretch if needed.

This skill of mindful attention to the present moment can be helpful when attention is distracted. It is the cornerstone of Zen Buddhism and has become integrated into psychotherapy. Turn to it (or any of the other mindfulness exercises in this book) often, and your ability to focus without distractions will improve. As mindfulness skills improve, what begins with deliberate dharana, focusing on the moment consciously, transforms into an automatic clarity and presence, attuned and focused, like an orienting reflex to be aware of yourself here and now.

Learning to Focus Attention Unconsciously

Enlist your unconscious processes to help with memory. Often, something more is there than what is consciously noticed, and these unconscious perceptions can enhance conscious focus. As priming research revealed (Mitchell, 2006; Squire & Kandel, 2000), other stimuli are registered that may be relevant and important, and yet are not consciously recognized. Unconscious preoccupations may interfere with conscious processing. Either way, drawing on unconscious perception is positive and beneficial, either to fill out what is consciously registered or to work on repetitive distractions that may interfere with focus.

Focus once again on the object used in earlier exercises. Instead of keeping your attention focused on it now, let your thoughts drift freely as you look at it. Allow your own thoughts and feelings to be stimulated as you contemplate and focus deeply. Let your associations roam freely around the object. Perhaps a symbolic meaning will be evoked for you. After several minutes, sit quietly for a moment. If your thoughts wandered away, where did they go? Can you reason from the new association back to the object to understand how your attention wandered and where it went? You may learn more about yourself as you explore how deliberate and spontaneous attention weave together.

Flexible Attention

As people age, they may get accustomed to fixed routines and feel reluctant to make changes, but keeping flexibility of attention is an important skill. People who suffer from psychological problems are often stuck in redundant patterns of thoughts and emotions. Attention is directed in a habitual pattern of focus. Eventually, they will tend to notice only those things that fit into the expected patterns, reinforcing the aberrant system. Long-term potentiation (LTP) of neuronal response may perpetuate the patterns. Training in flexible attention can begin a change process that ripples through the entire system, forming new neuronal connections to help elicit a change.

Alternating Attention Exercise

A simple place to begin is by developing the ability to shift attention from one thing to the next and then back again. You can utilize the interesting object of focus chosen in the previous exercise, or pick something new to focus on. Notice every detail about the object. Then, pick a detail to focus on. Look carefully at this detail and keep focused on it for 30 seconds or so. Close your eyes and visualize this detail. So, for example, if you have chosen the color of the object, just think of that color. Open your eyes, look at the object again, and pick a second detail, perhaps the shape of the object, such as a square shape. Focus attention on this second feature. Then close your eyes and focus on it in your imagination. Let other features fade, to be background. After several minutes, open your eyes and look at the first feature again. Think about it for a moment or two, close your eyes, and picture this feature. Then open your eyes and switch back to looking at the second feature. Alternate between the two, keeping attention focused selectively, first on one feature, and then on the other. Try the exercise with your eyes open and then with eyes closed. Finally, switch back and forth between features while keeping your eyes closed.

Mantra and Mudra Exercise for Memory Loss

This exercise is drawn from the Alzheimer's Research and Prevention Foundation performed at the University of Pennsylvania that used a form of mantra and mudra combined to help overcome memory loss associated with Alzheimer's disease and mild cognitive impairment (Newberg et al., 2010).

Sounds and hand movements were coordinated together from a comfortable sitting position. *Sit with your spine relatively straight and your eyes closed. Begin chanting the following sounds, repeating each syllable one after the other: Saa, Taa, Naa, and Maa. The meaning of these sounds in combination is "My highest or best self." As you say the sounds, focus your attention on the top of your head and imagine the sound flowing in through the top and out through the middle of your forehead. Speak the sounds for 2 minutes in a normal voice tone. Then whisper the sounds for two minutes. Then for 4 minutes, inwardly imagine yourself saying the sounds. Now, reverse the order, whispering for 2 minutes and then speaking aloud for 2 minutes, for a total of 12 minutes of practice. The first three tones should move down the scale, and then the final tone, Maa, moves back up one tone to sound the same note as Taa.*

Perform this simple corresponding mudra with each sound. For the first sound Saa, let your thumb touch your index finger as the other fingers curve gently around as pictured (Figure 11.11). *Then for Taa, touch the middle finger to the thumb, for Naa, touch the fourth finger to the thumb, and for Maa, touch the little finger to the thumb.*

Figure 11.11

PAIN CONTROL

Seniors are often bothered by chronic pain. They can use skills with yoga meditation and breathing to help ease their experience of pain and thereby enhance their quality of life. One client of ours had been diagnosed with cancer of an important endocrine gland. She was suffering such deep and debilitating pain that she was put on a strong dose of morphine, but as a result, she felt groggy and out of touch. She came to us to learn meditation to help cope with the pain. We taught her how to meditate and to redirect her focus away from the painful feelings. As she learned the skills, she found that she was able to reduce the dose of morphine so that she could enjoy her time with her family and participate in some of the activities she enjoyed doing.

Neurology and Psychology of Pain

People have more control over pain than they realize. A large component of the experience of pain is psychological, and this aspect can be controlled. Pain has its own pathway in the central nervous system. Pain information is carried rapidly along insulated (myelinated) fibers and slowly along uninsulated (unmyelinated) C-fibers. The axons ascend the spinal chord, and the signal is sent to the brain stem, through the medulla and pons, which control pain-related behavior such as crying out in pain. Then the pain information is distributed to the different thalamic areas and up to the cortex (Figure 11.12).

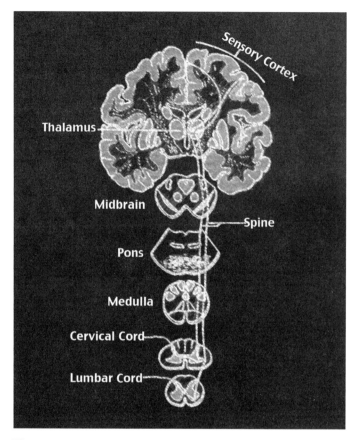

Figure 11.12

The psychological aspect comes through the cingulate cortex, which is activated by pain information, especially when people believe the stimulus will be painful. This area influences how intensely pain is experienced. Thus, psychological approaches that influence expectancy and handling of the emotional element involved in pain will have an effect on how the brain responds, encouraging a lowering of the sensation of pain. The body has natural capacities to respond to danger. The HPA (refer to Figure A-10) pathway activates to respond quickly to danger by running away or staying still until the danger has passed. When we feel pain, we may also feel afraid, because pain often is a signal of danger. Usually when people experience pain from an injury, illness, childbirth, and so on, there is no immediate danger, just the pain. Learning to not feel afraid of the body's built-in pain response can be accomplished using the many tools of yoga.

Pain may be very unpleasant and difficult to handle, but it is still just what it is, a sensation that is nothing to fear. By fearing the pain, something more is added. Instead, simply let the sensation be. The mind can intensify or lessen the sensation. So, for clients who are under a medical doctor's care, waiting for healing, or needing to endure, you can guide them to withstand the discomfort and patiently endure it as they wait for the process to run its course.

One way to manage pain is to recognize the difference between the sensation of pain and the reaction of fear in response to the pain sensation. The sensation of pain eases when the fear response is diminished. Therapy can show clients how to stop anticipating or imagining the pain. Then they will experience some moments with a little less pain. Other methods for dealing with pain are offered in Chapter 9, in the sections on withdrawing from an addictive substance, and can be adapted for seniors who are dealing with pain.

Exercise in Alteration of Pain

Stand, sit, or lie down in a position that produces the least pain possible for you. Focus on the sensation of pain, observe it, and try to contemplate it only as a sensation, and no more. What does it feel like? Is it hot? Pounding? Sharp? Dull? Describe it to yourself, noticing all of the details, locating its boundaries. What areas outside of the boundaries feel good? Imagine. Try to shift attention to the areas that feel better. Then, allow your awareness to fill out the perception of the body as a greater whole, to put the pain in a new perspective.

Distraction From Pain

A pleasant memory can be used to distract attention away from pain. Can you recall a time when you went on a vacation? Perhaps you visited a beautiful place, or maybe it was just a wonderful afternoon off from work when you could do exactly what you felt like doing. Visualize this experience now. Picture it vividly, recalling what the weather was like, how the surroundings looked, or perhaps what you were wearing. Recall other people who might have been there, what you did, and the pleasant feelings you had. Enjoy the experience for several minutes. You may be surprised to find that your pain goes away for a moment as you bring yourself fully into this pleasant memory. You may choose another experience that you prefer, with more meaning to you: perhaps time with someone you care deeply for, or again, perhaps engagement with meaningful work.

Acceptance

Although it is very unpleasant and uncomfortable, accept the pain sensation just for what it is. Do not let it hurt your feelings, so to speak. When you can let go of the hurt, your mind can be at peace, even though you are undeniably extremely uncomfortable. Your sensation is your awareness of the pain, not a punishment. You may have learned from early life experiences that pain is linked to punishment. Your body is not trying to punish you. Your nerves are doing their job— complaining, with good reason. Accept what is, do not resist, and the pain will be less disturbing. Be one with the pain; suffer with it, not from it. And perhaps then you can find meaning in your projects, and accomplish what matters to you now as well.

Renewal

Yoga breathing can be used to help you feel less pain and even regain feelings of comfort and renewal. People often tighten up against pain, which makes it worse. Allow your mind and body to be as calm as possible, relaxing the HPA pathway and shifting the balance more toward relaxation and comfort. Practice the complete breath (instructions given in Chapter 5). With each breath in, notice any tension in your body, and with each breath out, imagine the tension flowing out. You might find it helpful to visualize the air flowing in as clean, fresh, and even light in color and the air flowing out as dark and stale. Continue to breathe comfortably, and feel the relaxation and comfort spread with every breath.

CONCLUSION

The psychological problems seniors face can be made more difficult because of diminishing capacities that sometimes come with aging. But by using yoga methods, many capabilities can be enhanced, thereby offering seniors more tools for adapting to their situation. Furthermore, they can seek higher values for their lives that bring hope and renewal for a bright, active, and fulfilling future.

12

Freedom: Living From the Soul
for Clients and Therapists

*Understanding comes only through self-knowledge, which is awareness of
one's total psychological process. Thus, education in the true sense is the
understanding of oneself, for it is within each one of us that the whole of
existence is gathered.*

(Krishnamurti, 1953, p. 17)

The word *psychotherapy* comes from the Greek word *psyche,*
which means "breath, spirit, or soul" and *therpeuein,* "to serve or take care
of." At a deeper level, psychotherapy is care for the soul, and the source of
cure for the soul is in the soul's purity, the true Self. The process involves
turning attention inward towards the source, thereby finding a universe of
understanding. From the wellspring of this understanding come wisdom,
health, and fulfillment.

WHAT IS THE SOUL?

We have times when the mind is active with many thoughts, and times when
thinking wanes, with few thoughts. But something is beyond the flow of

thoughts, a light of truth that shines through. According to yoga theory, the true Self is the source of illumination that is always there, the soul. The soul "must belong to that which has light as Its own essence and, as such, can never decay or die, never become stronger or weaker" (Vivekananda, 1953, p. 295).

According to neuroscience, we are embodied beings. Our thoughts, feelings, and sensations are activated through the brain in the body that lives in an environment. We cannot separate the mind from the body, brain, or greater universe. Yoga theory adds another dimension: We are also *ensouled*, and to disregard the soul, the true Self within unity, is to leave out the source of wisdom.

The cognitive processes of the mind and brain may be what we know, but the soul is knowledge itself. The soul does not just partake in knowledge, it *is* knowledge. Carl Jung (1875–1961) offered an interesting explanation as to how the soul is knowledge itself with this example: Our eyes take in light waves and see them as color. The translation to color is seamless, linking the built-in way perceptions work with the laws of the light spectrum. All of the senses are similarly linked to the world, as are our cognitive faculties (Jung, 1978). We are directly linked to nature through universal laws. By turning inward to study our own sensations, perceptions, and cognition, which are lawful, we can learn to know nature's lawfulness. Each individual soul is like a drop of water that gives up its separateness, contributing it when it joins other drops to make up the ocean. Through truly knowing the part, our own drop of water, we can know the whole, the ocean.

The soul is the source for Samadhi. At one with the universe and at peace with ourselves, we can be wise and happy. But in order to know the soul to find wisdom and happiness, we must clear away the obscuring mental chatter of everyday concerns that distract us from the truth within. When we can see through all of the illusions, we are enlightened.

Clients are often stuck in the morass of illusions, alienated from their soul, the true self. They are disconnected from their inherent source of knowledge and happiness. The minds of clients are pushed and pulled by their conflicts. They feel lost and turn to therapy to guide them. Therapists know that there is something beyond those mental conflicts, a centered sense of self that each person can discover. We guide in turning clients' attention inward, to sense the wisdom that lies hidden. When clients learn to attune to their deeper inner sensing, they find an anchor in troubled waters, a way to steer their ship through treacherous storms.

From the Center

Being centered goes all the way down to the neuron's response of the receptor fields in the brain. On-center and off-center are always in interaction. The receptor field is arranged with a "center" area surrounded by a "surround" area. The firing response of these two areas is linked, such that when the center is activated, the surround is deactivated. So, in a visual receptor field, when a light shines on the center of an on-center cell, it fires, leading to activation, but when light shines on the surround area, the center is deactivated, decreasing the firing of the cell. Because of the center-surround relationship, cells can transmit information. Thus, the relationship to the center is built into our mind-brain system.

Therapy helps clients to regain their center. They are often functioning from the surround, looking somewhere outside for answers to what they feel or think. Taking in input is important, but when it comes to what someone feels, the truth is found by sensitively turning attention toward the center. From the attuned center, the relationship to all things surrounding becomes clear. Attention can be directed to any one of the senses, an emotion the client feels, or to a thought that is occurring. Any one experience can provide the link back to the center. Many of the exercises throughout this book have directed clients in these ways, as attention is taken from the outside concerns and turned inward. When they are successful in clearing away obstructions and sensitively following their experience to its roots, they will know themselves and recognize patterns. They will feel when they are on center or off and be able to do something about it.

The quality of certainty that goes along with the insight may not be easily articulated, but it is understood. The true self's knowledge is often wordless, a meditative moment. Samadhi is something to be experienced. There is no separation between self and soul in the center. Here, unity is found.

From the centered position, when there is no separation, actions are sincere and authentic. As karma yoga teaches, act wholeheartedly. Then each action taken is a meaningful expression of the soul, that unique essence of the individual. Doubts, ruminations, and second-guessing cease, and the client can proceed in endeavors with unwavering commitment. "The yogi, with mind controlled, always meditating thus on the Self (atma), arrives at my state, nirvanic ultimate, which is peace" (*Upanishads* in Woods, 1982, p. 25).

SOUL OF THE CLIENT: FOSTERING THE BEST

Diana began her therapy to help her lose weight, but as the treatment evolved, she realized that her weight problem was really part of a larger pattern of difficulty. She was divorced, with a young daughter who lived with her. She firmly believed that she was inadequate to do anything except get by. She was living without a sense of direction for her life, doing odd jobs. Her daughter had trouble keeping up at school. Diane believed her daughter was probably slightly below average in intelligence, so she accepted the poor performance as all that could be expected.

With each relationship, Diane progressively lost more of the boundaries of her identity in the other's experience. Her ex-husband believed in the powers of magic, so naturally she joined him in these beliefs. Together they had performed magical rituals as a religion when they were married, but now, she continued to practice rituals on her own for practical purposes, in the belief that they would bring her money and peace of mind, but to no avail. Her overeating had a somewhat similar pattern. Her current boyfriend worked in a health-food store and was a firm believer in health foods for a healthy life. She felt mystified that she had gained so much weight. After all, she was only eating natural foods that she bought at the health-food store, such as fresh fruit, hearty bread, and cheese. Therefore, she reasoned, she should have a healthy life. Her problem was that, unfortunately, she ate too much of these healthy foods, and so her weight was increasing more than her health!

Therapy began by learning how to meditate. She found dharana meditations difficult at first, because her tendency was to lose her focus and let her mind drift. But with practice, she began to be able to keep her attention steady. We worked on body awareness, to be able to sense her skin, her heartbeat, her emotions, and her thoughts. The control she gained through meditation gave her a deep sense of confidence in her own mind that sent ripples through her entire life. And just as she began to recognize that she had something missing, a gap in the network of admirable values she sincerely aspired to, she began to recognize a gap in her life, in its focus and meaning as a whole.

As she became more in touch with herself, she had a series of understandings about herself and other people in her life. She noticed something in herself that she had never felt before: motivation. She realized that she wanted to do something meaningful with her life. She recognized that she had been underachieving. As she got more in touch with herself, her other-oriented adjustment turned into a strong professional interest in the field of public health. From a confident center, she took a bold step forward and applied to graduate school to get a master's degree in public health, to become an administrator. Her ability to stay focused helped empower her to handle the pressures of school while being a single mom. She followed through to complete her degree and became a competent, fully licensed, and talented professional. Her daughter, who saw her mother study hard and take school seriously, performed better in her own schooling to become a top student in several subjects.

Diane had not realized that she had unrecognized potential. She had created a lifestyle with certain satisfactions, based in goals appropriate to lesser striving. But she was unfulfilled, shown symbolically in her compulsive symptom. She wanted more out of life and had the undeveloped talent to achieve it, experienced as a vague but compelling hunger. The clarity of inner vision that she gained from meditation gave her awareness of what she truly needed. And from the center, her true self was illuminated. Then, applying her yoga skills for focus and discipline, she was able to help fulfill her needs and beyond, to help others fulfill theirs.

The meditation, breathing, and postures taught throughout this book bring a certain feeling of confidence. It is not based on anything outside of the person's own efforts and gradually evolving skills. Sensing of the soul puts the client in touch with the wisdom within, and this offers tremendous support and a sense of confidence. At first, the therapist may need to point out progress, but as the client delves deeper into meditation, a felt sense within grows stronger. Before treatment, Diane did not have insight into her behavior or what her patterns were expressing, but after she developed her mental skills, her inner light shone through, and she could clearly see what she wanted and needed to do, for a more fulfilling and satisfying life.

Where to Place the Focus

At the heart of Indian philosophy and psychotherapy is the idea that perfection of the knower is the way to understanding; Refine yourself as the instrument of truth. As Aurobindo explained, "The capacity to know should be equal to the object to be known" (Sen, 1960, p. 186). We train ourselves to observe objectively in science in order to know the objects of the world. The best scientist has a refined eye, clear from bias. Yoga and psychotherapy also train in observational skills. The object of our gaze is the mental processes, and then delving deeper into the soul itself. We look as objectively and fully as we can with the belief that from the clear eye of the center we *will* know the true self. Then, from the personal clarity comes a reality-based perspective. The perfecting of the knower is the best way to truly understand oneself, and in so doing, to know the world. Knowledge chases ignorance as light chases darkness (Brunton, 1970, p. 147).

Aim for Higher Potential

Seek higher goals to which you aspire
Don't base your actions on lower desires
Happiness is not found in avoiding displeasure
Enlightenment is within, an invaluable treasure

C. Alexander Simpkins

Humanity has long believed that people can perfect themselves. In the West, the tradition can be traced back to the ancient Greeks, who pursued human excellence in art, sports, and thought. Aristotle offered the philosophical basis for this approach: "Every art and every inquiry, and similarly every action and pursuit, is thought to aim at some good, and for this reason the good has rightly been declared to be that at which all things aim" (Aristotle, *Nicomachean Ethics* Book 1 1094-1, in McKeon, 1948, p. 935). Aristotle goes on to ask, given that there is some good to which all things aim, "Will not the knowledge of it, then have a great influence on us?" (Book 1 1094-20, McKeon, 1948, p. 935). An archer improves in skill by knowing where and what the target is, and similarly we should try to understand the target of our inquiry.

For psychotherapy, the aim is the clients' problems. But what does this really entail? Clients often feel that their goal is not simply to take away their suffering. They want something more, to feel truly happy, engage deeply in loving relationships, and be engrossed in meaningful work. By opening treatment to point toward human potential, therapeutic change can lead to Samadhi.

Nonspecific Factors of Healing

Therapists may accept that people have vast potentials and that these potentials are available and found within. But if Samadhi is so readily available, what prevents clients from tapping their potential? On a fundamental level, clients lack the belief that they can do so. When they first come into the office, they are often demoralized and dispirited. They may feel hopeless that the future could be different and lack trust in themselves and others. Clients can certainly do more than they usually think they can. One of the first tasks of therapy is to enlist the powers of faith, hope, and trust to initiate a process.

Extensive research has found that faith, hope, and trust are factors nonspecific to any one form of treatment and are present in all that foster potential (Frank, Hoehn-Saric, Imber, Liberman, & Stone, 1978). These determinants, along with the therapeutic relationship and experiences of mastery, are the primary nonspecific factors that must be engaged for therapy to be effective (J. D. Frank & Frank, 1991). Recent research has shown a strong link between faith and health (Koenig, McCullough, & Larson, 2001). The brain seems to be hardwired for hope, faith, and even belief in a higher power (Ramachandran, Blakeslee, & Sacks, 1999). When these factors are included, treatment outcomes improve.

Enhancing of abilities and raising expectancies have a general, nonspecific positive influence that works side-by-side with specific treatments for improving psychological health. Both enhance each other. One of the early large meta-studies on psychotherapy effectiveness (Smith, Glass, & Miller, 1980) found that, in general, psychotherapy is effective. There was no definitive finding for which therapy is best, but rather that certain techniques might work better for a specific problem or client. All of the factors work together, both specific and nonspecific (C. A. Simpkins & Simpkins, 2001).

Placebo research has added further evidence for the power of hope, faith, and trust. What people expect about a treatment can strongly influence how well that treatment works. Pain-reducing effects from a placebo can be nearly as effective as pain medication. Studies of pain illustrate the point. A large meta-analysis including 1,183 participants from 12 studies found that the expectation of pain relief stimulates the release of opioids in the brain (Sauro & Greenberg, 2005). Opioids are neurotransmitters that are endogenous to the brain and act similarly to how opiate drugs relieve pain. Additional evidence that the brain releases natural opioids when expecting pain relief was found when subjects were given naloxone. Naloxone is an opioid antagonist that blocks the brain's opioids, and the subjects who took naloxone lost the analgesic effect of the placebo. This kind of research shows that human beings have untapped potentials built into the mind-brain-body system. Why not harness these potentials for our treatments?

The Value of Values

Developing human excellence can be enhanced with values to guide the course. Positive psychology is a growing movement in our field that aims to understand and facilitate human excellence and bring it into the realm of psychotherapy. "Applied positive psychology is the application of positive psychology research to the facilitation of optimal functioning" (Linley & Joseph, 2004). The process is facilitative, fostering the best in clients by encouraging them to live in accordance with an explicit set of values that point toward positive individual traits. Values are defined as "Social-cognitive representations of motivational goals. They are desirable goals that vary in importance and serve as guiding principles in people's lives" (Sagiv, Roccas, & Hazan, 2004, p. 68). The yamas and niyamas serve as guidelines to channel actions toward higher goals. They help shape the direction to travel, like the track for a bobsled, and the yoga techniques provide the vehicle for the journey.

So, values provide a framework that moves us in the right direction. For therapy, this means engaging the powers of the placebo, inspiring expectant hope and faith, and entering into a process that will transcend limitations and free abilities. Once abilities are freed, values keep these abilities moving in healthy directions. The therapeutic process opens the possibility and then guides on the path by providing tools along the way. Then, as clients clear away illusions and become the true Self, living from the soul, they become one with the greater universe and through that union, find freedom and release. "What it [enlightenment] brought was an inexpressible Peace, a stupendous silence, an infinity of release and freedom" (Rishabhchand, 1960, p. 213).

DRAWING ON THE SOUL OF THE THERAPIST

There are many things that belong to, or are prerequisites for doing good analytic work. . . . But basic even to these prerequisites is a certain kind of attentiveness to the patient.

(*Horney, 1987, p. 18*)

Nourishing the Soul of the Therapist

Meditation is a known method to help therapists reduce the stress that accompanies the helping professions. The healthy therapist knows how to work on personal difficulties as they arise, and meditation can serve as a method to come back to center. The regular practice of the different forms of meditation presented in this book can help you to draw on your intuitive grasp, to apply your therapeutic wisdom to yourself as needed. One client, an oncology nurse, had to deal with the death of patients with whom she often formed a strong bond. She found meditation a resource that helped her return to her own center, her source for calm and resilience.

Meditation should be practiced regularly, not just to reduce stress and calm the mind, but to stay attuned to your soul. The true Self is the source for clear vision, and through meditation, it becomes accessible for therapeutic work. Light from the center shines through to provide perception that can cut through illusion to grasp reality. The therapist who works from the soul is present in the moment: aware and open.

Begin From an Ethical Framework to Guide the Way

Professional psychotherapists have codes of ethics, our yamas and niyamas so to speak, for how to deal with clients. From a yoga view, professional ethics can serve as guidelines. By deeply understanding and sincerely living in accord with ethics, freedom is found. As instincts are honed to be one with values, action can be trusted to be correct and true. Then, therapists can intuitively apply their procedures in creative ways, knowing that they are true to the code.

The training requires study and thought about the ethics of your field. When you truly know them and have thought them through to their roots, you know how you feel about each standard. We encourage the self-study of tapas to investigate deeply. Apply your intelligence and intuition to enhancing your understanding of the deeper intent of the code. As the sensitive person that you undoubtedly are, you will find your way to make the ethical code of your field a positive source of strength and a guide for technique.

In addition to the ethics of good therapy, there is a sense of purity in that the therapeutic intent is aimed toward the good of the client. The intent that you have for the client is not from your own wishes. In this sense, it is selfless. You are not trying to embody yourself in the client, but rather to foster the client to become his or her personal best. When therapists find themselves intertwining their own wishes and needs with those of the client, meditation can help to distinguish between these two sets of needs and to clear away whatever is being imposed. The meditative process helps you to disentangle from your own self-needs while being present for the client's therapeutic needs.

Developing Intuition

Intuition is a primary quality that therapists engage in with clients in every session. We often count on it to just be there, and often it spontaneously arises, captivating us in the moment. How can we enhance intuition, this primary quality of good therapeutic work? One way is to ensure that our perceptions are open and accurate. As has been shown throughout this book, the qualities of attention, concentration, and focus are many, and they can be refined through training. Therapists can develop their powers of intuition to become well-tuned instruments of healing by enhancing and refining their attentional abilities.

The ability to focus attention on the client is important. As clients speak, therapists need to keep attention both focused and free-floating. Skilled therapists know how to narrow their attention enough to stay in touch with what the client is communicating without restricting attention so much that they miss their own intuitive associations or relevant links from their training. Here is where the practice of meditation offers helpful ways to train attention. There are many times when being able to narrow attention is invaluable for noticing subtle cues in behavior, alterations in voice tones, or significant nuances of meaning. Being able to follow the thread of the client's thought also requires focus of attention that cuts through the meanderings of the client's flow of ideation. Training these skills through your own dharana meditation will serve you well in honing your attention abilities.

But focus may be restrictive. There are times when the free-floating attention of dhyana is vital, allowing you to see beyond the given, into the broader heartfelt intentions and meanings, which are often unknown to the client. When you can allow a deep contemplation in open-ended attention, insight fills the room. In such moments, therapist and client come to a shared realization. By narrowing and opening the focus at will, you develop your mental capacities on many levels. Through the interplay with the client in the present moment, a therapeutic Samadhi can take place.

ATTAINMENT OF FREEDOM

Having kindled the impulse toward ultimate freedom and adopted an appropriate spiritual path, the practitioner gradually sheds ignorance and simply awakens as the ever-present Real.

(Feuerstein, 2003, p. 575)

The mind and body, when working together, can develop enhanced abilities that lead to liberation from limitations and problems. With the light of wisdom, freed from inner conflict, comes a tremendous feeling of release. The hidden wellspring of freedom in the real Self can now be found, experienced, and drawn from. Zen Buddhism calls enlightenment "nothing special," because it is not a something that is added like a present received on a birthday. Rather, it is our birthright, there because we all share in the divine nature of the universe. The miracle, so to speak, is the recognition that it *is* there and anyone *can* experience it. Even the most troubled individual has the capacity within for peace and harmony, happiness and fulfillment. The therapist acts as a catalyst to help the client recognize the possibility and then guides the client in developing the skills to resolve problems, dispel illusions, and maintain the inner tranquility to fully realize it. And so, enlightenment is where? Here. Enlightenment is when? Now. Uncover and discover what is deep within, the capacity for wisdom, love, and peace.

Clearing Meditation

Sit quietly now in any pose that you find most comfortable. Allow the flow of thoughts to slow and then still, as you sit quietly now in this moment. Through the open, quiet moment, an inner light shines through, a vast illumination stretching out before you. Step into the light and nothing holds you back. Let yourself feel the glow of your own light now, and in its empty open warmth, feel calmly at peace with yourself. Leave your inner struggles behind, and express your potential as you will, with a calm and steady mind!

> Open to openness
> For insight clear
> Seek space within
> Then center here.
> For vision of truth
> The outer world conceals
> Happiness and freedom
> The true self reveals

C. Alexander Simpkins

Appendix I: Warming Up for Supplemental Practice

The practice of yoga teaches how to listen, feel, and sense. It gently and gradually points people back to the fundamentals of breathing, sitting, standing, and moving. From this firm foundation, everything in life becomes easier and more natural. Attending to the inside can make a difference on the outside. Self-awareness grounds people in their life and world, to intuitively know what to do and have the self-discipline to do it. Often clients will want to supplement their therapy between sessions by doing some of the meditations along with breathing and asanas they learn in the office. This appendix offers guidelines for warming up before performing asanas. We speak directly to clients, since they will be doing the exercises on their own.

WARM-UP EXERCISES

Before you engage in any of the postures in this book, it is important to warm up your body. You will derive the most benefit from warm-ups by paying close attention to the movements as you perform them. Whenever you do warm-ups, be sure to bring your attention to them as well.

When you begin to stretch, start from wherever you are. Do not try to push beyond what is comfortable. Do the exercises slowly, without straining. You will make progress if you practice carefully and gradually. You will enjoy the benefits that you can achieve from gentle, sensitive stretching.

Upward Stretch

Begin by standing upright, feet together. Raise your open hands overhead, extending your fingers, and stretch your arms gently upward as you inhale. Let your rib cage lift as your whole body extends up a bit, and then exhale while you let your arms bend at the elbows and slowly lower back to your sides. Repeat several times.

Head Roll

Keep your arms resting down at your sides. Limber your neck muscles and upper spine by tilting your head sideways so that your right ear moves closer to your right shoulder. Then gently roll your head forward bringing your chin toward your chest. Continue to move your head around to the left, so that your left ear moves toward your left shoulder, and then let your head tilt back slightly. Continue to roll around in a circle in this way three times.

Shoulder Roll

Keep your arms down at your side. Lift your shoulders slightly and gently roll them forward, up, back, and down. Continue to roll your shoulders around 3 times in one direction and then 3 times in the reverse direction. This exercise helps relieve tension from sitting long hours at a desk.

Forward Bend

Inhale as you raise your arms up over your head again and then slowly lower your body forward. Let your arms hang down toward the floor and let your head relax. Do not strain beyond a comfortable forward bend. Raise and lower 3 times.

Bent Elbow Twist

Move your legs about a foot apart and bend your arms, raising them to shoulder height. Place one hand on top of the other and inhale, as you stand comfortably upright. Then gently pivot your arms around to the right, allowing your body to stretch around too, as you exhale. Come back to center and inhale and then pivot to the left for a stretch on the other side as you exhale again. Repeat 3 times on each side.

Side Stretch

Now place your legs about two shoulder widths apart with your feet facing straight ahead. Inhale as you extend your arms out sideways from your shoulders, holding them parallel to the floor. Then extend your right hand overhead while exhaling, and lean over sideways to the left, to give you a gentle side stretch. Keep your legs straight. Lower your arm back to extend outwards as you return to an upright position, facing front, and inhale. Then exhale as you raise your left arm overhead and then stretch to the other side. Don't push too hard or stretch too deeply on either side. Keep in mind that you are just trying to limber and warm up your muscles.

Chest Stretch

Return to standing upright with your legs together and clasp your hands behind your back, with arms extending downward. Press your shoulder blades toward each other as you press your hands together and inhale. Then relax your shoulders and arms as you exhale. Repeat three times.

Lower Back Stretch

Lie on the floor on your back and inhale. Then bring your knees up toward your chest as you exhale. Hold your legs below the knees and pull gently, allowing a light stretch of your lower back. Release your legs and inhale again. Then repeat 2 more times.

Leg Swing

Limber your legs by gently swinging your left leg forward and then back, slowly and carefully. Repeat with the right leg. You can keep your hands on your hips or hold on to a stable chair back, kitchen counter, or wall, if you feel unsteady. Keep the leg swings controlled, relaxed, and easy. Repeat 3 or 4 times on each side as you breathe normally.

Appendix II: A Quick Tour
Through the Brain

COMPONENTS OF THE NERVOUS SYSTEM

Begin Small: Neurons

The brain is made up of neurons. Neurons are the functional units in the brain and throughout the nervous system. There are more than 180 billion neurons, with at least 80 billion involved in cognitive processes. Each neuron connects with hundreds of other neurons, and so we have vast potentials for an enormous amount of interactions occurring simultaneously (Figure A.1).

Neurons have two main functions: They process certain chemicals within them, and they communicate with other neurons. This communication process of inputs, integration, and outputs occurs across the synaptic gap between neurons. When the gap is close enough, the electrical signal can simply leap across and keep going, but more often, the gap is too large for this to happen. With the larger gaps, the electrical signal is converted into a chemical, known as a neurotransmitter, and the neurotransmitters swim across the gap to then be converted back into an electrical impulse when they reach the other side (Figure A.2).

We have several different kinds of neurotransmitters. Glutamate is an excitatory neurotransmitter that is found throughout the nervous system. GABA (gamma-aminobutyric acid) is inhibitory and, like glutamate, is

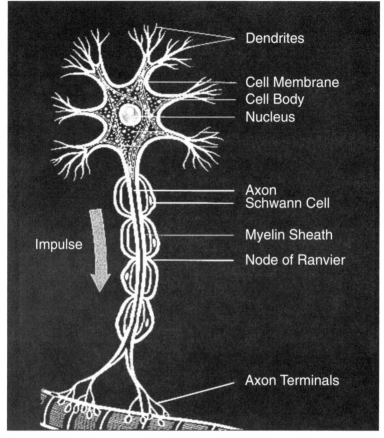

Figure A.1

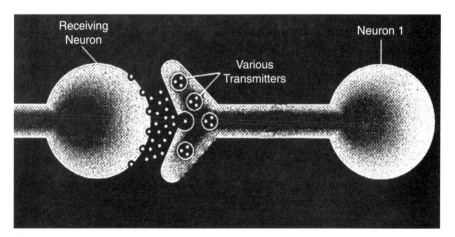

Figure A.2

found everywhere in the nervous system. Certain neurotransmitters are more specific in what they communicate. For example, dopamine is related to pleasure and reward. Serotonin involves emotionality and sleep patterns, norepinephrine influences alertness, and endorphins alleviate pain. The neurotransmitter system usually has everything it needs already built in, but when the neurotransmitters are out of balance, drug therapy and psychological treatments such as meditation, hypnosis, and psychotherapy can stimulate or inhibit processes to stimulate a better balance. Medications for psychological problems such as depression and anxiety are just acting to stimulate the neurons to produce more of certain neurotransmitters or to block the action of other neurotransmitters.

The transmission across the synapse either activates the neuron to fire or deactivates it from firing. When neurons fire together repeatedly, these neurons tend to become wired together, known as Hebb's rule (Hebb, 1949), forming a stronger synaptic connection. This firing and wiring strengthening, known as LTP (long-term potentiation), explains, at a neuronal level, how learning and memory occur. It also helps account for neuroplasticity.

The Central Nervous System and Peripheral Nervous System

All of the neurons combined make up the nervous system, consisting of the central nervous system (brain and spinal cord) and the peripheral nervous system (autonomic nervous system, cranial nerves, and spinal nerves). The peripheral nervous system extends through the whole body and communicates information to and from the central nervous system. The autonomic nervous system interacts closely with the central nervous system, often automatically and unconsciously (Figure A.3).

The neurons of the autonomic nervous system include two key systems: the sympathetic nervous system and the parasympathetic nervous system. The sympathetic nervous system prepares the body for vigorous action. The parasympathetic nervous system acts as an opposite to the sympathetic nervous system's activations. So, when the sympathetic activation constricts blood vessels or inhibits digestion during exercise, the parasympathetic system relaxes vessel walls and stimulates digestion when the workout is over. Both systems work together to help foster appropriate responses. These systems of activation and deactivation are involved in emotions such as fear

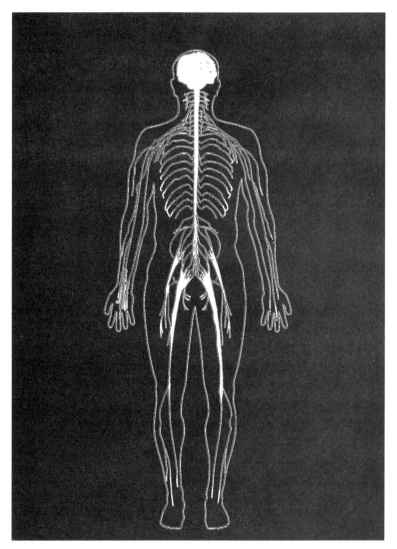

Figure A.3

and anger, as well as participating in responses to stress and feelings of enjoyment. Together, these two systems maintain the control that keeps the mind, brain, and body in balance. Yoga breathing, postures, and meditations can shift the balance in the autonomic nervous system.

Brain Structures and Functions

The brain orchestrates the nervous system. It is often described in terms of its structures and functions. Unconscious processing tends to travel a short,

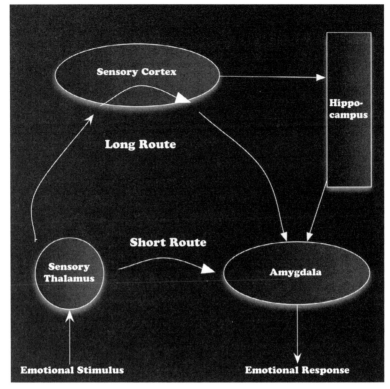

Figure A.4

subcortical path through the lower brain areas, known as bottom-up processing, which does not engage the higher-level processing cortex. For awareness of emotions, sensations, and cognitions, the information usually travels a long path, sometimes called top-down processing, involving higher parts of the cortex (Figure A.4).

Lower Brain Areas: Brain Stem and Cerebellum

At the base of the brain is the brain stem, the transition between the spinal cord and the brain. This area is important in regulating vital body functions such as breathing, heart rate, and other automatic functions. These lower brain areas coordinate their action with many other regions of the brain (Figure A.5).

The cerebellum (Latin for *little brain*), located at the back of the neck, has two hemispheres with functional sections in each, known as lobes. The cerebellum interacts closely with other parts of the brain through loops

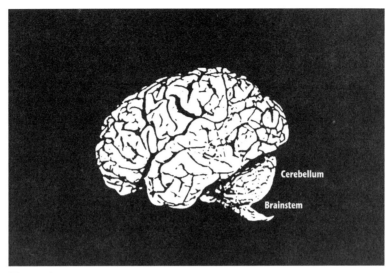

Figure A.5

of interaction. It serves a variety of functions, including the regulation of higher cerebral processes in motor planning, cognition, involuntary functions, and problem solving. It also regulates posture and the command of movement. We have all experienced the effort required to learn new movements, such as playing a sport or mastering a dance pattern. During the learning period, the cerebellum is active. Once movement control is mastered, the cerebellum becomes less active, and other parts of the brain get involved.

Interior Brain Areas: Basal Ganglia and Limbic System

The region that spans the area from the brain stem to below the cortex in the interior of the brain is the limbic system for emotions (Figure A.6) and the basal ganglia for voluntary movement and coordination (Figure A.7). The basal ganglia form a C-shape of four interconnected structures: the substantia nigra, the caudate nucleus, the putamen, and the globus pallidus. These structures are also involved in planning movement, performing movements in sequence, and maintaining learning. This area is also part of predictive control, attention, and working memory.

The limbic system has been given much attention for therapy because it is intimately involved in regulating emotion, fear conditioning,

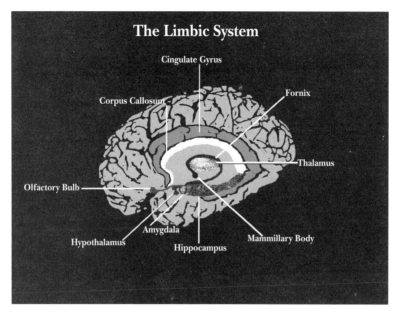

Figure A.6

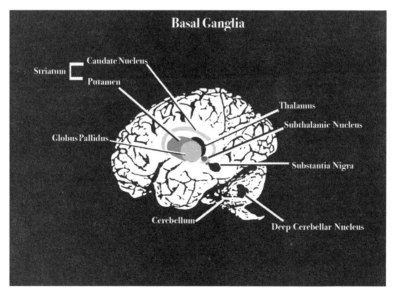

Figure A.7

fight-or-flight and stress responses, as well as learning and memory. Many structures play a central role in the limbic system. The most central ones include the amygdala for emotions, the hippocampus for learning and memory, the hypothalamus for regulating many autonomic functions including biological rhythms and stress, and the thalamus as a gateway for sensory information. Several other structures are considered important for some aspects of emotion; and these are the olfactory cortex, involved in the sense of smell, the pituitary gland regulating hormones, and the nucleus accumbens, important for reward, laughter, pleasure, addiction, and the placebo effect. Two cortical areas are also strongly linked to the limbic system: the cingulate gyrus for monitoring conflicts and the orbitofrontal cortex (part of the prefrontal cortex). All of these structures interconnect and interact together, although some contribute more to one function than to another. With so many varied brain structures all closely interacting functionally with each other as well as with higher cortical functions, it makes sense as to why emotions play such an important role in every aspect of living.

Higher Brain Areas: The Cerebral Cortex

The cerebral cortex is the outer layer of the hemispheres with many convolutions, *gyri*, and folds, *sulci*. Folding increases the surface area of the cortex, so that more than two-thirds of the surface is hidden from view. The cortex is sometimes referred to as the higher part of the brain. Each hemisphere is divided into four lobes: the frontal, parietal, temporal, and occipital. The lobes monitor different functions, although they are all interrelated, interacting together. The fibers that connect the two hemispheres are called the corpus callosum, which helps the two hemispheres communicate with each other (Figure A.8).

Frontal Lobes

The frontal lobes account for nearly one-third of the cerebral cortex. The prefrontal cortex is located at the front of the frontal lobes behind the forehead. The fact that the prefrontal areas have extensive links throughout the brain shows how interrelated brain functions really are. Areas of the prefrontal cortex are involved in executive functions that include planning, higher-level decision making, sequencing, and goal-directed behavior. Independent thinking is processed in this area as well. Another part of the prefrontal cortex processes personality characteristics, such as

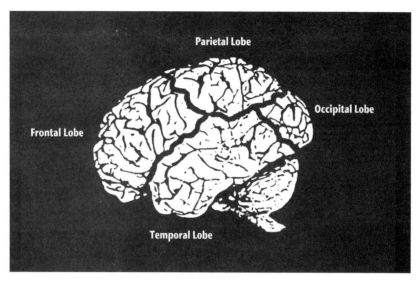

Figure A.8

the experience of empathy, socially appropriate behavior, and emotional control.

The primary motor area is located in the back (posterior) area of the frontal lobes. It is important for control of movement. This area has a map of the body on it. Larger portions of the cortical map are devoted to areas that are used more, such as the hands and face. The nonprimary motor cortex, located in front of the primary motor cortex, includes a premotor area and a supplementary motor area. These areas are involved with movement and coordination in general, such as stance, gait, and initiation of voluntary movement sequences. Mirror neurons are located in the motor area of the frontal lobe as well. The mirror neurons are involved in understanding and empathizing with the intentions and actions of others and help with social understanding.

One other important area located in the frontal lobes is the cingulate gyri, also called the cingulate cortices. This area is involved in motivated behavior, spontaneity, and creativity. Complex behavior and attention, or conflict monitoring, are also processed in the cingulate gyri. This area is primary during the emotional reaction to pain and in the regulation of aggressive behavior. It has also been found to play an important role in maternal attachment, as evident in behaviors like nursing and nest building in animals.

The Parietal Lobes

Behind the frontal lobes and close to the cingulate gyri are the parietal lobes. These lobes are involved in sensation and perception of touch, pressure, temperature, and pain. Sensory information from the body is correlated there during perception or cognition of a sensation. The parietal lobes are activated when locating objects in space and mapping the relationship of the body to the world. The back (anterior) portion of the parietal lobes is the sensory strip. The body is mapped on the sensory strip for sensations, similar to how the primary motor cortex is where movement is mapped for the body.

The Temporal Lobes

The temporal lobes house the primary auditory cortex. They are located near the temples and moderates auditory information. Wernicke's area, on the left hemisphere side, plays a larger role in understanding spoken language. Although most of the visual processing occurs in the primary visual areas in the occipital lobes, some visual processing is performed in the temporal lobes, involving perception of movements and face recognition.

The Occipital Lobes

The occipital lobes are located in the posterior region of the brain. Axons coming from visual input from the eyes pass through the thalamus and are directed to the primary visual cortex. The visual cortex is also sometimes called the *striate cortex* because of its striped appearance. Human beings rely on their vision quite heavily, and this is revealed in the complexity of this region of the brain. There are more than 32 zones for visual processing differentiating aspects of seeing such as color, texture, and movement. All are located in the occipital lobes.

HOW THE BRAIN AREAS WORK TOGETHER

So, how do all of these brain areas function? Senses provide a window to the world. First, the receptor organs (such as the eyes, fingertips, nose, tongue, or ears) detect a stimulus. Each sensory system has its own pathway that sends the signal to the cortex. The signal registers on receptor fields for the particular sensory modality in a cortical map, located on the cortex. Maps can change depending on what stimuli are experienced. Maps that are used more often tend to grow larger. Attention, regulated in the frontal lobes, is what helps us to notice important stimuli and ignore others, such as attending to reading while ignoring rain sounds on the roof.

Pathways

The central nervous system is a complex collection of structures and functions that are organized in pathways. Thoughts, feelings, and behaviors are intimately involved in the flow of these pathways, dynamic systems of interactions between brain structures and the flow of energy and neurotransmitters.

Several pathways through the nervous system help coordinate the mind-brain-body balance. One pathway processes sensory input and has a special pathway to process painful stimuli. A reward pathway regulates positive emotions and drives toward fulfillment, satisfaction, and enjoyment (Figure A.9). The fear pathway, also called the HPA (hypothalmic-pituitary-adrenal) pathway, provides the capacity to respond to threat and then return to homeostatic balance (Figure A.10). When overactivated, the fear pathway becomes a stress pathway. Regulatory systems control the appetite and the

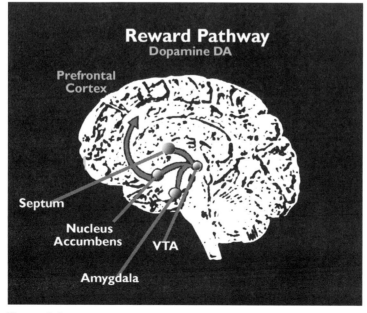

Figure A.9

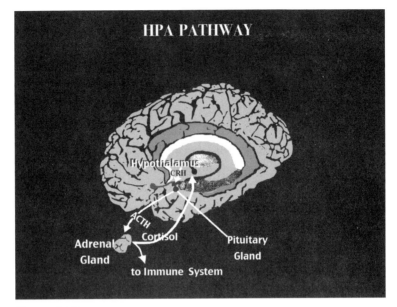

Figure A.10

sleep-wake cycle as well. When any of these systems are out of balance, disorders and problems tend to develop. All of these systems can be altered using the therapeutic yoga techniques included in this book.

References

Abela, J. R. Z., & D'Alessandro, D. U. (2002). Beck's cognitive theory of depression: The diathesis-stress and causal mediation components. *British Journal of Clinical Psychology, 41,* 111–128.

Abou-Nader, T. M., Alexander, C. N., & Davies, J. L. (1990). The Maharishi technology of the unified field and reduction of armed conflict: A comparative longitudinal study of Lebanese villages. In R. A. Chalmers, C. Clements, H. Schenkluhn, & M. Weinless (Eds.), *Scientific Research in the Transcendental Meditation and TM-Sidhi Program: Collected Papers,* Vol. 4. Vlodrop, Netherlands: Maharishi Vedic University Press.

Alexander, C. N., Rainforth, M. V., & Gelderloos, P. (1991). Transcendental meditation, self-actualization, and psychological health: A conceptual overview and statistical meta-analysis. *Journal of Social Behavior and Personality, 6,* 189–247.

Alexander, C. N., Swanson, G. C., Rainforth, M. V., Carlisle, T. W., Todd, C. C., & Oates, R. M. (1993). Effects of the transcendental mediation program on stress reduction, health, and employee development: A prospective study in two occupational settings. *Anxiety, Stress, and Coping: An International Journal, 6,* 245–262.

Allard, T. T., Clark, W. M., & Merzenich, M. M. (1987). Syndactyly results in the emergence of double-digit fields in somatosensory cortex in adult owl monkeys. *Society for Neuroscience, 11,* 965.

Allport, G. W. (1961). *Pattern and growth in personality.* New York, NY: Holt, Rinehart, and Winston.

American Psychiatric Association. (2000). *Diagnostic and statistical manual of mental disorders* (4th ed., DSM-IV). Arlington, VA: American Psychiatric Publishing.

American Psychological Association. (2008). *Stress in America: Mind/body health: For a healthy mind and body, talk to a psychologist*, October 7, 2008. Washington, DC: American Psychological Association.

American Psychological Association. (2010). http://www.apa.org/topics/addiction/index.aspx.

Antonuccio, D. O., Danton, W. G., & DeNelsky, G. Y. (1995). Psychotherapy versus medication for depression: Challenging the conventional wisdom with data. *Professional Psychology: Research and Practice, 26*(6), 574–585.

Barlow, D. H., Chorpita, B. F., & Turovsky, J. (1996). Fear, panic, anxiety, and disorders of emotion. In D. A. Hope (Ed.), *Nebraska Symposium of Motivation,* Vol. 43: *Perspectives on anxiety, panic, and fear.* Lincoln: University of Nebraska Press.

Bavelier, D., Tomann, A., Hutton, C., Mitchell, T., Liu, G., Corina, D., & Neville, H. (2000). Visual attention to the periphery is enhanced in congenitally deaf individuals. *Journal of Neuroscience, 20*(17), 1–6.

Bears, M. F., Connors, B., & Pardiso, M. A. (1996). *Neuroscience exploring the brain.* New York, NY: Williams & Wilkins.

Begley, S. (2007). *Train your mind, change your brain: How a new science reveals our extraordinary potential to transform ourselves.* New York, NY: Ballantine.

Benson, H. (1974). Decreased alcohol intake associated with the practice of meditation: A retrospective investigation. *Annals of the New York Academy of Science, 233,* 174–177.

Bentler, S. E., Hartz, A. J., & Kuhn, E. M. (2005). Yoga helps chronic fatigue: A prospective observational study of treatments for unexplained chronic fatigue. *Journal of Clinical Psychiatry, 66*(5), 625–632.

Bhatia, M., Kumar, A., Kumar, N., Pandey, R. M., & Kochupilla, V. (2003). Electrophysiologic evaluation of Sudarshan Kriya: An EEG, BAER, and P300 study. *Indian Journal of Pharmacology, 47,* 157–163.

Blair, R. J. (2004). The roles of the orbital frontal cortex in the modulation of antisocial behavior. *Brain and Cognition, 55,* 198–208.

Bonura, K. B. (2007). The impact of yoga on psychological health in older adults. http://etd.lib.fsu.edu/theses/available/etd-05082007-000113/unrestricted/KBBonura2007.pdf.

Brazier, A., Mulkins, A., & Verhoef, M. (2006). Evaluating a yogic breathing and meditation intervention for individuals living with HIV/AIDS. *American Journal of Health Promotion, 20*(3), 192–195.

Breedlove, S. M., Rosenzweig, M. R., & Watson, N. V. (2007). *Biological psychology: An introduction to behavioral, cognitive, and clinical neuroscience.* Sunderland, MA: Sinauer Associates.

Briones, T. L., Klintsova, A. Y., & Greenough, W. T. (2004). Stability of synaptic plasticity in the adult rat visual cortex induced by complex environment exposure. *Brain Research, 20*(1018), 130–135.

Brooks, C. (1982). *Sensory awareness: The discovery of experiencing.* Santa Barbara, CA: Ross Erikson.

Brown, R. P., & Gerbarg, P. L. (2005). Sudarshan Kriya yoga breathing in the treatment of stress, anxiety, and depression, Part I: Neurophysiologic model. *The Journal of Alternative and Complementary Medicine, 11*(1), 189–201.

Brunton, P. (1970). *The inner reality.* London, England: Rider & Co.

Buckenmeyer, J., & Freltas, D. (2007). Factors affecting student achievement and related behaviors. Retrieved October 3, 2010, from http://www .yogakids.com/toolsforschools/Docs/YogaKids%20Tools%20Schools%20 -Study%20Report.pdf

Capeza, R., & Nyberg, L. (2000). Neural basis of learning and memory: Functional neuroimaging evidence. *Current Opinion in Neurology, 13,* 415–421.

Chaudhuri, H., & Spiegelberg, F. (Eds.). (1960). *The integral philosophy of Sri Aurobindo.* London, England: George Allen & Unwin.

Christensen, A. (1997). *The American Yoga Association's new yoga challenge: Powerful workouts for flexibility, strengthen, energy, and inner discovery.* Chicago, IL: Contemporary Books.

Churchland, P. M. (1995). *The engine of reason, the seat of the soul: A philosophical journey into the brain.* Cambridge, MA: MIT Press.

Churchland, P. S. (1986). *Neurophilosophy: Toward a united science of the mind-brain.* Cambridge, MA: MIT Press.

Colcombe, S. J., Erickson, K. I., Rax, N., Webb, A. G., Cohen, N. J., & McAuley, E. (2003). Aerobic fitness reduces brain tissue loss in aging humans. *Journals of Gerontology, Series A, Biological Sciences and Medical Sciences, 58*(2), 176–180.

Cook, I. A., Shapiro, D., Leuchter, A. F., Abrams, M., & Ottaviani, C. (2005). Yoga augmentation and remission in partial responders to antidepressant medications. Poster presented at the NCDEU Annual Meeting, Boca Raton, FL, June 6–9, 2005.

Cranson, R. W., Orme-Johnson, D. W., Gackenbach, J., & Dillbeck, M. C. (1991). Transcendental meditation and improved performance on intelligence-related measures: A longitudinal study. *Personality and Individual Differences, 12*(10), 1105–1116.

Curiati, J. A., Bocchi, E., Freire, J. O., Arantes, A. C., Braga, M. R., Garcia, Y., ... Fo, W. J. (2005). Influence of yoga & ayurveda on self-rated sleep in a geriatric population. *Journal of Alternative and Complementary Medicine, 11*(3), 465–472.

Dantzker, J. M. (2006). Bursting on the scene: How thalamic neurons grab your attention. *PLoS Biology, 4*(7), e250.

Das, N., & Gastaut, H. (1955). Variations in the electrical activity of the brain, heart, and skeletal muscles during yogic meditation and trance. *Electroencephalography and Clinical Neurophysiology, Supplement, 6,* 211–219.

Davidson, R., Goleman, D., & Schwartz, G. (1976). Attentional and affective concomitants of meditation: A cross-sectional study. *Journal of Abnormal Psychology, 85,* 235–308.

Davies, J. L., & Alexander, C. N. (1989). Alleviating political violence through reduction of collective stress: Impact assessment analysis of the Lebanon war. Paper presented at the annual meeting of the American Political Science Association, Atlanta, GA.

Desikachar, T. K. V. (1995). *The heart of yoga: Developing a personal practice.* Rochester, VT: Inner Traditions International.

Deutsch, E. (Trans.). (1968). *The Bhagavad Gita.* New York, NY: Holt, Rinehart, & Winston.

Devi, I. (1959). *Yoga for Americans.* Upper Saddle River, NJ: Prentice-Hall.

Dhar, H. R. (2002). Meditation, health, intelligence and performance. *Medicine update. Apicon, 12*(202), 1376–1379.

Dillbeck, M. C. (1980). Test of a field theory of consciousness and social change: Time series analysis of participation in the TM-Sidhi program and reduction of violent death in the U.S. *Social Indicators Research, 22*(4), 399–418.

Dillbeck, M. C. (1982). Meditation and flexibility of visual perception and verbal problem solving. *Memory & Cognition, 10*(3), 207–215.

Dillbeck, M. C., Assimakis, P. D., Raimondi, D., & Orme-Johnson, D. W. (1986). Longitudinal effects on the transcendental meditation and

TM-Sidhi program on cognitive ability and cognitive style. *Perceptual and Motor Skills, 62*(3), 731–738.

Dillbeck, M. C., Cavanaugh, K. L., Glenn, T., Orme-Johnson, D. W., & Mittlefehldt, V. (1987). Consciousness as a field: The transcendental meditation and TM Sidhi program and changes in social indicators. *Journal of Mind and Behavior, 8,* 67–104.

Dillbeck, M. C., & Orme-Johnson, D. W. (1987). Physiological differences between transcendental meditation and rest. *American Psychologist, 42*(9), 879–881.

Dohrenwend, B. P., & Dohrenwend, B. S. (1981). *Stressful life events and their concepts.* Brunswick, NJ: Rutgers University Press.

Epel, E. S., Blackburn, E. H., Lin, J., Dhabhar, F. S., Adler, N. E., & Morrow, J. D. (2004). Accelerated telomere shortening in response to life stress. *Proceedings of the National Academy of Sciences (USA), 101*(49), 17312–17315.

Esiri, M. (1994). Dementia and normal aging: Neuropathology. In F. A. Huppert, C. Brayne, & D. W. O'Connor (Eds.), *Dementia and normal aging* (pp. 385–436). Cambridge, UK: Cambridge University Press.

Feifer, S. G. (2009). Mood and anxiety disorders in children. In S. E. Feifer & G. Rattan (Eds.), *Emotional disorders: A neuropsychological, psychopharmacological and educational perspective* (pp. 123–146). Middletown, MD: School Neuropsychology Press.

Feuerstein, G. (2003). *The deeper dimension of yoga: Theory and practice.* Boston, MA and London, England: Shambhala.

Fodor, J. A. (1983). *The modularity of mind.* Cambridge, MA: MIT Press.

Frank, J. D., & Frank, J. B. (1991). *Persuasion and healing.* Baltimore, MD: Johns Hopkins University Press.

Frank, J. D., Hoehn-Saric, R., Imber, S. D., Liberman, B. L., & Stone, A. R. (1978). *Effective ingredients of successful psychotherapy.* New York, NY: Brunner/Mazel.

Gage, F. H., Eriksson, P. S., Perfilieva, E., & Bjork-Eriksson, T. (1998). Neurogenesis in the adult human hippocampus. *Nature Medicine, 4*(11), 1313–1317.

Galamtino, M. L., Galbavy, R., & Quinn, L. (2008). Therapeutic effects of yoga for children: A systematic review of the literature. *Pediatric Physical Therapy, 20*(1), 66–80.

Gandhi, M. (1960). *An autobiography or The story of my experiments with truth*. Bombay, India: Ghandi Book Centre.

Ganzel, B. L., Morris, P. A., & Wethington, E. (2010). Allostasis and the human brain: Integrating models of stress from the social and life sciences. *Psychological Review, 117*(1), 134–174.

Gauthier, L. V., Taub, E., Perkins, C., Ortmann, M., Mark, V. W., & Uswatte, G. (2008). Remodeling the brain: Plastic structural brain changes produced by different motor therapies after stroke. *Stroke, 39,* 15–20.

Gazzaley, A., Cooney, J. W., Rissman, J., & D'Esposito, M. (2005). Top-down suppression deficit underlies working memory impairment in normal aging. *Nature Neuroscience, 8*(10), 1298–1300.

Gelderloos, P., Walton, K. G., Orme-Johnson, D. W., & Alexander, C. N. (1991). Effectiveness of the transcendental meditation program in preventing and treating substance misuse: A review. *International Journal of the Addictions, 26*(3), 293–325.

Golomb, J., Kluger, A., de Leon, M. J., Ferris, S., Convit, A., Mittelman, M.,... George, A. (1994). Hippocampal formation size in normal human aging: A correlate of delayed secondary memory performance. *Learning and Memory, 1,* 45–54.

Granath, J., Ingvarsson, S., von Thiele, U., & Lundberg, U. (2006). Stress management: A randomized study of cognitive behavioral therapy and yoga therapy. *Cognitive Behavior Therapy, 35*(1), 3–10.

Grant, J. E. (2008). *Impulse control disorders*. New York, NY: W. W. Norton.

Green, E., & Green, A. (1977). Self-regulation: East and West. In E. Green & A. Green, *Beyond biofeedback* (pp. 197–218). New York, NY: Knoll.

Greenough, W. T., Black, J. E., & Wallace, C. S. (1987). Experience and brain development. *Child Development, 58,* 539–559.

Hagelin, J. S., Rainforth, M. V., Cavanaugh, K., Alexander, C. N., Shatkin, S. F., Davies, J. L., . . . Orme-Johnson, D. W. (1999). Effects of group practice of the transcendental meditation program on preventing violent crime in Washington, D.C.: Results of the national demonstration project, June–July 1993. *Social Indicators Research, 47*(2), 153–201.

Haug, H. (1985). Are neurons of the human cerebral cortex really lost during aging? A morphometric evalution. In J. Traber & W. H. Gispen (Eds.), *Senile dementia of the Alzheimer type* (pp. 150–163). Berlin, Germany: Springer.

Hebb, D. O. (1949). *The organization of behaviour*. New York, NY: Wiley.

Hempel, H., & Ott, U. (2006). Effects of hatha-yoga: Autonomic balance, absorption, and health. Unpublished manuscript.

Horney, K. (1987). *Final lectures.* New York, NY: W. W. Norton.

Iyengar, B. K. S. (2001). Alcoholism; drug addiction. In B. K. S. Iyengar, *Yoga: The path to holistic health* (pp. 347–348, 353–355). London, England/ New York, NY: Dorling Kindersley.

Iyengar, B. K. S. (2001). *Yoga: The path to holistic health.* London, England/ New York, NY: Dorling Kindersley.

Jack, C. R., Jr., Peterson, R. C., Xu, Y., O'Brien, P. C., Smith, G. E., & Ivanik, R. J. (2000). Rates of hippocampal atrophy correlate with change in clinical status in aging and AD. *Neurology, 55*(4), 484–489.

Jack, D. R., Jr., Shiung, M. M., Weigand, S. D., O'Brien, R. C., Gunter, J. L., & Boeve, B. E. (2005). Brain atrophy rates predict subsequent clinical conversion in normal elderly and amnestic MCI. *Neurology, 65*(8), 1227–1231.

Janis, I. (1971). *Stress and frustration.* New York, NY: Harcourt Brace Jovanovich.

Jenkins, W. M., Merzenich, M. M., Ochs, M. T., Allard, T., & Guic-Roble, E. (1990). Functional reorganization of primary somatosensory cortex in adult owl monkeys after behaviorally controlled tactile stimulation. *Journal of Neurophysiology, 63,* 82–104.

Jensen, P. S., & Kenny, D. T. (2004). The effects of yoga on the attention and behavior of boys with attention deficit/hyperactivity disorder (ADHD). *Journal of Attention Disorders, 7*(4), 205–216.

Jerath, R., Edry, J. W., Bames, V. A., & Jerath, V. (2006). Physiology of long pranayamic breathing: Neural respiratory elements may provide a mechanism that explains how slow deep breathing shifts the autonomic nervous system. *Medical Hypotheses, 67*(3), 556–571.

Johansson, B. (1991). Neuropsychological assessment in the oldest-old. *International Psychogeriatrics, 3* (Suppl.), 51–60.

Johnson, S. (2008). *Hold me tight: Seven conversations for a lifetime of love.* New York, NY: Little, Brown.

Jung, C. G. (1978). *Psychotherapy and the East.* Princeton, NJ: Princeton University Press.

Kasser, T. (2004). The good life or the goods life? Positive psychology and personal well-being in the culture of consumption. In P. A. Linley &

S. Joseph (Eds.), *Positive psychology in practice* (pp. 55–67). Hoboken, NJ: Wiley.

Katz, R., & McGuffin, P. (1993). The genetics of affective disorders. *Progress in Experimental Personality & Psychopathology Research, 16,* 200–221.

Kaufman, A. S., Reynolds, C. R., & McLean, J. E. (1989). Age and WAIS-R intelligence in a sample of adults in the 20–74 year age range: A cross sectional analysis with educational level controlled. *Intelligence, 13,* 235–253.

Khalsa, D. S., & Newberg, A. (2007). Mind body medical techniques and memory loss reversal. *Alzheimer's Disease and Associated Disorders, 6,* 10–14.

Khumar, S. S., Kaur, P., & Kaur, S. (1993). Effectiveness of shavasana on depression among students. *Indian Journal of Clinical Psychology, 20,* 82–87.

Kobasa, S. C. (1979). Stressful life events, personality, and health: An inquiry into hardiness. *Journal of Personality and Social Psychology, 42,* 707–717.

Koenig, H. G., McCullough, M. E., & Larson, D. B. (2001). *Handbook of religion and health.* New York: Oxford University Press.

Koob, G. F. (2003). Neuroadaptive mechanisms of addiction: Studies on the extended amygdala. *European Neuropsychopharmacology, 13*(6), 442–452.

Krishnamurti, J. (1968). *The first and last freedom.* Wheaton, IL: The Theosophical Publishing House.

Kuhn, H. G., Dickinson-Anson, H., & Gage, F. H. (1996). Neurogenesis in the dentate gyrus of the adult rat: Age-related decrease of neuronal progenitor proliferation. *Journal of Neuroscience, 16*(6), 2027–2033.

Kumar, V. K., & Pekala, R. J. (1988). Hypnotizability, absorption, and individual differences in phenomenological experience. *International Journal of Clinical and Experimental Hypnosis, 36* (2), 80–88.

Lazar, S. W., Kerr, C. E., Wasserman, R. H., Gray, J. R., Greve, M., Treadway, T., . . . Fishi, B. (2005). Meditation experience is associated with increased cortical thickness. *NeuroReport, 16*(17), 1893–1897.

Lazarus, R. S. (1977). Psychological stress and coping in adaptation and illness. In Z. J. Lipowski, D. R. Lipsitt, & P. C. Whybrow (Eds.), *Psychosomatic medicine* (pp. 11–26). New York, NY: Oxford University Press.

Lazarus, R. S. (1991). *Emotion and adaptation.* New York, NY: Oxford University Press.

Lazarus, R. S., & Folkman, S. (1984). *Stress, appraisal, and coping*. New York, NY: Springer.

Ley, R. (1999). The modification of breathing behavior. Pavlovian and operant control in emotion and cognition. *Behavioral Modifications, 23*, 441–479.

Linley, P. A., & Joseph, S. (2004). Applied positive psychology: A new perspective for professional practice. In P. A. Linley & S. Joseph (Eds.), *Positive psychology in practice* (pp. 3–12). Hoboken, NJ: Wiley.

Lupien, S. J., de Leon, M., de Santi, S., Convit., A., Tarshish, C., & Nair, N. P. (1998). Cortisol levels during human aging predict hippocampal atrophy and memory deficits. *Nature Neuroscience, 1*(1), 69–73.

Lutyens, M. (Ed.). (1970). *The only revolution by J. Krishnamurti*. New York, NY: Harper & Row.

Lutz, A., Slagter, H. A., Dunne, J. D., & Davidson, R. J. (2008). Attention regulation and monitoring in meditation. *Trends in Cognitive Science, 12*(3), 163–169.

Mahesh, Maharishi Yogi. (1990). *Enlightenment and invincibility*. Fairfield, IA: Maharishi International University Press.

Manjunath, N. K., & Telles, S. (2005). Influence of yoga and ayurveda on self-rated sleep in a geriatric population. *Indian Journal of Medical Research, 121*(5), 693–690.

Martin, K. C., Bartsch, D., Bailey, C. H., & Kandel, E. R. (2000). Molecular mechanisms underlying learning-related long-lasting synaptic plasticity. In M. S. Gazzaniga (Ed.), *The new cognitive neurosciences*. Cambridge, MA: MIT Press.

Martin, K. C., & Zukin, R. S. (2006). RNA trafficking and local protein synthesis in dendrites: An overview. *Journal of Neuroscience, 5*(26/27), 7131–7134.

McCloskey, G., Hewitt, J., Henzel, J., & Eusebio, E. (2009). Executive functions and emotional disturbance. In S. G. Feifer & G. Rattan (Eds.), *Emotional disorders: A neuropsychological, psychopharmacological and educational perspective* (pp. 65–104). Middletown, MD: The School of Neuropsychology Press.

McEwen, B. S., & Magarinos, A. M. (1997). Stress effects on morphology and function of the hippocampus. *Annals of the New York Academy of Sciences, 821*, 271–284.

McGuire, E. A., Gadian, D. G., Johnsrude, I. S., Good, C. D., Ashburner, J., Frackowiak, R. S. J., & Frith, C. D. (2000). Navigation-related structural change in the hippocampi of taxi drivers. *Proceedings of the National Academy of Sciences (USA), 97*(81), 4398–4403.

McKeon, R. (Ed.). (1948). *The basic works of Aristotle.* New York, NY: Random House.

Medina, J. F., Christopher Repa, J., Mauk, M. D., & LeDoux, J. E. (2002). Parallels between cerebellum and amygdala dependent conditioning. *National Review of Neuroscience, 3,* 122–131.

Merzenich, M. M., Nelson, R. J., Kaas, J. H., Stryker, M. P., Jenkins, W. M., Zook, J. M., . . . Schoppmann, A. (1987). Variability in hand surface representations in areas 3b and 1 in adult owl and squirrel monkeys. *The Journal of Comparative Neurology, 248,* 281–296.

Michalsen, A., Grossman, P., Acil, A., Langhorst, J., Ludtke, R., Esch, T., . . . Dobos, G. J. (2005). Yoga reduces stress and anxiety among distressed women. *Medical Science Monitor, 11*(12), 555–561.

Miller, B. S. (1986). *The bhagavad-gita: Krishna's counsel in time of war.* New York, NY: Bantam.

Miller, B. S. (1998). *Yoga, discipline of freedom: The yoga sutra attributed to Patanjali.* New York, NY: Bantam Dell.

Mitchell, D. B. (2006). Nonconscious priming after 17 years: Invulnerable implicit memory? *Psychological Science, 17*(11), 925–929.

Nakashima, G. (1981). *The soul of a tree.* Tokyo, Japan: Kodansha International Ltd.

Nespor, K. (2001a). Yoga and coping with harmful addictions (part 1). *Yoga Magazine, 12*(5), 39–47.

Nespor, K. (2001b). Yoga and coping with harmful addiction (part 2). *Yoga Magazine, 12*(6), 38–47.

Newberg, A. B., & Iversen, J. (2003). The neural basis of the complex mental task of meditation: neurotransmitter and neurochemical considerations. *Medical Hypotheses, 61*(2), 282–291.

Newberg, A. B., Wintering, N., Khalsa, D. S., Roggenkamp, H., & Waldman, M. R. (2010). Meditation effects on cognitive function and cerebral blood flow in subjects with memory loss: A preliminary study. *Journal of Alzheimer's Disease, 20,* 517–526.

Niranjanananda Saraswati, S., & Alexander, C. N. (Eds.). (1994). *Self-recovery: Treating addictions using transcendental meditation and Maharishi ayur-veda*. Binghamton, NY: Haworth Press.

Ouchi, Y., Okada, H., Yoshikawa, E., Nobezawa, S., & Futatsubashi, M. (1999). Brain activation during maintenance of standing postures in humans. *Brain, 122*(2), 329–338.

Pilkington, K., Kirkwood, G., Rampes, H., & Richardson, J. (2005). Yoga for depression: The research evidence. *Journal of Affective Disorders, 89*(1), 13–24.

Piver, S. (2008). The surprising self-healing benefits of meditation. *Weil Lifestyle*. www.drweil.com/drw/u/ART02791/self-healing.

Place, U. T. (1999). Is consciousness a brain process? In W. G. Lycan (Ed.), *Mind and cognition* (pp. 14–29). Oxford, UK: Blackwell.

Pons, T. P., Garraghty, P. E., Ommaya, A. K., Kaas, J. H., Taub, E., and Mishkin, M. (1991). Massive cortical reorganization after sensory deafferentation in adult macaques. *Science, 252*(5014), 1857–1860.

Porges, S. W. (1992). Vagal tone: A physiologic marker of stress vulnerability. *Pediatrics, 90*(3), 498–504.

Porges, S. W. (2009). Reciprocal influences between body and brain in the perception and expression of affect: A polyvagal perspective. In D. Fosha, D. J. Siegel, & M. Solomon (Eds.), *The healing power of emotion: Affective neuroscience, development and clinical practice* (pp. 27–54). New York, NY: W. W. Norton.

Pramanik, T., Sharma, H. O., Mishra, S., Mishra, A., Prajapati, R., & Singh, S. (2009). Immediate effect of slow pace bhastrika pranayama on blood pressure and heart rate. *The Journal of Alternative and Complementary Medicine, 15*(3), 293–295.

Prasad, K. V. V., Sunita, M., Raju, P. S., Reddy, M. V., Sahay, B. K., & Murthy, K. J. Y. (2006). Impact of pranayama and yoga on lipid profile in normal healthy volunteers. *Journal of Exercise Physiology Online, 9*, 1–6.

Prochaska, J. O., DiClemente, C. C., Velicer, W. F., & Rossi, J. S. (1993). Standardized, individualized, interactive and personalized self-help programs for smoking cessation. *Health Psychology, 12*(5), 399–405.

Prochaska, J. O., DiClemente, C. C., & Norcross, J. C. (1992). In search of how people change: Applications to addictive behaviors. *American Psychologist, 47*(9), 1102–1114.

Radhakrishnan. (1977). *Indian philosophy*, Vol. I & II. London, England: George Allen & Unwin.

Raju, P. T. (1948). The universal in the Western and the Indian philosophy. In W. R. Inge, L. P. Jacks, M. Hiriyanna, E. A. Burtt,. & P. T. Raju (Eds.), *Radhakrishnan comparative studies in philosophy* (pp. 379–408). New York, NY: Harper & Row.

Ramachandran, V. S., Blakeslee, S., & Sacks, O. (1999). *Phantoms in the brain: Exploring the mysteries of the human brain.* New York, NY: Harper Perennial.

Ramachandran, V. S., Rogers-Ramachandran, D. C., & Stewart, M. (1992). Perceptual correlates of massive cortical reorganization. *Science, 258*(5085), 1159–1160.

Raskin, S. A., Borod, J. C., & Tweedy, J. (1990). Neuropsychological aspects of Parkinson's disease. *Neuropsychology Review, 1,* 185–221.

Raub, J. A. (2002). Psychophysiologic effects of hatha yoga on musculoskeletal and cardiopulmonary function: A literature review. *Journal of Alternative Complementary Medicine, 8*(6), 797–812.

Raz, A., Lieber, B., Soliman, F., Buhle, J., Posner, J., Peterson, B. S., & Posner, M. I. (2005). Exological nuances in functional magnetic resonance imaging (fMRI): Psychological stressors, posture, and hydrostatics. *Neuroimage, 25,* 1–7.

Raz, A., Soliman, F., Fan, J., Flombaum, J., Durston, S., & Posner, M. I. (2000). Sitting up versus lying down in a scanner: Cognitive performance issues. New York, NY: Joan and Stanford I. Weill Medical College of Cornell University.

Restak, R. M., & Grubin, D. (2001). *The secret life of the brain.* Washington, DC: National Academies Press.

Rishabhchand. (1960). The philosophical basis of integral yoga. In H. Chaudhuri & F. Spiegelberg, *The integral philosophy of Sri Aurobindo* (pp. 213–222). London, England: George Allen & Unwin.

Rolls, E. T. (2004). Consequences of sensory systems in the orbitofrontal cortex in primates and brain design for emotion. *The Anatomical Record, Part A: Discoveries in Molecular, Cellular, and Evolutionary Biology, 28*(1), 1212–1225.

Rossi, E. (2002). *The psychobiology of gene expression: Neuroscience and neurogenesis in hypnosis and the healing arts.* New York, NY: W. W. Norton.

Sagiv, L., Roccas, S., & Hazan, O. (2004). Value pathways to well-being: Healthy values, valued goal attainment, and environmental congruence. In P. A. Linley & S. Joseph (Eds.), *Positive psychology in practice* (pp. 68–85). Hoboken, NJ: Wiley.

Salthouse, T. A., Babcock, R. L., Skovronek, E., Mitchell, D. R. D., & Palmon, R. (1990). Age and experience effects in spatial visualization. *Developmental Psychology, 26,* 128–136.

Sarang, S. P., & Telles, S. (2006). Changes in P300 following two yoga-based relaxation techniques. *International Journal of Neuroscience, 116*(12), 1419–1430.

Sauro, M. D., & Greenberg, R. P. (2005). Endogenous opiates and the placebo effect: A meta-analytic report. *Journal of Psychosomatic Research, 58,* 115–120.

Schilpp, P. A. (Ed.). (1952). *The philosophy of Sarvedpalli Radhakrishnan.* New York, NY: Tudor.

Schneider, A. M., & Tarshis, B. (1986). *An introduction to physiological psychology.* New York, NY: Random House.

Schofeld, W. (1964). *Psychotherapy, the purchase of friendship.* Englewood Cliffs, NJ: Prentice-Hall.

Schoville, W. B., & Milner, B. (1957). Loss of recent memory after bilateral hippocampal lesions. *Journal of Neurological Neurosurgery Psychiatry, 20,* 11–22

Seligman, M. E. P. (1990). *Learned optimism.* New York, NY: Knopf.

Seligman, M. E. P. (1992). *Helplessness: On depression, development, and death.* New York, NY: W. H. Freeman.

Seligman, M. E. P. (2002). *Authentic happiness: Using the new positive psychology to realize your potential for lasting fulfillment.* New York, NY: Free Press.

Selye, H. (1974). *Stress without distress.* New York, NY: Signet Books.

Sen, I. (1960). The Indian approach to psychology. In H. Chaudhuri & F. Spiegelberg (Eds.), *The integral philosophy of Sri Aurobindo* (pp. 184–191). London, UK: George Allen & Unwin.

Shaffer, H. J., LaSalvia, T. A., & Stein, J. P. (1997). Comparing hatha yoga with dynamic group psychotherapy for enhancing methadone maintenance treatment: A randomized clinical trial. *Alternative Therapies in Health and Medicine, 3*(4), 57–66.

Shannahoff-Khalsa, D. (2006). *Kundalini yoga meditation: Techniques specific for psychiatric disorders, couples therapy, and personal growth.* New York, NY: W. W. Norton.

Shannahoff-Khalsa, D. S., & Beckett, L. R. (1996). Clinical case report: Efficacy of yogic techniques in the treatment of obsessive compulsive disorders. *International Journal of Neuroscience, 46,* 53–59.

Shapiro, D., Cook, I. A., Davydov, D. M., Ottaviani, C., Leuchter, A. F., & Abrams, M. (2007). Yoga as a complementary treatment of depression: Effects of traits and moods on treatment outcomes. *Evidence-based Complementary and Alternative Medicine.* eCAM, doi: 10.1093/ecam/nel114.

Shen, K. (2003). Think globally, act locally: Local translation and synapse formation in cultured aplysia neurons. *Neuron, 49*(3), 323–325.

Simpkins, C. A., & Simpkins, A. M. (2001). *Timeless teachings from the therapy masters.* San Diego, CA: Radiant Dolphin Press.

Simpkins, C. A., & Simpkins, A. M. (2003). *Yoga basics.* Boston, MA: Tuttle.

Simpkins, C. A., & Simpkins, A. M. (2009). *Meditation for therapists and their clients.* New York, NY: W. W. Norton.

Simpkins, C. A., & Simpkins, A. M. (2010). *The dao of neuroscience: Combining Eastern and Western principles for optimal therapeutic change.* New York, NY: W. W. Norton.

Simpkins, C. A., & Simpkins, A. M. (2010). *Neuro-hypnosis: Using self-hypnosis to activate the brain for change.* New York, NY: W. W. Norton.

Sivananda, S. (1958). *Autobiography of Swami Sivananda.* Rishikeah, Himalayas: The Yoga-Vedanta Forest Academy.

Slagter, H. A. (2007). Mental training affects distribution of limited brain resourses. *PLoS Biology, 5,* e138.

Slueck, M., & Gloeckner, N. (2005). Yoga for children in the mirror of the science: Working spectrum and practice fields of the training of relaxation with elements of yoga for children. *Early Child Development and Care, 175*(4), 371–377.

Smith, M. L., Glass, G. V., & Miller, T. I. (1980). *The benefits of psychotherapy.* Baltimore, MD: Johns Hopkins University Press.

Snowdon, D. A., Greiner, L. H., Kemper, S. J., Nanayakkara, N., & Mortimer, J. A. (1999). Linguistic ability in early life and longevity:

Findings from the Nun Study. In J. M. Robine, B. Forette, C. Franceschi, & M. Allard (Eds.), *The paradoxes of longevity*. Berlin, Germany: Springer.

Sovik, R. (2000). The science of breathing—The yogic view. *Progressive Brain Research, 122,* 491–505.

Squire, L., Bloom, F. E., McConnell, S. K., Roberts, J. L., Spitzer, N. C., & Zigmond, M. J. (2003). *Fundamental neuroscience* (2nd ed.). New York, NY: Academic Press.

Squire, L. R., & Kandel, E. R. (2000). *Memory: From mind to molecules*. New York, NY: Henry Holt.

Steffensen, E. H., Brookhart, J. M., & Gesell, R. (1937). Proprioceptive respiratory reflexes of the vagus nerve. *Proceedings of the National Academy of Sciences (USA), 116*(17), 517–526.

Subramanya, P., & Telles, S. (2009). Effect of two yoga-based relaxation techniques on memory scores and state anxiety. *BioPsychoSocial Medicine, 3*(8), doi:10.1186/1751-0759-3-8.

Sulekha, S., Thennarasu, K., Vedamurthachar, A. Raju, T., & Kutty, B. (2006). Evaluation of sleep architecture in practitioners of Sudarshan Kriya yoga and Vipassana meditation. *Sleep and Biological Rhythms, 4*(3), 207–214.

Sung, B. H., Roussanov, O., Nagubandi, M., & Golden L. (2001). Effectiveness of various relaxation techniques in lowering blood pressure associated with mental stress. *Journal of Sports Medicine, 35*(3), 185–186.

Susman, E. J. (2006). Psychobiology of persistent antisocial behavior: Stress, early vulnerabilities, and the attenuation hypothesis. *Neuroscience and Biobehavioral Reviews, 30,* 376–389.

Thompson, W., Thompson, L., & Gallagher-Thompson, D. A. (2004). Pilot study of yoga and meditation intervention for dementia caregiver stress. *Journal of Clinical Psychology, 60*(6), 677–687.

Tsujimoto, S. (2008). The prefrontal cortex: Functional neural development during early childhood. *The Neuroscientist, 14*(4), 345–358.

Vaitl, D., & Ott, U. (2005). Altered states of consciousness induced by psychophysiological techniques. *Mind and Matter, 3,* 9–30.

Vishnu-devananda, S. (1995). *The complete illustrated book of yoga*. New York, NY: Three Rivers Press.

Vivekananda. (1953). *The yogas and other works*. New York, NY: Ramakrishna-Vivekananda Center.

Wacholtz, A. B., & Pargament, K. I. (2005). Is spirituality a critical ingredient of meditation? Comparing the effects of spiritual meditation, secular meditation, and relaxation on spiritual, psychological, cardiac, and pain outcomes. *Journal of Behavioral Medicine, 28*(4), 369–384.

Wallace, R. K., Dillbeck, M. C., Jacobe, E., & Harrington, B. (1982). The effects of the transcendental meditation and TM-sidhi program on the aging process. *International Journal of Neuroscience, 16*(1), 53–58.

Weiss, J. M., & Simson, P. G. (1985). Neurochemical basis of stress-induced depression. *Psychopharmacology Bulletin, 21,* 447–457.

West, J. B., Dollery, C. T., & Naimark, A. (1964). Distribution of blood flow in isolated lung: Relation to vascular and alveolar pressures. *Journal of Applied Physiology, 19,* 713–724.

Whitehorn, J. C. (1956). Stress and emotional health. *The American Journal of Psychiatry, 112*(10), 773–781.

Williams, A. L., Selwyn, P. A., Liberti, L., Molde, S., Njike, V. Y., McCorkle, R., . . . Katz, D. L. (2005). Efficacy of frequent mantram repetition on stress, quality of life, and spiritual well-being in veterans: A pilot study. *Journal of Palliative Medicine, 5,* 939–952.

Woods, E. (1982). *Yoga.* New York, NY: Penguin.

Woods, J. H. (1927). *The yoga system of Patanjali: Or the ancient Hindu doctrine of concentration of mind.* Delhi, India: Motilal Bankarsidass and The Harvard University Press.

Yapko, M. D. (2009). *Depression is contagious.* New York, NY: Free Press.

Yoga Journal. (2008). www.yogajournal.com/advertise/press_releases/10.

Zillmer, E. R., Spiers, M. V., & Culbertson, W. C. (2008). *Principles of neuropsychology.* Belmont, CA: Thomson Wadsworth.

Index

Meditation (*continued*)
  on posture and breathing, 148
  on something else, 189
  for relationships, 178
  samyama, meditative last three
    limbs, 69, 70
Memory, 36–41, 134, 172
  conscious memory, 38–39
  declarative memory, 38–40
  memory with children, 211–216
  memory enhancement with aging,
    231–236
  nondeclarative memory, 40
Michalsen, A., 12
Mild cognitive impairment,
  220–221
Miller, B. S., 50, 133
Mind and brain
  balance under stress, 182
  change, ix-x
  relationship, 23–24, 37,
    159, 178
Mitchell, D. B., 39, 234
Molafson, H. M., 40
Mudras, 6, 235–236

N

Nervous system, xi, 6, 14, 16, 19, 24,
  25, 26, 27, 28, 29, 30, 116,
  121, 130, 133, 136, 138,
  140, 153, 162, 181, 196,
  207, 218, 236, 256–259,
  266
Nespor, K., 14
Neurogenesis, 32–36
Neurons, 24, 32, 34, 37, 182, 218,
  232, 256–258, 264
Neuroplasticity, 14–15, 23, 32–36,
  87, 152

Neuroscience research
  body postures, 28–29
  breathing, 26–28
  executive control, 25
  memory and learning, 31–36
  polyvagal theory, 27
  remapping the brain, 33–36
Neurotransmitters, 117, 134, 157,
  158, 181, 186, 221, 247,
  256–258, 266
Newberg, A. B., 16, 28, 235
Niranjanananada Saraswati, S., 14
Niyamas, 76–80, 87–89
  for addiction, 185–186
  ishvara pranidhana, 80
  pranitara, 79–80, 185
  shaucha, 78–79, 154
  santosha, 78, 79, 185,
  for stress, 121–123
  tapas, 78, 79, 185, 249
Non-specific factors of healing,
  247–248

O

Obsessive compulsive disorder
  (OCD), 136, 154–155
Occipital lobes, 18, 28, 29, 30, 263,
  265
Open focus meditation, 31–32, 129,
One-pointed awareness, 129
Orme-Johnson, D. W., 9, 10, 21
Ott, U., 10, 18
Ouchi, Y., 29

P

Pain control, 236–239
  neurobiology of pain, 235–238
  psychology of pain, 236–238
Panic disorder, 136, 149–151